CU00758464

Promising Practices in 21st Century Music Teacher Education

Promising Practices in 21st Century Music Teacher Education

Edited by
Michele Kaschub and Janice Smith

OXFORD
UNIVERSITY PRESS

Oxford University Press is a department of the University of Oxford.
It furthers the University's objective of excellence in research, scholarship,
and education by publishing worldwide.

Oxford   New York
Auckland   Cape Town   Dar es Salaam   Hong Kong   Karachi
Kuala Lumpur   Madrid   Melbourne   Mexico City   Nairobi
New Delhi   Shanghai   Taipei   Toronto

With offices in
Argentina   Austria   Brazil   Chile   Czech Republic   France   Greece
Guatemala   Hungary   Italy   Japan   Poland   Portugal   Singapore
South Korea   Switzerland   Thailand   Turkey   Ukraine   Vietnam

Oxford is a registered trademark of Oxford University Press
in the UK and certain other countries.

Published in the United States of America by
Oxford University Press
198 Madison Avenue, New York, NY 10016

© Oxford University Press 2014

All rights reserved. No part of this publication may be reproduced, stored in a
retrieval system, or transmitted, in any form or by any means, without the prior
permission in writing of Oxford University Press, or as expressly permitted by law,
by license, or under terms agreed with the appropriate reproduction rights organization.
Inquiries concerning reproduction outside the scope of the above should be sent to the
Rights Department, Oxford University Press, at the address above.

You must not circulate this work in any other form
and you must impose this same condition on any acquirer.

Library of Congress Cataloging-in-Publication Data
Promising practices in 21st century music teacher education / Michele Kaschub and Janice
Smith, editors.
pages cm
Includes bibliographical references and index.
ISBN 978-0-19-938474-7 (alk. paper) — ISBN 978-0-19-938475-4 (alk. paper)
1. Music—Instruction and study.   2. Music—Instruction and study—Technological
innovations.   I. Kaschub, Michele, 1967– editor of compilation.   II. Smith, Janice, 1952–
editor of compilation.
MT1.P792 2014
780.71—dc23
2014003492

9 8 7 6 5 4 3 2 1
Printed in the United States of America
on acid-free paper

CONTENTS

Promising Practices in 21st Century Music Teacher Education

PART I

Current Challenges and New Opportunities

1 }

Music Teacher Education in Transition
Michele Kaschub and Janice Smith

What does it mean to be a music educator in the twenty-first century? This question must be answered from philosophical and sociological perspectives predicated on fluid conceptions of the nature of music, the potentially differing values assigned to that music, and the multitude of ways that humans interact with music in contemporary culture. Further, the changing nature of teaching and learning must be considered in terms of several constructs: (1) the relational structures and the power they have; (2) synchronous and asynchronous temporal organizations; and (3) physical and virtual spatial constructs. The implications of these factors—as well as other influential variables external to the core interactions of the educational enterprise—produce overarching tensions. These tensions will be viewed by some as barricades, and by others as a call to action. Some of the tensions inherent in the evolution of music, musical practices, and teaching and learning in music will be addressed in this chapter and in the early chapters of this book. The remainder of the book will provide models of teacher preparation programs that place these tensions in responsive and constructive balance to advance the definition of "twenty-first-century music educator."

The Changing Nature of Music and Musical Experiences

Humans are music-making creatures. Historical artifacts suggest that the ability to create and respond to music has been an indelible part of what it means to be human. Early musical experiences were completely dependent on live performance. While this remains a special engagement with music still actively sought by many people, twenty-first-century musical experiences are not limited to live performance and are available in multiple auditory and physical contexts.

Although sounds have been mechanically produced for repeated playback since the 1400s, the invention of sound recordings similar to those heard today took place only 140 years ago. The excitement that surrounded the invention of recording technology and the distribution of recordings through radio broadcasts and gramophone ownership led to a new type of musical valuing. In describing the achievement of the gramophone, Hubert (1893) wrote "Bear in mind that these phonograms do not deteriorate by constant use, the same music coming out the hundredth time as perfectly as the first" (p. 153). This evolution in musical engagement certainly allowed for a change in value systems, since listeners could hear the same performance as frequently and as many times as they desired. Within Western classical traditions, the eagerness to hear the latest work by a renowned composer was replaced by the desire to listen to a recording of a work multiple times.

This technology, and the new values accorded to it, had significant impact on fledgling school music programs. In 1893 Hubert posited that "[The phonograph] will become a great teacher of music, as even the phonographic echo of the piano, of singing, or of the orchestral work, will be sufficient to furnish pupils with precise models" (p. 153). The availability of such models has indeed proven to be a beneficial teaching tool, but not one without consequences. In both Hubert's time and current practice, students' desire to hear and work with familiar music has been a powerful factor in student and community expectations, and subsequently in curriculum design.

In addition to broadening the dimension of access to music, the gramophone also altered the interpersonal nature of the musical experience. The performers' ability to nuance interpretation in response to audience reactions ceases to exist when a live performance becomes a recorded performance. Even when the television eventually afforded audiences a visual component within listening experiences, the direct interaction between performer and audience remained absent.

The emergence of real-time performance in technologically shared spaces is beginning to return a degree of direct interaction to the audience-performer relationship. Though physical spaces may be continents apart, acoustic spaces may be shared within the collaborative platform. Further, contemporary practices are moving beyond the audience-performer dichotomy. Some of the most popular technologically shared spaces allow individuals to collaborate in ways that call for them to simultaneously fill not only the roles of listener and performer, but that of creator as well.

The historic changes highlighted above parallel the innovations that currently challenge music education. Previous generations of music educators did not ignore these challenges. Indeed, when given access to new tools, they adapted their curricular offerings. Music appreciation courses exist because these early technological advances made it possible to experience music even when live performance was not readily accessible. What new curricular offerings will twenty-first-century music educators be able to create to make best use of new musics, tools, and practices?

Creating Music

There are multiple opportunities for humans to engage in the creation of music throughout their lifespan. Young children seek to use their voices and easily accessible sounds from within their environment to create music. As children grow into adulthood, their sound choices often shift from what is readily available to that which is socially accepted, expected, and broadly popular. The musical choices and practices adopted at this time typically carry through to adulthood.

Over the past several decades, the proliferation of "accessible sounds" has been unprecedented. From toys imbued with sound-making components to more advanced electronics such as smartphones and tablets, people of all ages now have greater access to more sophisticated sound-making sources than ever before. It is important to note, however, that novice creators of any age may know what products they want to create even though they may not possess the skill set necessary to fully achieve their intentions. The capacities associated with composition, namely feelingful intention, expressivity, and artistic craftsmanship (Kaschub & Smith, 2009), exist in all people to a certain degree. These capacities can be increased in both breadth and depth through interaction with music educators who are prepared and willing to guide their development.

The value of creativity should not be underestimated. Beyond the obvious importance of composition to musical evolution, improvisation, listening, and other forms of generative music-making allow learners to develop a specific set of tools. Creative engagement with music allows students to develop problem finding, solution testing, and evaluative skills which are highly sought by businesses in nearly every sector of the market (Andrew et al., 2010). Most importantly for music education, these skills can lead to significant innovations that impact the evolution of both music and musical experiences.

Performing Music

Creating music is not the only aspect of musical interaction that has experienced rapid change. The nature of performance has expanded as well. While large instrumental and choral ensembles do exist in schools and to some extent in society at large, the vast majority of people do not choose to participate in these types of music-making experiences, either in K–16 schools or beyond them. Performance-oriented musicianship, like many other aspects of contemporary culture, is shifting toward individual activity or perhaps engagements that involve just a few people assembled in informal, social, and often digital contexts.

Given this shift away from music making that requires large numbers of people to gather in spaces where specialized equipment can be housed, emphasis has shifted toward sound-making tools that are highly portable and easy to use in smaller common and domestic spaces. Guitar sales continue to rise (Berk, 2012) while smartphone and tablet applications that can be used to originate or manipulate music grow increasingly popular. These tools foster both user control and autonomy in the musical interaction. They allow users to explicate and illuminate feelingful sound potentials via intentional, personal interpretation. Many more individuals have the means to influence personal and shared musical experience. They can do this by shaping and presenting the connections between sound and feeling through performance on traditional and newer instruments (Väkevä, 2010). However, the capacity for artistic mediation, as well as the ability to imagine and implement artistic interpretations, can often be enhanced with assistance from supportive and musical teachers.

In addition to the changes in tools used to generate music, performance venues also continue to evolve. Concert halls, theaters, stadiums, and the clubs where jazz and popular musicians typically perform once dominated the performance landscape. Now newly emerging "stages" are growing in popularity. Web-distributed performances that can reach audiences all over the world are attracting millions of users. Virtual choirs and orchestras, collaborative music ensembles in disparate locations, and musical flash mobs all have contributed to the evolving and expanding definitions of musical performance and what constitutes a performer.

Listening to Music

While the roles that music fulfills in society have remained somewhat similar, autonomous control of musical interaction has dramatically shifted from collective and shared listening experiences to the engagements of a single listener. Individuals are increasingly able to make choices about how they will use music to suit their interests and needs. The majority of music listening experiences were once planned and programmed by individuals fulfilling particular societal roles, such as ensemble conductors, music directors within religious organizations, radio DJs. Now, individual listeners increasingly experience their choice of music through earbuds. It is this listener who determines what will be heard and the level of attention that will be devoted to the listening experience.

It is important to emphasize that the values brought to the listening experience by these individuals are influenced by cultural and societal values. While some listeners will pursue a passion for preserving music and performance practices grounded in historical conventions, others will be interested in discovering all that is new—even if "new" is relative within a specific genre, style or tradition. In both cases, a mindful educator can help listeners broaden their range of exposure and explore the depths of feelingful capacity found within their personal listening choices. With such guidance, the listener's capacity for artistic audiation[1] will continue to increase as he or she more completely apprehends the principles and elements of music. This allows the person to construct and refine personal musical meanings and values.

It is clear that people have an infinite capacity to create, perform, and listen to music in ways that both respond to and influence music's continuing presence in human culture. These evolutions and changes have significant import for those charged with guiding the development of young learners in contexts that are facing similar evolutions and changes. Therefore, the nature of teaching and learning must be revisited.

The Changing Nature of Teaching and Learning

Music education, in the formal sense, has a far shorter history than that of musical experience. The breadth of human musical engagement has steadily evolved from initial vocalizations and percussive sounds through an ever-increasing range of acoustic and electronic instruments. Musicians have always learned from, copied, and extended the work of other musicians. Beyond school-based music learning opportunities, young musicians often pursue private music lessons, participate in church choirs or community youth ensembles, and join their peers in the formation of other music groups. Through these activities, students develop a broad range of musical skills and habits that may or may not align with formalized music education practices as presented within schools (Jaffurs, 2004; Westerlund, 2006). Indeed, school music has tended to adopt the pervasive "one size fits all, everybody needs to know" model, despite the fact that "one size" rarely "fits all."

For some students, especially those who are not interested in joining and participating in large performing ensembles, other types of interactions with music are often highly valued. The educational and musical needs of these students extend beyond the preparation provided to most music teachers. This tension is increasingly apparent as access to music and ways of learning about music continue to proliferate.

DIVERSE NATURE OF STUDENTS AND SCHOOLS

Another tension within the realm of teaching and learning is the diverse nature of students and the schools they attend. While some rural and private schools have maintained a fairly homogeneous student population, many urban and suburban schools now have students from varying familial, sociocultural, and musical backgrounds. These multiplicities have the potential to expand the types of music and the musical functions that students and others in the community experience. Music educators who value a wide array of musical styles and experiences can find a welcome place in these schools and communities. A demonstrated eagerness to learn and to value musics of different cultural origins should be a prerequisite for a teaching certificate.

Ethnomusicologists have explored the uses and functions of music in various societies. In the mid-twentieth century Alan Merriam wrote about the functions of music in his book *The Anthropology of Music* (1964). His list can still provide guidance for the ways people interact with music. That list includes communication, emotional expression, symbolic representation, aesthetic satisfaction, entertainment, physical response, encouraging conformity to social norms, validating social institutions and religious rituals, contributing to the continuity and stability of culture, and contributing to the integration of society (pp. 209–227). Since there is so much diversity in contemporary American culture, music educators must be prepared to interrogate the issue of whose social norms, whose institutions, and whose cultures are to be privileged in schools. Again, "one size fits all" models of teacher education cannot possibly succeed in preparing teachers to meet the needs of such diverse student bodies.

KEY CONSIDERATIONS IN PREPARATION OF MUSIC TEACHERS

Because teacher education programs cannot possibly address every eventuality that teachers will encounter, prospective teachers need experiences in generating, sharing, and applying new knowledge about teaching and learning in a variety of settings and contexts. These experiences offer a breadth of experience that can serve as a springboard for adapting to newly emerging contexts. Teachers must be prepared to be learning facilitators and must develop the ability to continuously expand their own learning. These skills will allow them to better serve the needs of their students.

Prospective music educators must be prepared to provide learning opportunities tailored to the needs of all students. These include specialized populations who speak limited English or who have conditions that impact the ways in which they learn. In order to do this, pre-service teachers need to be able to identify the key factors that impact the design and implementation of effective opportunities to learn.

Educators must be scholar-practitioners who spare no effort in attempting to understand the needs of all students so that they can effectively nurture the students' musical intelligences and interests. This assumes that pre-service teachers will develop a working knowledge of how to read and interpret the research being done in education broadly and in music education in particular. They must know how to conduct personal research in a variety of contexts for the improvement of instruction. Finally, they need a basic understanding of assessment in music education and how to create valid, reliable assessments for in specific music learning contexts.

Most of the preceding ideas have been discussed in education circles and music education at least since the start of the new millennium. While these ideas are not new, they have not necessarily had widespread acceptance by the music education profession. In many ways, music education has become tradition-bound. Many other aspects of schooling have moved forward toward a more pluralistic, inclusive future. Pockets of innovation in music education have evolved, yet the dominant model in most schools in the United States is still that of the performing ensemble. Even in elementary general music settings, it is often assumed that the students are being prepared for a future in an ensemble, rather than as life-long music makers and consumers. In a world where there is instant access to music and music instruction, preparation as a conductor for an ensemble needs to be a smaller part of what it means to be a future music educator.

What follows is an explication of some of the tensions in the learning environment: (1) the relationships between music teachers and students and the power issues entangled in that relationship; (2) the changing spaces where music education is taking place; (3) the external factors that influence music education, schools, and learning; (4) the need for educational change as juxtaposed with the requirements for licensure; and (5) the need to work within existing school and community structures as changes occur.

RELATIONAL CONSTRUCTS AND POWER WITHIN THE LEARNING ENVIRONMENT

The teacher-leader role that dominates nearly all of education is further amplified in music education by the power historically granted to the conductor as ensemble leader. As a musical authoritarian, the conductor is endowed with the responsibility to be "all knowing" and makes all musical decisions from repertoire selection, to interpretation, to all aspects of performance. Continuing with this model, music educators have naturally emphasized ensemble teaching. This focus on ensembles has enabled music education to maintain a teacher-dominated model well beyond the point where other branches of education have sought to soften the boundaries between teacher and learner.

Teaching practices that place students in more powerful roles where they have the opportunity to influence curriculum and to construct personal meaning have grown steadily since the work of Vygotsky (1978) gained influence in the late 1970s. As the work of constructivist educators broadened in scope and reach, music educators such as Boardman (2001), Greene (1996), and Wiggins (2000, 2004) provided strong arguments for altering the design and implementation of educational experiences. Social nature, shared learning, the autonomy of teachers and students, and the notions of psychological constructivism as written about by Phillips (2000) are highlighted within this body of work.

Given these new and evolving learning contexts, music educators must be prepared to honor individual learning while still maintaining the social interactions and constructs that are necessary for collaborative music making. These constructs include those traditionally required for ensemble-based music making, but applied in broader circumstances. Further, newly evolving contexts for interaction with music make it obligatory for teachers to consider how they might address collaborative learning that occurs in multiple physical spaces. For example, the asynchronous production of music may involve many creators, performers, and listeners who are privy not only to a final product, but to every step of the process from germinal idea to magnum opus.

The definitions of teacher, learner, and learning environment are in constant evolution. While teachers in traditional settings may retain a degree of their role as keepers of knowledge, immense quantities of information are now widely accessible without a teacher. What is less accessible is the knowledge that teachers bring of societal roles and role expectations (Reimer, 2003). Teachers are increasingly facilitators of experience. They manage data and assessments as they collaborate with students, teaching peers, and community members to design, adapt, and arrange curriculum in a manner that creates opportunities for students to engage in entrepreneurial learning.

Entrepreneurial learners are willing to take educational and musical risks in order to further their own learning. They are willing to try new things. The ability to assess a situation, identify problems or potentials, and engage with those challenges and opportunities is the very foundation of knowledge acquisition and meaning making. It is not sufficient for the teacher to identify and solve problems while instructing students to follow along or execute particular musical skills and performances. Entrepreneurial learning requires teachers and students to collaborate as travelers on a shared journey. This journey may take place in a wide variety of spaces.

The Changing Space where Learning Occurs

In addition to reframing the roles of student and teacher in traditional learning contexts as discussed above, technology now makes possible new teaching and learning spaces. Web-based formats allow collaborators to inhabit separate physical spaces as they work in real time. Within these formats, students have ready access to information. Teachers then can provide guidance and support as students experience "need to know" or "ready to learn" moments. Asynchronous spaces with access to websites such as YouTube allow learners to search through millions of how-to videos and seek guidance when questions arise as they engage with any number of topics and activities. This immediate access, which exists outside the formal bounds of schools, creates yet another environment that may hold potential for enhanced learning opportunities. How will future music educators interact in these spaces? More importantly, how will they acquire experience in doing so?

Musicians have traditionally learned from other musicians. While individual lessons were the mainstay of the Western classical tradition, studying with a master performer has been the model in other traditions as well. People are drawn to this manner of learning because music making with others is an intrinsically rewarding activity. Seeking out a more experienced person and working with them to learn something new is likely to continue because of the distinctiveness of that face-to-face human interaction.

There is something special about the experience of being in the same space, at the same time, and sharing meaningful sounds together. Those engaged in such processes often feel them very deeply. Obviously, individual music making can be very satisfying as well. Performers who are often thought of as spending considerable time working alone, such as guitar players and pianists, often find whole new worlds of musical engagement and satisfaction when they collaborate with musicians. Working with other performers, whether face-to-face or virtually, constitutes another type of learning environment.

Schools have not always allowed for this model of individual master/apprentice lessons or chamber music instruction, perhaps because of its cost. These models have existed and continue to exist in communities and spaces outside of school-based music programs. Private music schools, community-based ensembles, and individual private teachers all contribute to this type of learning. In the past ten years, this has taken a new direction as interactive media have begun to allow collaboration in digital spaces.

Beginning with "how to" videotapes and progressing through DVDs, YouTube, and real-time streaming media, musicians have learned from each other without being in the same geographic location. Economic, social, and technological transformations are linking learners and their teachers in unprecedented ways. Collaborative improvising, composing, performing, and sharing of musical creations are all possible. Instant feedback on musical decisions from a number of sources is easily available. However, not all sources of feedback are equally informed and knowledgeable, as anyone can assume the role of the teacher. Consequently, the nature and usefulness of the feedback to the learner can vary widely.

In technologically mediated formats, virtual ensembles can be formed and an impressive array of media may be included. None of this requires a school, a certified teacher, or formal assessment and grading. People can choose to learn what they want to learn, when they want to learn it, and—to a large extent—from whom they wish to learn. This individualization of instruction can lead to very fragmented command of a skill or material. However, it has the possible advantage of being more tailored to the learner's desires, interests, and immediate needs.

There will be increasing convergence between the settings where learning takes place and who determines what will be learned. Students and teachers who succeed will need dispositions that include an openness to change and a desire to continually engage in learning. This particularly applies to teachers who will succeed in their chosen profession. How will future professional educators strike a balance between honoring traditions, connecting to contemporary practices, and encouraging innovative explorations?

EXTERNAL FACTORS INFLUENCING EDUCATIONAL CHANGE

Many veteran teachers bemoan the differences they see in students today, compared with how they remember their students from years ago. Indeed, students are different. As a whole, they are more diverse, technologically aware, collaborative, and possibly more independent. More societal transformation is inevitable. Such change does not go away. However, the students themselves may— if institutionalized education does not evolve. Home-schooling is an increasingly viable option for some. Other learners just put in their time until they can leave school to pursue learning what they want to learn on their own terms.

Unfortunately, students can choose to not learn much of anything beyond that which is already familiar and comfortable. How will they be motivated to learn things that may not be of immediate interest? Should they learn things for which they see no immediate value? How can we help them persist when materials or skills become challenging? What can we learn from gaming and social media that can help with persistence? Finally, what does it mean to be educated?

These and many other questions about education will need to be addressed in the broader arena of general education, as well as the changing context of music education. Some efforts are underway to do exactly that, but there are mitigating external factors that work against the forces for change in the ways and places education takes place. These factors include the political forces, accreditation requirements for teacher education programs and the pressures of preK–12 standards and the current excessive emphasis on standardized testing.

Political Factors

Given that most adults have experienced a dozen or more years of schooling, many feel that they have some expertise on what schooling should be like and what the purpose of schooling is. Agendas from conservative and liberal perspectives feature educational goals that range from abolishing public education to providing higher education for everyone—and everything in between. It has long been fashionable to blame education in general and teachers in particular for the ills of society. Interestingly, though, parents often feel their own children's teachers are doing well at providing an education (Levine & Wagner, 2007). Within music education, teachers are often highly valued by parents and students while being simultaneously marginalized by school administrators and policy makers.

There is little agreement in American society on what the definition of education should be and what it means to be educated. Goals such as national defense, global competition, civic participation, and achieving the American dream all have their political proponents. Every group with a political agenda has touted ways to "fix" education, but few have truly examined the changing nature of learners or where learning best occurs.

Institutions of higher learning are hard pressed to keep pace with the rapid changes taking place in society and in education. The nature of learners, learning environments, and the values that shape personal learning experiences are all in transition. However, there have been some serious attempts made to meet the evolving needs of learners through distance learning, blended classes, online classes, and massive open online courses (MOOCs). Some of the better options have been thoughtfully created by reputable colleges and universities (New, 2013). While these initiatives hint at what might become future best practices, they are still being refined. Unfortunately, there have also been less careful efforts that have served to point out some of the pitfalls of these approaches (Bowan, 2013).

Accreditation

Teacher education programs are typically reviewed at the national, state, and local levels every few years. The best known of these accreditors have been the National Council for Accreditation of Teacher Education (NCATE) and the Teacher Education Accreditation Council (TEAC). These two very powerful accreditors have recently merged to become the Council for the Accreditation of Educator Preparation (CAEP), which holds significant power over institutions in terms of curriculum, faculty, financing, space, support staff, and myriad other factors that impact what people experience as they prepare to enter the field of education.

In addition to CAEP approval, many schools of music also seek accreditation from the National Association of Schools of Music (NASM). They certify a wide range of music programs, including music teacher education programs, and offer a handbook replete with programmatic guidelines. Further, regional accrediting bodies, such as the Middle States Association for Schools and Colleges, weigh in on the requirements for higher education programs, while state and local edicts govern how teachers are prepared in terms of courses taken, tests completed, and classroom teaching experiences.

Change at any of these levels can be exceedingly slow. It is relatively easy to make changes to individual courses, but the requirements imposed by accreditation panels along with those set forth by politicians at state and federal levels sometimes negatively impact the preparation that pre-service music teachers receive. In some circumstances, these changes are implemented without regard for the findings of educational research or the accepted standards of best practice. This is particularly true of educational policies that assume that the arts are the handmaidens of other curricular areas. Professional music educators are increasingly expected to demonstrate how their subject matter addresses the "common core" of learning, how music study improves school test scores and a myriad of other goals that have little to do with music as an art form or means of human self-expression.

Learning Standards and Standardized Testing

Governmentally mandated, standardized testing has replaced competency-based assessments in many educational settings. These tests, usually heavily focused on what students know, give much less attention to what students are able to do—perhaps because knowledge is easier and less expensive to assess than are skills. In a test-dominated educational environment, creativity and individual achievement are quickly forfeited in favor of high test scores. Curriculum has become assessment driven. The requirement to pass tests determines the content that is taught. "Will this be on the test?" is no longer just a question from the students, but from their teachers as well. The students are only part of the equation as they pass (or fail) the tests. This is the antithesis of the promises enumerated above by advancing technologies. The individual interests and proclivities of students are ignored in favor of standardization.

Voluntary standards for preK–12 music education were adopted by the Music Educators National Conference (MENC), now called the National Association for Music Education (NAfME), in the 1990s (MENC, 1994). At that time, there was a push to create standards in all curriculum areas and then to establish benchmarks and assessments. (Standardized national assessment programs were not part of these initiatives.) Individual states, often simply paralleling national models, also generated standards for all curriculum areas. It soon became apparent that these voluntary standards were a wonderful guide, but that there were not enough hours in the day to meet all of the standards in all of the curriculum areas for most students, let alone for all students.

In an attempt to meet the spirit of the standards, many music educators diligently tried to add composition, improvisation, and the other specified areas of music instruction to their curriculums, though little guidance was available as to how to do so. Teacher education institutions also responded by emphasizing the national and state standards. Still, actual curricular change in many preK–12 schools was limited. This was variously seen as due to community performance expectations, scheduling issues, and other more traditional considerations. Many practicing teachers also felt unprepared to teach any music content or skills that went beyond the performing ensemble or the traditional elementary general music curriculum. These issues led to criticism of the standards as unattainable for all but a few exceptional programs, while music teacher education programs were caught in a rift between traditional performance-driven practice and what the standards sought to establish as a future vision.

Music Teacher Education Programs: Admission, Teacher Testing, and Practitioner Assessment

Although it is not the intent of this book to fully examine or offer solutions to the challenges of college music program admission requirements, teacher testing, or practitioner assessment, it is important to note that these issues do exist and do pose significant challenges to the field of music education and teacher education in general. Who is accepted into music education programs varies widely from institution to institution and from state to state. Students can easily shop for the institution that will allow them entry. Still, the bases used for determining who is to be admitted determine where preparation begins. How do we know that prerequisite skills, knowledge, and performance abilities measured in the admission process actually identify the students who will become responsive and innovative twenty-first-century music educators?

ADMISSION TO MUSIC TEACHER EDUCATION PROGRAMS

Admission to schools of music, and by extension music education programs, is often grounded in conservatory models that rely on performance auditions and theory placement exams. Music education faculty may augment these measures with interviews; but more often than not it is the performance audition that determines acceptance. Beyond that, there are the admission requirements of the college or university itself. These policies and procedures restrict access to music programs and prevent learners of diverse musical interests and preferred learning styles from gaining access to formalized music teacher preparation programs. For example, to what extent is mastery of operatic singing a valuable skill in the world of teaching in schools? Similarly, is the ability to play a Beethoven piano sonata a necessary prerequisite for teaching in an elementary general classroom?

Yet students who have other desirable twenty-first-century music skills, such as experience with electronic instruments, experience in gospel choirs (but not classical voice), or extensive performance on electric bass or even electric guitar, often struggle to find a music education program that will admit them. When non-classical musicians are admitted to these programs, they are frequently required to adopt and master a classical instrument or vocal style and follow the curriculum associated with those instruments and practices. Yet these are not the sounds and musical engagements that first drew the student to study music and may not align with the musical passions that the student had hoped to share through the act of teaching others. How can we best facilitate the desire to learn exhibited by these students and enable them to join our profession?

Moreover, built into admissions procedures are biases based on much more subtle qualities, including gender and race. Julia Eklund Koza (2004) has written eloquently on this subject. She writes, "Stringent and restrictive notions of what constitutes musical competence, together with narrow definitions of legitimate musical knowledge, shut out potential teachers from already underrepresented culture groups and are tying the hands of teacher-educators at a time when greater diversity, both perspectival and corporeal, is needed in the music teaching pool" (p. 85). Koza then argues that raising performance "standards restricts admission to those who have had access to private study, and that only certain kinds of music performance are considered acceptable by music schools in academe. This tension between tradition and expanding opportunities for music making is in great need of rebalancing and correction if music teaching is to become more responsive to students.

Once students are admitted, the same issues arise during the course of their programs. Higher education has become increasingly focused on issues of retention, graduation rates, and getting people through programs in four years. This business model proves challenging to music programs because music students typically have to demonstrate skills that are developed over time and with repeated practice. It is often impossible to meet the many requirements for a music education degree, let alone those for licensure, in four years. Yet programs are viewed less favorably when students take longer complete their programs.

The pressure of tracking program completion rates creates additional obstacles. Students who are not financially able to attend full-time or who must work while attending college are seen as less focused or committed to earning a degree. These candidates are less attractive applicants because their longer program trajectories negatively impact completion counts. Similarly, students of diverse or nontraditional backgrounds may be excluded unfairly based on the presumption that they are less equipped for the rigors of academic study. Unfortunately this can lead to a teacher candidate cohort that is predominantly white and upper middle class, who then go to work in schools where the student body is quite different.

As a simple example, how many African American orchestra teachers are there? Similarly, how many women percussionists are in teacher education programs? It is fair to assume that students who do not see themselves as "like their teachers" may not pursue the music instruction being offered by those teachers. The lack of diversity in the pool of music teacher candidates is problematic. Western classical training perpetuates and privileges this bias. Re-visioning teacher education practices must include the ways in which people are admitted to programs, provided with training, and licensed. The changing nature of music teacher certification (or licensure) also poses considerable challenges to curricular evolution.

TEACHER TESTING FOR CERTIFICATION

There has been a significant shift in the requirements for certification of music educators over the past few decades. The former standard, of offering three certificates (commonly K–8 classroom music, 5–12 vocal music, and 5–12 instrumental music) at the state level, has now been replaced. The vast majority, some thirty-eight states at the time of writing, now offer preK–12 certification in music. (Certification requirements for music teachers in each state may be viewed at http://www.ets.org/praxis.) The tensions and challenges outlined above suggest this is no longer appropriate, if indeed it ever was.

Despite this shift in the implied definition of "prepared to teach music," music teacher education programs remain largely the same. Curricular changes are limited to minor course re-visions or occasional course additions to accommodate requirements imposed by accrediting bodies or legislatures. These updates occur in patchwork fashion rather than in a wholesale re-visioning of teacher preparation. Schools of music and music departments have their own traditions and cultures and it is very difficult to convince entrenched interests that change is necessary. These internal debates prove a daunting challenge for even the most passionate music teacher-educator. Indeed, the very nature of institutionalized practice—and the now commonly heard edict to limit program credit hour requirements to the 120 hour bachelors degree—forces adherence to a somewhat rigid and limiting frame.

In addition to the challenges faced by traditional teacher education programs, projected and current teacher shortages have spurred the creation of alternative routes to certification in many states. These routes have not come into being without their own set of internal and external conflicts and negotiated compromises, and arguably not without considerable impact on traditional teacher education programs as well as school music programs (Hellman et al., 2011). The very creation of these alternative programs has called into question what is really required within teacher education programs. What preparation is required to make an excellent music teacher? Certainly this question requires constant attention, but from a purely practical standpoint and regardless of the route to certification, music teacher-educators must remain focused on the foundational components of our profession—music and education—and must continue to prepare teachers who are well versed in the knowledge, skills, and understandings relevant to both halves of our "music educator" title.

Programs that offer minimal training to musicians with performance degrees in an attempt to make them instant teachers do not adequately prepare those performers for the life of a professional educator. Not only is their expertise narrowly defined, but they often lack any concept of how to interact with or inspire young musicians. They may justify the challenges they experience by blaming students for "not wanting to learn". Similarly, they do not have experience with or understand the nature and structure of schools. Further complicating this scenario is the fact that administrators typically lack skill and knowledge required to properly supervise music teaching and programs. While excellence is usually easy to recognize, it is much more difficult for administrators to identify mediocre or poor programs in music and provide the necessary guidance and assistance to bring about needed improvement.

PRACTITIONER ASSESSMENT AND PERFORMANCE EVALUATION

A major purpose of teacher evaluation should be to insure that students are receiving the best possible instruction. It should also be used to support novice teachers, provide constructive feedback for teachers who are continuously seeking to improve their practice, and to affirm the work of teachers who excel. Ideally, the processes of teacher supervision should also facilitate sharing of the expertise teachers develop through their interactions with students.

The assertion by Stronge and Tucker that "without high quality evaluation systems, we cannot know if we have high quality teachers" (2003, p. 3) is somewhat presumptuous. Individuals have always been able to define strong and weak teachers, but they did so through a degree of consensual assessment rather than through broadly adopted prescriptive measures. In recent times, pressure to fully and formally document and report teacher quality has become a key focus of the perennial political debate surrounding educational systems, reforms, and practices. It is no longer acceptable to say someone is a good teacher without being able to quantify why it is so. "Value added teaching," narrowly defined as increased student test scores, is one of the more recent catch phrases in pedagogical assessment.

Teacher evaluation systems should be focused on accountability and improvement. They should consider the professional development of teachers, the mission of schools, and the overarching educational regulations. Such measures usually contribute to the professional development of teachers in ways that influence how students experience school (Stronge, Helm, & Tucker, 1995). They are summative as they seek to determine how teachers, students, and schools compare with identified benchmarks.

However, such benchmarks, often mandated by legislative action, fail to include the measures that educators find most useful: those that are more formative in nature and that emphasize ongoing processes and improvements over time rather than fixed products. Moreover, these benchmarked and aggregated test data provide no feedback on the progress of individual students. Schools are labeled "failing" while students and their teachers are making actual progress.

Music educators are increasingly and unfairly burdened with prescribed summative measures, particularly those that focus on student test scores in the areas of language arts and mathematics (Hamann et al., 2011). These measures are used to determine music teachers' effectiveness though they are not directly involved in offering instruction in those areas. Moreover, music educators are being required to include literacy and numeracy content in their classes. It is not uncommon for prospective teachers to be asked in interviews how they will contribute to raising the school's test scores.

Appropriate assessment tools can contribute to the development of high-quality music education professionals. To achieve this goal, it is important to consider what criteria define high-quality music educators and how those qualities might be documented. Unfortunately, much of the current emphasis in teacher assessment focuses solely on student test scores and ignores the very nature of quality music instruction.

There are some hopeful signs on the horizon, but they are being accompanied by a fair amount of resistance. Pre-service teachers in states where the commercial edTPA program—developed by Stanford University and Pearson Publishing—has been adopted are being required to submit videos of their teaching and written reflections on them. This assessment has specific assignments and rubrics for music.

This holds some promise for valid, reliable, authentic, high-quality assessments for prospective music educators. The process is new enough that it remains to be seen if it will live up to this promise and meet this potential for improving music teacher quality on a broad basis. As with any assessment, the underlying assumptions of what teachers should know and be able to do are key to its validity. Those assumptions have yet to be thoroughly interrogated by the music education profession. Music teacher-educators need to examine whether these commercial licensure systems benefit students, teachers, programs, and larger institutional objectives.

A few basic questions need to be answered:

(1) Do these assessments increase and enhance the educational opportunities and experiences of students—both the college students who take them and the preK–12 students they then proceed to educate?

(2) Do pre-service teachers experience an increase in content and pedagogical knowledge?

(3) Do pre-service teachers become more familiar with teaching methods and materials?

(4) Do pre-service teachers further develop the skills necessary to match instructional techniques to learner needs and to improve teacher-student interactions?

(5) What are the inherent dangers when many states use a single commercial product developed by a company that stands to profit from its adoption? Is it appropriate for teacher education to allow a for-profit entity to codify the expectations for music teacher knowledge, skills, behaviors, and interactions with students? And at what point does the "teach to the test" mentality return to usurp future curricular innovation?

These questions are predicated on assumptions about the criteria for high-quality educational interactions. The questions, and the tests pre-service teachers take, are subject to many of the same tensions that this book delineates.

Assessment of certified teachers soon may be influenced by the models of evaluation used for the licensure pre-service educators. However, this type of assessment process is expensive and time-intensive. Clear answers to the efficacy of the process and its value for improving education are needed. As with much of the material in this book, a balance must be sought between the tensions of the time needed to complete the assessments, their cost, and the benefits to students, teachers, and schools.

TENSIONS IN RESPONSIVE AND CONSTRUCTIVE BALANCE

As we explore curricular adaptations, innovations, and re-inventions, it is important to consider the balance of positive benefits and perhaps negative impacts that such changes may bring about. Yet, there is a need to hold these tensions in responsive and constructive balance rather than to be stymied by the specter of potential obstacles. Central to achieving this critical stance is our ability to consider unity and uniformity, standards and standardization, and diversity of thought and action.

There is a difference between unity, which gives our profession strength, and uniformity, which dampens our ability to respond to evolutions in both music and the ways that people interact with music. In unity, music teacher-educators must strive to provide the best possible preparation for pre-service teachers and the best possible professional development opportunities for practitioners. However, we need not be uniform in our approach to that goal. The broad ideas presented in this book are not intended to fit wholesale within any single music teacher preparation program. They are offered to spark the imagination of music teacher-educators as they create programs tailored to specific contexts, populations, and student needs.

Pursuing a similar vein, it is possible to have standards, and indeed our standards for music teachers must be carefully considered and well designed. However, strict standardization of every component of teacher education is not necessarily the best way to attain the high levels of competence we seek if we intend to embrace the multitude of musics and musical practices now available to our students. Consequently, it is vitally important that music teacher-educators remain deeply involved in the work of the accreditation organizations. Teacher preparation programs across the country should share similar overarching goals while allowing those goals to be achieved through the means appropriate to regional, local, and even institutional circumstances.

Additionally, there is an incredible reserve of creativity, strength, and wisdom to be found within our profession. Our current model of ensemble-dominated music programs does not reflect the breadth of our collective imagination. Music education remains positioned as an inverted triangle, precariously teetering from side to side, invested fully in less than 23 percent of the school population.[2] By calling upon our impressive strengths and innovative capacity, music education can flip this triangle and set it firmly on its base—the broader population. To do this, music teacher education must embrace the breadth of interests, multitude of practices, and ever-present evolutions within music and culture. This will allow music education to create a responsive balance of curricular offerings to meet the needs of our increasingly diverse student population.

Finally, some of the wisdom brought to bear on music teacher education is found in the diverse perspectives, beliefs, and experiences of the authors who have contributed to this book. The thought-provoking models they offer partnered with a reflective readership open to the idea that music teacher education can evolve may provide the impetus the profession needs to move from discussions of current shortcomings into the actions that create the very future of music teacher education. Drawing on the wisdom of those willing to critically examine current practices, embrace new approaches, and share their experiences, this collection offers an approach to music education that honors historical practice, partners seamlessly with contemporary practice, and embraces the notion that further innovations will come.

Notes

1. In our use, the phrase "artistic audiation" signifies a process that extends beyond the ability to recognize and identify rhythms and the keyality of sounds that are not, and may never have been, physically present (Gordon, 1975). The word "artistic" is key in our conception as it denotes the purposeful use and imaginative application of aural skills in the act of meaning making.

2. The National Center for Education Statistics, designating music and performing arts as an "extra-curricular activity," reports that 23 percent of high school seniors participated in a music or performing arts group in 2010. http://nces.ed.gov/programs/coe/indicator_exa.asp. Retrieved February 2, 2013.

References

Andrew, J., Manget, J., Michael, D., Taylor, A., & Zablit, H. (2010). *Innovation 2012.* Boston, MA: Boston Consulting Group.

Berk, B. (2012, April 10). Guitar sales strumming the right chords. *Music & Sound Retailer.* Retrieved from http://www.msretailer.com/msr/guitar-sales-strumming-the-right-chords/.

Boardman, E. (2001). Generating a theory of music instruction. *Music Educators Journal, 88*(2), 45–53.

Bowan, W. L. (2013). The potential for online learning: Promises and pitfalls. *Educause Review, 48*(5). Retrieved from http://www.educause.edu/ero/article/potential-online-learning-promises-and-pitfalls.

Conner, M. L. (2004). Informal learning. 1997–2008. Retrieved from http://marciaconner.com/resources/informal-learning/.

Fruedenthal, H. (1976). Preface. *Educational Studies in Mathematics, 7*(3), 189–190.

Gordon, E. (1975). *Learning theory, patterns, and music.* Buffalo, NY: Tometic Associates.

Green, L. (2002). *How popular musicians learn: A way ahead for music education.* Burlington, VT, and Aldershot, UK: Ashgate.

Green, L. (2008). *Music, informal learning and the school: A new classroom pedagogy.* Burlington, VT, and Aldershot, UK: Ashgate.

Greene, M. (1996). A constructivist perspective on teaching and learning in the arts. In C. Fosnot (Ed.), *Constructivism: Theory, perspectives, and practice* (pp. 120–144). New York: Teachers College Press.

Hamann, K., Orzolek, D., Butler, A., Conway, C., Hash, P., Taggart, C., & Thompson, L. (2011). Music teacher evaluation: The state perspective. Panel presentation at the 2011 Symposium of the Society for Music Teacher Education, University of North Carolina, Greensboro.

Hellman, D. S., Resch, B. J., Aguilar, C. E., McDowell, C., & Artesani, L. (2011). A research agenda for alternative licensure programs in music education. *Journal of Music Teacher Education, 20*(2), 78–88.

Hubert, P. G. (1893, May/October). What the phonograph will do for music and music-lovers. *Scribner's Monthly, 46*, 152–154.

Jaffurs, S. E. (2004). The impact of informal music learning practices in the classroom, or how I learned to teach from a garage band. *International Journal of Music Education, 22*(3), 189–200.

Kaschub, M., & Smith, J. P. (2009). *Minds on music: Composition for creative and critical thinking.* Lanham, MD: Rowman and Littlefield Education.

Koza, J. E. (2010). Listening for whiteness: Hearing racial politics in undergraduate school music. *Landscapes: the Arts, Aesthetics, and Education, 7,* 85–95.

Levine, P., & Wagner, M. (2007). Parents' perceptions of students' school, teachers, and school programs. Retrieved from http://www.seels.net/designdocs/wlw2/SEELS_W1W2_chap7.pdf.

Merriam, A. P. (1964). *The anthropology of music.* Evanston, IL: Northwestern University Press.

Music Educators National Conference (MENC). (1994). *The school music program: A new vision.* Reston, VA: R & L Education and the National Association for Music Education.

New, J. (2013, February 4). MOOCs and tablet computing are top tech trends in 'Horizon Report.' *Chronicle of Higher Education.* Retrieved from http://chronicle.com/blogs/wiredcampus/moocs-and-tablet-computing-are-top-tech-trends-in-horizon-report/42143.

Phillips, D. (Ed.). (2000). *Constructivism in education.* Chicago: University of Chicago Press.

Reimer, B. (2003). *A philosophy of music education: Advancing the vision* (3rd ed.). Englewood, NJ: Prentice-Hall.

Stronge, J. H., & Tucker, P. D. (2003). *Handbook on teacher evaluation: Assessing and improving performance.* Larchmont, NY: Eye On Education.

Stronge, J. H., Helm, V. M., & Tucker, P. D. (1995). *Evaluation handbook for professional support personnel.* Kalamazoo: Center for Research on Educational Accountability and Teacher Evaluation, Western Michigan University.

Väkevä, L. (2010). Garage band or GarageBand®? Remixing musical futures. *British Journal of Music Education, 27*(1), 59–70.

Vygotsky, L. S. (1978). *Mind in society: The development of higher psychological processes* (M. Cole, V. John-Steiner, S. Scribner, & E. Souberman, Eds.). Cambridge, MA: Harvard University Press.

Westerlund, H. (2006). Garage rock bands: A future model for developing musical expertise? *International Journal of Music Education, 24*(2), 119–125.

Wiggins, J. (2000). *Teaching for musical understanding.* New York: McGraw-Hill.

Wiggins, J. (2004). Letting go—Moving forward. *Mountain Lake Reader, 3,* 81–91.

2 }

Considering both Curriculum and Pedagogy
David A. Williams

The University of South Florida (USF) is a large, public university in Tampa that enrolls slightly fewer than 48,000 students. The School of Music at USF has historically offered quite traditional undergraduate and graduate programs, including degrees in performance, education, and composition. The school serves roughly 350 undergraduate majors and another 150 graduate majors. About half of the undergraduates consider themselves to be music education students, and there are normally about forty music education graduate students in masters and doctoral programs.

Before our recent curricular changes, the undergraduate music education program looked very similar to programs at most other institutions in the United States. Pre-service teachers experienced a music curriculum of approximately fifty credit hours that included seven semesters of private instruction on their primary instrument and concurrent participation in appropriate large ensembles, a standard four-semester sequence of music theory, three semesters of music history and literature, covering a wide span of Western European musical practice, four semesters of class piano, and a basic conducting course.

In addition, students took a typical sequence of music education courses including an introduction class, instrumental, choral, and elementary methods and techniques courses, and a full semester of student teaching experience. The state of Florida also requires a variety of courses for all education majors in order to qualify for state certification. Almost annual changes occur to this list of required course work from the state, but generally twelve to fifteen credit hours are required in areas such as teaching diverse populations, educational technology, competencies and strategies for English speakers of other languages, and the teaching of reading and literacy skills. It is most common for specific courses to be required in order to satisfy these requirements. There is generally little or no opportunity for music courses to be substituted.

Along with general education course requirements for all university students, the total number of credit hours for the undergraduate music education

25

degree program has fluctuated between 130 and 134. With the exception of a few select degrees, all undergraduate programs in Florida state colleges and universities are limited to no more than 120 credit hours. Music education programs are allowed 134 credit hours.

The USF undergraduate music education program produced graduates prepared to teach the typical band, choral, and orchestra programs, as well as standard general music classes. For some time, however, there had been a very strong feeling among the music education faculty that we needed to better prepare our students for the musical realities they would face in twenty-first-century schools. As part of existing coursework, we did our best to lead discussions and devote class time to exploring possibilities that went beyond the traditional ensembles and classes, but it simply was inadequate.

Planning for Change

It became apparent to our music education faculty that without considerable opportunities to practice newer, unfamiliar teaching models, very few students would leave our program with much interest in modifying their approach to preK–12 music, let alone have the confidence and ability necessary to do so. In order to provide significant opportunities to practice alternative music methods, it was essential that we make curricular changes. There was a strong sense that something substantial had to happen in order to make significant lasting changes in the skills and dispositions of our students.

As is probably true of most teacher preparation programs, almost all our students shared some common experiences. First, they came mostly from successful, traditional music programs. They personally enjoyed these programs and flourished in them. More often than not, they had decided to major in music education in large part because of their desire to bring this same enjoyment to others. Second, they seemed uninterested in the large mass of students who were not part of the music programs at schools from which they came. They were oblivious of the musical needs of these students. Music education students had never contemplated why these contemporaries of theirs were not participating in school music programs. They also seemed unaware that most high school students simply were not interested in "serious" musical involvement. Rarely, if ever, had our students considered the limitations of the program offerings as the deterrent to participation.

RATIONALE

With all this as a backdrop, the music education faculty spent the better part of two years discussing, considering, and planning for curricular change. All of our decisions were made with an understanding of two parameters we faced: (1) no additional hours could be added to the curriculum without the elimination of something that already existed; and (2) any proposed changes would have to be approved by a vote of the full School of Music faculty. We knew that the elimination of any aspect of existing curriculum was certainly going to be troubling and potentially divisive for some segment of the faculty.

As we considered the possibilities of curricular change, we realized that we were actually interested in more than just curriculum. We came to feel that the most significant change we might make was helping our students to understand and practice new pedagogical models—pedagogies that we felt could be used with almost any music curriculum. So our focus became twofold: (1) to develop a new curriculum that would help our students become competent and confident as they worked with a broader conception of musicianship than that with which they were familiar; and (2) to provide time for students to practice pedagogies that were significantly different than the traditional large ensemble model.

Before going into the details of our new curriculum, it is important to consider why we took two years for the planning stage. We recognized that what we were doing was going to be seen as radical and controversial by our rather conservative music faculty. Because of this, we purposely proceeded slowly and made sure to not only consider change, but to also develop a research-supported, philosophical rationale for everything were going to suggest.

ALLIANCES

We also spent time talking with carefully selected music faculty members, both alone and in small groups, to introduce them to our work. We were trying to create allies and build support for change. We learned something very important by doing this. While we worked hard to remain focused on the broad outlines of curricular change, individual faculty outside of music education were more apt to pinpoint any curricular aspect that directly affected the area in which they taught. As an example, ensemble conductors paid little attention to proposed changes in music theory, but they had strong opinions concerning any proposal related to ensemble participation by music education students. Interestingly, conductors did not raise any objections to the addition of specialized ensembles for music education majors as long as the addition would not affect participation requirements for traditional ensembles. A cynical person might think these members of faculty were more interested in protecting their course enrollments than in what might be best for students. Regardless, faculty tunnel-vision was a reality with which we had to cope.

We also enlisted input from several preK–12 music supervisors in our immediate area who historically had hired a significant number of our graduates. The input of these supervisors was invaluable because they responded to our ideas and made further suggestions. In contrast to many of our university colleagues, every aspect of our proposals was of interest to them. We made several adjustments to our plans because of input we received.

Four Elements of the Original Proposal

REPEATED PRACTICE

The first proposal we brought to the School of Music faculty reflected four important factors. First, we wanted to not only expose students to new and different ways of thinking about musical possibilities for preK–12 schools, but to also provide them with significant experiences to practice working with them. We wanted to remove the blinders from students' eyes. They came to us focused only on band, choir, and/or orchestral settings. We knew our students should see additional possibilities, and feel a level of proficiency with courses involving instruments and musical styles outside the traditional ensembles. This would require positive experiences with instruments such as acoustic and electric guitars, with an assortment of digital devices, and with a variety of instruments from other cultures. Additionally they needed a familiarity with the musical styles that made use of these instruments. This demanded the use of, and familiarity with, a variety of popular music styles.

The necessary element of repeated practice by the students with new curricular concepts was a strong part of our proposal. We took our cue from traditional curriculum where students experience methods and techniques in classes and then participate in repeated opportunities to practice those methods through both ensemble participation and practicum experiences. It is this sustained practice that enables students to build the essential skills that help them confidently approach their first year as a teacher of an ensemble.

These types of repeated experiences are doubly important for students when they are with musical practices in which they have not previously participated.

For example, a student who has never engaged in a hip-hop group would no doubt find it difficult teaching a class devoted to hip-hop performance. A one-time assignment devoted to this genre would probably not be sufficient for most students to build enough competence. Students require repeated opportunities to practice concepts and situations, with which they have had little previous background.

DIGITAL MEDIA

Second, we felt it important that students become knowledgeable about— and proficient with—as much electronic and digital music technology as possible. New musical devices and new ways to make music have completely changed the music industry and most popular forms of music making. It is exceedingly detrimental to students to continue to ignore this reality in college music classes.

However, it is also a mistake to assume that students know more about music technology than we do, or that they will figure it out on their own. The exciting thing about technology is how quickly it develops and changes. The frustrating thing about technology, of course, is how quickly it develops and changes. Students need our help to find their way through the multiple possibilities of musicianship development made possible with new technologies. At the same time, we knew that learning how to learn to use new devices and applications should be the focus. Flexibility and adaptability are essential skills when dealing with ever-changing technologies.

We became convinced that a sufficient level of mastery was not possible from a single, separate music technology class. Instead, we decided to infuse music making through technology into as many classes as possible. Again, this was to provide many opportunities to build competence and skill.

CONCEPTIONS OF MUSICIANSHIP

Third, we wanted to broaden our students' conceptions and definitions of musicianship. Nearly all of our students came to us with years of musicianship built up in a specific, time-honored way. This is the Western European orchestra model, based on group performance and individual practice. When they were asked what was required to be considered a musician, student responses would involve "performance ability"—especially performance based in that particular stylistic practice.

This belief was amazingly strong. For example, when presented with the question of rock performers as musicians, responses would often include sarcasm and cynicism, sometimes reluctantly concluding that rockers were "kind of like" musicians, but often lacking knowledge required of real musicians, which they defined as the ability to read musical notation, and significant understanding of music theory. When the names of popular musicians who also had classical music training were brought into the discussion (such as Rick Wakeman or Keith Emerson) students generally agreed this training would qualify them as real musicians.

Broadening this view is surprisingly difficult for most students. It is, after all, the view espoused by many ensemble directors and private instructors with which these students work closely and for whom there is a vested interest in preserving their hegemony firmly rooted in historic practices.

Composition and Improvisation

In trying to broaden this conception of musicianship we focused on three particular features. The first involved the creative aspects of musicality—especially composition and improvisation. We felt that ongoing and systematic experiences with musicianship concentrating on creativity were necessary, to expose students to new and different ways of thinking about musical possibilities for preK–12 students, and that they would build essential skills that would help them confidently approach their first year as a teacher.

Aural Transmission

The second feature emphasized aural transmission. While musicianship as traditionally practiced in music education stresses notational skills, the greater majority of musics in the world are aurally based and seldom rely on the traditional form of Western music notation with which our students are so familiar. Understanding music from an aural basis is important if students are to experience an expanded sense of musicianship. Playing by ear has often been disparaged in the conservatory model of music education; yet it requires true musical skill and competence. Our dependence on notation systems should be a source of embarrassment for the profession. Instead, only jazz musicians have been required to create in the absence of notation. Classical performers were often required to memorize a score for performance but not to create in the absence of notation.

Most popular musics, folk musics, and World musics emphasize other aspects of the musical experience, including movement, dancing, lighting, visual effects, socializing, interaction between musicians and between the audience and the musicians.

Social Background

This third feature of broader musicianship involved focusing attention beyond the acoustic properties of performance to its social and cultural aspects. The Western European model that we traditionally practice in music teacher education programs places almost exclusive attention on the production of sound. Merit is measured solely on the quality and accuracy of sound produced by the performer. This is rarely true in other musical settings.

PEDAGOGY

The final factor associated with our first proposal had to do with pedagogy. As mentioned above, we felt it was important to help our students learn and employ pedagogies that were significantly different from that of the traditional large ensemble model. There was a clear consensus among the music education faculty that pedagogical changes were at least as important as curricular changes when we looked ahead to what our students would need as they moved on to teaching positions.

Much of our thinking about pedagogy was guided by the work of Lucy Green (2008), material on constructivist learning theories (Bruner, 1977; Piaget, 1970; Dewey, 1998), and from previous research involving established practices in other countries (examples include, Byrne & Sheridan, 2000; Finney & Philpott, 2010; Folkestad, 2006; Georgii-Hemming & Westvall, 2010; Hallam, 2005; Karlsen, 2010; Price, 2005, 2006; Wright & Kanellopoulos, 2010).

We wanted to include aspects of informal teaching and learning, and student-centered learning, that involve high degrees of student autonomy over such things as music choice and instruments. We also wanted them to experience authentic learning and performance practices taken from vernacular musics in the United States and around the world. This would require learning music by ear and aural-based compositional practices in small groups. Our interest was to provide students with other pedagogical models and repeated opportunities to practice those models.

It is important to note that our intent was not to replace traditional methods and pedagogies, but instead to augment these with new experiences for our students. While much has been written recently concerning the possibility that some of our traditional methods might be outdated (Bartel, 2004; Kratus, 2007; Williams, 2011), we were not yet at a point where we were ready to dismiss these altogether. Instead of eliminating them, we made decisions that would reduce study in some of traditional areas in order to make room for new experiences. Again we were interested in opening our students' minds to additional possibilities for music education programs and in providing them with repeated opportunities to practice with models involving electronic and digital technologies, broader concepts of musicianship, and different pedagogical approaches.

The Specifics of Our Proposal

Our initial proposal to the School of Music faculty began with the following "background" information, which some may find useful when proposing their own curricular changes:

> Through a several decades-long process examining the status and aims of music education in the schools, we realize that we must enact changes in our undergraduate curriculum to address the changing needs for musical understanding in American public school students.

We acknowledge that music-making has changed more dramatically than our prevailing instructional methods reflect. Recent research suggests approximately 90% of students presently do not participate in secondary school music programs.

We continue to be, first and foremost, concerned with achieving the highest levels of musicality, and in order to build on that which is well-represented in our current curriculum we accept that we must focus on increasing skills, knowledge and understanding in the following three areas:

- Composition and improvisation abilities, as well as requisite aural skills.
- World musics and the American music traditions.
- Technologies and its uses in current music making and music teaching models.

These areas have been identified by NASM as well as our professional organization, National Association for Music Education, as areas in which teacher education programs can be improved and expanded. We intend to join others in leading change in our profession. Thus, we propose the following changes to our curriculum, which our music education faculty has spent over a year refining.

We then proposed the following additions, deletions and changes to the existing music education curriculum:

Proposed additions:

Three-semester sequence of progressive music education methods
Three-semester sequence of creative performance chamber
   ensemble
An American roots music history course
Elective hours to program (none had existed previously)

Proposed deletions:

Three semesters of major ensemble
Three semesters of primary instrument applied
Fourth semester of music theory sequence
One semester of current Western European music history sequence
Music education forum (catch-all class before student teaching)
One semester of general music methods

Proposed changes:

World drumming section added to current percussion techniques
   course

Reduced theoretical bases in "Intro to music ed" course, replaced
with grounding in progressive methods

This provoked heated exchanges at the faculty meeting where it was proposed. As would be expected, most faculty retreated into camps and formed alliances to protect their academic areas. The ensemble directors defended ensemble requirements. Studio teachers argued for applied lessons. Music theory and music history faculty criticized changes in their areas. All of these arguments were predicated on the claim to know "what is best for the students." None actually admitted that their area might not be vitally important to future teachers.

However, there were some faculty members interested in our justifications for the proposal as a whole. For example, there was a noticeable reaction to the data concerning high school music class enrollment. We had data from our "home" county (Hillsborough County), which is one of the ten largest school districts in the United States. It showed that only 8.8 percent of high school students were enrolled in band, choir, and orchestra classes. The data for neighboring counties revealed about a 5 percent enrollment in these ensembles. Some faculty questioned the accuracy of our figures, but the point was not lost on anyone. A low percentage of students take ensemble classes.

It was nearly a semester following this first meeting before our proposal came to a vote. During that time many small group meetings took place and a lot of discussion ensued. For perhaps the first time, issues faced by music education faculty and music education students were at the forefront of discussions with colleagues The long-term good that has resulted is substantial. There is a much greater understanding of what music education students must know and be able to do in order to flourish in their chosen careers. There is also a greater understanding of the external curriculum requirements that constrain our offerings in music education and how all aspects of the music curriculum impact other areas.

As a result of this time and dialogue, our proposal was revised. While it took two votes, it was eventually passed by the School of Music faculty. The accepted proposal contained the following changes:

Adapted additions:

Two-semester sequence of progressive music education methods
(down from three)
Two-semester sequence of creative performance chamber ensemble
(down from three)
An American roots music history course (history of blues and rock)
Six elective hours to program (none had existed previously)

Adapted deletions:

One semester of major ensemble (proposed three the first time)
One semester of primary instrument applied (proposed three the
   first time)
Fourth semester of music theory sequence
Music education forum (catch-all class before student teaching)
One semester of general music methods

Adapted changes:

Reduced theoretical bases in "Intro to music ed" course, replaced
   with grounding in progressive methods
Reworked music history sequence
Reduced the credit-hour requirement for student teaching (this was
   not a reduction in experience for students—only in credit hours,
   which ironically helped student teaching qualify as a university
   exit course)

By seeking reductions in certain requirements, namely major ensembles, applied lessons and music theory, the music education faculty were not suggesting that these experiences were unimportant for future teachers. However, we did argue that we needed to make decisions based on what would best enable pre-service music teachers to find success, especially given the reality of credit-hour restrictions. We all knew decisions concerning priorities needed to be made. This went well beyond ensembles and lessons. We could have made a very long list of courses and experiences that would be valuable for music education students. However, only so much can be done within the undergraduate framework time constraints.

One point worth highlighting here is that we took the position that we were the best qualified to make judgments regarding the needs of pre-service music educators. We based our decisions on research, discussions with practicing music educators, and much thought and discussion among ourselves. We were taking a broad view of a total curriculum and not just the perspective of specific content areas such as theory and private instruction—or even music education. We emphasized to other faculty in our discussions with them that, after weighing all the variables, we were presenting the most reasonable and supportable approach to curriculum reform at this time. We also stressed that this "time" was different from when traditional music education curriculums were founded and it was an injustice to continue to train future music teachers as if our culture and our students needs had remained unchanged.

Progressive Music Education Methods Classes

Our most significant curricular changes were the addition of two semesters of a course we call "Progressive music education methods," and of two semesters of a related ensemble named "Creative performance chamber ensemble." Students are required to take the corresponding level of these concurrently. We went through several name changes for the ensemble aspect of this curricular tandem before settling on a name that included the terms "performance" and "chamber." The final name, while long, was in part a political move. Adding a course that involved "chamber music performance" was hardly questioned at all by our performance faculty. In fact, we received kudos for our interest in chamber music. Of course, what most faculty think of as chamber music really was not what we intended to add, but the name turned out to be a real ally in getting the curriculum approved. Small changes in names can sometimes make a notable difference in people's perceptions.

The following is the course description for the first-level progressive methods course:

> This course will provide students a grounding in methods for music education settings outside the traditional general, band, choir and string programs. The course is intended to challenge students to engage in two modes of music learning that differ from notation based instruction. These two modes are systematic aural transmission and informal learning, which together form the way most popular musicians acquire their performing and musicianship skills. This methodology is based on partnerships of students, shared responsibilities among student-centered groups, and acknowledgement by the classroom teacher for respect and value of students' pre-existing interests, abilities, and preferences. In particular, student preference and knowledge become the primary starting points from which students expand outwards into different musical styles, genres and cultures. Topics may vary from semester to semester as new possibilities of music methods materialize. Potential topics include concepts of informal learning principles in music, development of creativity in music, theoretical principles of popular musics, computer and digital music technology, sound engineering and recording, multiple-arts approaches, and sound amplification. The course will include a combination of lecture, discussion, modeling, and "hands-on" activities such as singing, playing instruments, and moving. The course will also include several practicum sessions and activities with area preK–12 schools. Students should wear clothing that is comfortable and allows freedom of movement. Additionally, some class sessions will include visiting artists and musicians.

The second level of the progressive methods course continues the same activities, which allows students significant time to experience all the various possibilities. This includes playing acoustic and electric guitar, electric bass guitar, electronic keyboards, acoustic and electric drum kit performance, vocals, iPad music-making, DJing, songwriting, beat making, looping, recording, and editing. In these methods classes students learn fundamental and advanced techniques that they then put into practice in the chamber performance ensemble classes. Student groups have now presented both formal and impromptu performances in a variety of settings both on and off campus.

In these new methods and ensemble courses students are free to delve into any musical style that interests them, so long as they learn through aural copying and also by creating original material. The range and choice of styles have been broad. It is important to note that both the new methods and the ensemble courses are now situated in a different pedagogy that extends beyond the content of the curriculum. The same pedagogical approach can be used to investigate music from any style (including classical music) and could involve any musical instruments. At times students have chosen to include traditional wind and string instruments in their music making. For example, one collaboratively created piece made use of an electronic drum kit, an electronic keyboard, iPad, bass guitar, cello, bass recorder, flute, tambourine, and vocals. It also included costuming, acting, dance, and storytelling.

Another interesting aspect of this new pedagogy is that students are not identified as a performer of a particular instrument. Instead, students gain experience with a variety of musical roles and will sometime perform on multiple instruments in one piece of music. Every student becomes a composer, arranger, multi-instrument performer, vocalist, producer, recorder, mixer, and editor. Some find particular satisfaction in roles they had never before experienced. Consequently this strengthens and broadens their personal identity as musicians.

While this pedagogy is focused on these new courses and ensembles, it is also finding its way into some of our more traditional music education courses. Our winds techniques courses, for example, now involve a good deal of student autonomy. The students in this class now work in collaborative small group settings, create original compositions, and engage in aural copying.

Changes in Other Music Education Classes

Our other significant curricular change provided a two course broadening of traditional music education themes. The first is our reworked introduction to music education course. We moved this from a sophomore level class to a freshmen class. Now most students interested in music education get this course in their first year at USF. We refocused the course to emphasize the importance of change for the profession. The course also provides an overview of curricular offerings and pedagogical approaches these students will experience later in the new pedagogy classes and ensembles.

As is typical in introductory music education classes, a large amount of class time also is spent sampling the settings that will be visited later in great detail. We do this primarily through video conferencing technologies such as GoToMeeting, which allows us to visit a wide range of music classes. This includes those where students can see atypical music classes in action. This is where we begin to broaden our students' conceptions toward a more progressive look at music education. We ask them to begin considering the possibilities for curricular expansion in preK–12 schools.

This introductory course is closely followed by the Blues and Rock History class. In this course the students learn the historical and social background for today's popular music. It is perhaps a little disconcerting to find how little students know about the music to which they regularly listen. They are often surprised to find there are historical antecedents and evolutions that led directly to current trends and favorites. These two courses serve as the foundation for the Progressive Methods and Creative Ensemble course sequence.

There were more changes to make and more improvements to achieve. We have recently been fortunate to have student teaching certified as an exit course by the university. This has freed up additional credit hours for our program so we are now working toward adding a three-semester sequence of preK–12 onsite teaching experiences for our students before their student teaching semester. Our goal is to get music education majors working with preK–12 students on a weekly basis over an extended number of semesters. Some of these will occur before the existing practicum experiences associated with the various methods classes. They do not replace these practica but are in addition to them.

Another area in which we find we need to reconceive the skills needed by music education students is that of piano keyboard competency. We have conceived separate piano skills courses specifically for music education students. These courses are designed to replace the traditional keyboard skills courses that our students had taken with other music majors. The new sequence of keyboard skills courses includes the following:

- reading and playing chord sheets,
- using the keyboard in songwriting,
- creating accompaniments,
- improvisation from lead sheets,
- using the keyboard as a MIDI controller,
- recording and editing accompaniments for student performance,
- using a MIDI keyboard as a performance synthesizer,

- jazz and pop harmony,
- blues progressions,
- comping, and
- reading and transposing changes.

We feel these are skills all music students might need in their professional lives, but at this point they are being considered only for music education students. Change comes slowly to conservatory training.

Considering Admission Procedures

In the near future, we also want to address issues associated with the admission of students into our music education program. As is true at many institutions, admission to the School of Music is primarily the purview of performance faculty and ensemble directors. This may be the most important change we could make at our institution. We are convinced there are high school students that would potentially make outstanding music teachers that either do not consider music education as a career or are not admissible to the School of Music for a variety of reasons. These reasons usually include a lack of classical performance background and a lack skill with typical music notation. This is a complex issue that will no doubt take much time and negotiation. However, having the ability to admit students who already possess exceptional musical ears and skills with non-classical music making might help the music education profession connect with the large numbers of secondary school students who presently do not enroll in school music programs.

The task of developing the undergraduate curriculum is never finished and we continue to revise and refine ours. The process of curriculum change at USF has been a long, and not always enjoyable, experience. It can be very stressful. However, the improvements in our program have been worth the effort. We already see changes in the skills and dispositions of our students. We are optimistic that they will be able to effect meaningful change in the preK–12 settings where they will be employed and to reach larger percentages of secondary students by gradually implementing exciting new classes. Change is always incremental, but what better place to begin than with the next generation of teachers.

References

Bartel, L. (2004). *Questioning the music education paradigm*. Research to practice: A biennial series, Vol. 2. Toronto: Canadian Music Educators Association.

Bruner, J. (1977). *The process of education*. Cambridge, MA: Harvard University Press.

Byrne, C., & Sheridan, M. (2000). The long and winding road: the story of rock music in Scottish schools. *International Journal of Music Education, 36*, 46–58.

Dewey, J. (1998). *Experience and education* (60th anniversary ed.). Indianapolis, IN: Kappa Delta Pi.

Finney, J., & Philpott, C. (2010). Informal learning and meta-pedagogy in initial teacher education in England. *British Journal of Music Education, 27*(1), 7–19.

Folkestad, G. (2006). Formal and informal learning situations or practices versus formal and informal ways of hearing. *British Journal of Music Education, 23*(2), 135–145.

Georgii-Hemming, E., & Westvall, M. (2010). Music education—a personal matter? Examining the current discourses of music education in Sweden. *British Journal of Music Education, 27*(1), 21–33.

Green, L. (2008). *Music, informal learning and the school: A new classroom pedagogy.* Burlington, VT, and Aldershot, UK: Ashgate.

Hallam, S. (2005). *Survey of musical futures.* A report from the Institute of Education, University of London for the Paul Hamlyn Foundation.

Karlsen, S. (2010). BoomTown Music Education and the need for authenticity—informal learning put into practice in Swedish post-compulsory music education. *British Journal of Music Education, 27*(1), 35–46.

Kratus, J. (2007). Music education at the tipping point. *Music Educators Journal, 94*(2), 42–48.

Piaget, J. (1970). *Science of education and psychology of the child.* New York: Oxford University Press.

Price, D. (2005). *Musical futures: An emerging vision.* London: Paul Hamlyn Foundation. Retrieved from www.musicalfutures.org.

Price, D. (2006). *Supporting young musicians and coordinating musical pathways.* London: Paul Hamlyn Foundation.

Williams, D. A. (2011). The elephant in the room. *Music Educators Journal, 98*(1), 51–57.

Wright, R., & Kanellopoulos, P. (2010). Informal music learning, improvisation and teacher education. *British Journal of Music Education, 27*(1), 71–87.

3 }

Starbucks Doesn't Sell Hot Cross Buns

EMBRACING NEW PRIORITIES FOR PRE-SERVICE
MUSIC TEACHER PREPARATION PROGRAMS

Frank Abrahams

In this chapter, I propose a re-visioning of music teacher education that challenges views of music teaching and music learning. Preparing twenty-first-century pre-service music teachers to engage children in music-making experiences in schools requires new notions of what music teachers should know and understand, as well as a reconceptualized view of musical literacy. For example, what constitutes musical literacy for the child whose music is delivered from a cell phone through a pair of earbuds? What are the musical understandings children need to select music and organize it into categories called playlists? Rarely, if ever, do those playlists center on the traditions of musical form, meter, key, and instrumentation. Is this traditional information still important to teach pre-service music teachers, or might we assume they can access it on their laptops, tablets, or smartphones should they need to do so?

It is time to rethink the music teacher preparation programs that privilege historical icons of the music education canon as well as music and musical experiences that children in schools perceive as irrelevant to their lives and their communities. The reality is that Starbucks doesn't sell hot cross buns. Many children sing or play a song about them, but do not know what they actually are. Instead, they know about lattes, rainbow (M&Ms) cookies, mixing ice creams at the neighborhood creamery, and snacking on Lunchables. They live in a world rich with computers, videogames, digital music players, and cell phones. Children text, tweet, instant message, Skype, and have a wide circle of friends on social networking sites. They bypass cable TV and watch television on their own schedule freely streamed from the Internet onto their laptops. Children routinely post and view self-produced video clips on YouTube. Ten years ago, college students took classes in technology to learn how to create a *PowerPoint* presentation, to cut and paste text, or to notate a musical composition on Finale. Now, they make those presentations for their professors. Today, college students may take classes online where they can learn at their own pace, on their own time, and in their own physical space. As a result, students think and processes information in ways that are fundamentally different from those who are teaching them. Coursework and experiences should therefore provide pre-service music teacher candidates with behaviors, enduring understandings, and the opportunity to develop a critical consciousness. These are the tools they will need to ensure that their own students will have rich, creative, and fulfilling musical lives now and in the future.

Three Stories

ASHANTE: A STUDENT TEACHER

Ashante had been student teaching in a high school band program for nine weeks. During her semester at the school, she worked with a cooperating teacher who had built the program from a handful of students to an impressive wind ensemble that performs challenging literature. At this particular school, student teachers are observed once by an administrator, and in Ashante's case the school principal was scheduled to visit Wednesday morning's rehearsal. Ashante planned a rehearsal that was typical of those she and her cooperating teacher led each day. To begin, she asked the students to tune. As soon as they took their seats, the students played a bit by themselves to warm-up, much in the way professional orchestral musicians do when they enter the stage for a concert. After a few moments, Ashante asked the first-chair clarinet player to sound a concert B-flat on her smartphone, and the band tuned. In the middle of the first piece, an alto saxophone player asked about a fingering. "Look it up on your phone," Ashante said. The player did, and found the fingering chart on the web. It was just the information he needed. This was routine for Ashante. She believed that students had the technology in their phones to tune and to find a fingering. For this particular observation, Ashante had invited the composer of one of the pieces the band was learning to visit the rehearsal on Skype, speak to the students about the piece, and critique their performance. Unfortunately, the school blocked Skype on the school computers, so Ashante used her own laptop to project the composer's visit onto the screen in the front of the rehearsal room. The session with the composer lasted thirty minutes of the 120-minute rehearsal. Students asked wonderful questions of the composer. At the end, Ashante moved the students into groups of like instruments and challenged them to reflect on the composer's comments and to come up with ways that they might incorporate the composer's suggestions into their own performance and the performance of their section. The students had insightful comments and terrific ideas to share. Ashante tried several student ideas with the band at the end, and most agreed that the performance was improved. At the conclusion of the rehearsal, Ashante asked students to email her a blog reflection on the rehearsal, instructing them to comment on what they had learned and how they would apply the learning in future rehearsals.

In the post-observation conference, Ashante was severely reprimanded, as was the cooperating teacher, by the principal. You see, Ashante broke all the rules. Students were not permitted to use mobile phones in school. Teachers were not permitted to use their personal computers inside the school building. Skype was a banned site. A negative letter was sent to Ashante's college supervisor, and the principal requested that Ashante be transferred to an elementary position to finish her student teaching block.

JOEL: A JUNIOR MUSIC EDUCATION MAJOR

Joel was a junior music education major. He was one of the more popular and active students on campus. He played the leading role in the fall musical, sang in one of the auditioned choirs on campus, and was a member of the college chapter of Phi Mu Alpha Sinfonia, the professional music fraternity. For the collegiate National Association for Music Education (NAfME) chapter, he was the group photographer. Last spring, as a sophomore, Joel worked as a substitute music teacher in a school for children with language learning challenges. Joel's assignment was to teach the school drum circle. Although his applied concentration at college was voice, Joel had played percussion in high school. He had also taken a week-long workshop in Afro-Brazilian drumming the summer before and was anxious to share what he knew with his students. Watching him teach was a joy. He was a natural with the children, and they loved drum circle because of his care for them and his enthusiasm for world drumming.

This semester, Joel enrolled in a choral methods course. For Monday night, his assignment was to present a warm-up to his classmates at the beginning of class. Joel had sung in the college choirs for two years—ensembles steeped in the Western choral tradition—and had studied classical voice, singing lieder by Schubert, sixteenth- and seventeenth-century Italian songs, English art songs, and arias from operas of the classical period. But, on this night, Joel tried something different. He began with the Harlem Shake,[1] which he had seen on YouTube, hoping that it would meet the goals of the physical part of the warm-up. The response from the class was unanimously positive. They were engaged, focused, and had fun. The response from the professor was one of horror. "What is the matter with you?" the professor scolded. "Have you learned nothing in your time at college? Have you learned nothing about singing in your voice lessons? Do you want to ruin the voices of your peers and your future students? How could this possibly prepare students to sing the Palestrina motet that we are working on next? Did you not read the chapter on warm-ups in the course textbook?" Joel never got to the exercises for moving from smaller range to wider, softer to louder, slower to faster, and listening for matching tone quality. Instead, he failed the warm-up assignment.

ERIC: AN EIGHT-YEAR-OLD STUDENT

Eric, my eight-year-old grandson, is a millennial, born in the twenty-first century. He lives in a world of social media, smartphones, tablets, and remotes. At five, he could program the DVR on the television, and now at eight, he can easily send a text, download a game from the Internet, buy a song on iTunes, and more. Last Thanksgiving, he was at the house for a family holiday dinner. He had arrived with his parents early in the afternoon so that his mother might help my wife prepare the meal.

"Grandpa," he said. "Wanna hear a rap I wrote?"

"Sure," I answered, and he pulled a sheet of paper from his pocket and proceeded to perform a wonderful Thanksgiving rap. He had the rhyme scheme down pat, and the movement was perfect.

"Wow," I said. "That's fantastic."

"Well, it would be much better if I had a beat to go with it. Would you help me find one on YouTube?"

"Of course" I said, and for the next two and a half hours, we searched YouTube looking for the perfect beat. It felt like we heard hundreds. With each example, Eric listened carefully, and I could see he was mouthing the text silently as he checked out each example. "This one is too slow. That one is too fast. This one doesn't have the right feel," and so forth. Finally, he found the one that was just right, and we bookmarked it on my laptop. Then, as each guest arrived for dinner, Eric performed the rap, complete with movement and beat. (Actually, by the end of the evening, we all knew the rap and could perform it as well).

"Eric," my wife asked, "does your music teacher know you compose and perform raps?"

"Grandma, are you for real? He [the music teacher] is not interested. All we do in music class is clap back patterns or slap our thighs [patsch]."

"Do you know why?" asked my wife.

"He says we need to learn to keep a steady beat. But, really Grandma, we can already keep a steady beat."

"Do you ever sing anything?" my wife asked.

"We sing about sweet Betsy from Pike. Do you know where Pike is?" No one at the dinner table could answer.

"What else do you sing?" asked my son, who was also with us at dinner.

"Hot Cross Buns" Eric answered.

"Did you ever eat a hot cross bun?" my son asked.

"Nope" replied Eric. And, curiously, while we all knew what they were, no one else at the table had ever had ever eaten one either.

In what ways should Ashante's band program connect to the millennials she is teaching? In what ways should the music education program at Joel's school prepare him to meet the needs of students like Eric and add meaning and value to their musical lives? In what ways might Ashante, Joel, and Eric combat the hegemonic practices of schooling that champions the powerful and silences the powerless, that marginalizes minorities by privileging a musical tradition that may not represent who they are but prepares them instead for a musical life of the past? The ideas that follow provide some suggestions for Ashante, Joel, and Eric and for those who prepare pre-service music teachers.

A New Sociology for Music Education

For those who will teach children of the twenty-first century, the efficacy of music education in schools is something that requires thoughtful debate and discourse. The new sociology, then, embraces four new fundamentals.

1. Music education is a discipline that empowers musicianship and in the process transforms both the students and their teacher. It is a field of study to enrich and change the knowings, understandings, and perceptions that students and teachers have as individuals and as members of society.

A purpose of music education, I teach my students, is to foster musicianship (Abrahams, 2005). The Brazilians use the word "musicalization" to mean the act of becoming musical. Music teacher preparation programs should prepare students to foster engagements *with* music rather than *about* it. The goal is to nurture each student's musical ability and potential.

Howard Gardner (1983) identified music as one of various potentials each human possesses. In fact, he suggested that musical potential is an intelligence, akin to the ability to speak or write or perform mathematical computations. Paulo Freire (1970) spoke about reading and writing the world. By this he meant an ability that went deeper than decoding the words and forming them into phrases and sentences. His belief was that the ability to read and write empowered students to perceive and process issues of social justice, marginalization, gender, and the like. School music programs should provide students with the tools they need to read and write the world in music. Music teacher preparation programs need to provide teaching strategies for future music teachers to learn to do this. For Eric, it means the ability to discriminate, compare, and contrast various beats to go with his rap. For Ashante, it means guiding students to discover how to use the smartphones, tablets, and laptops that they routinely carry with them to find and apply information they need on demand, that is, when they need it. It means helping Joel make the connections in his own teaching so that the understandings he shares with his students are long lasting.

2. Music education in schools provides opportunities for teachers and students to interact in authentic musical experiences, which are acknowledged as important and meaningful to both of them. Music education is a domain where students can hone twenty-first-century skills of critical thinking, critical acting, critical feeling, collaboration, communication, creativity, and community.

Like Eric in the vignette above, students may not find relevance in the experiences and content of their school music class. They may not see how playing recorder and learning songs about things that are not common to their culture or heritage add value to their lives. Some have difficulty relating to a music teacher who is unfamiliar with their musical preferences and resent teachers who do not value their music or impose music on them. Pre-service music teachers would be well served if they could find ways to connect what students bring into the classroom with the goals of their curriculum. In short, the music lesson should begin in the student's world and their experience of reference. For example, if a lesson for young children is designed to introduce various families of instruments of the symphony orchestra, which they may never have seen or heard, the lesson might begin by sharing the experiences students have at their own birthday parties. Different categories of people come to birthday parties. Some are friends and some are family. How can children tell them apart? Members of families all share similar characteristics. Everyone in Emily's family has red hair, for instance. Every one of her friends lives on the same street. All of her parents' brothers are called uncle and so forth. A lesson on rondo form might begin with a field trip to the corner to watch traffic lights and to study the pattern and sequence with which the red, yellow, and green lights change. Determine what repeats and what is different. Investigate to uncover a recurring pattern. A middle school lesson on music and culture might begin with students bringing to class a recording of music that represents who they are (Abrahams & Head, 2005) or they may be invited to teach the class a song that someone in their family taught them. The caveat is that the song must be representative of their family heritage. Discussions of meaningfulness and critical reflection should be included throughout the lesson experience.

3. A musical education nurtures a student's musical potential. Such potential includes musical imagination, musical intellect, musical creativity, and musical performance.

The ability to think in music should be a goal of a musical education. Imagination, intellect, creativity, and performance are the component parts of that ability and are already embedded in the National Standards for Music

Education (Consortium of National Arts Education Associations, 1994). For instance, musical imagination occurs when students meet standards 8 and 9 (understanding music's connection to other subjects and to history and culture); musical intellect is engaged through standards 5 and 6 (reading, notating, listening to, analyzing, and describing music); musical creativity is nurtured in standards 3 and 4 (improvising, composing, and arranging music); and musical performance is implied in standards 1 and 2 (performing varied repertoire through singing or playing instruments). Yet, the conceptualization that follows in this chapter goes beyond the knowing and doing suggested by the original nine. Instead, its core is the ability of students to understand music in ways that connect to how they learn and how they artistically engage with music in their lives outside the school building. It connects mind, body, and spirit in the pursuit of artistic expression. Those who are studying to be music teachers need opportunities to experience music through the lenses of imagination, intellect, creativity, and performance. They must learn how to contribute to a change in the students' perception of who they are and provide the energy that fuels the people they may become.

4. Music education in schools is a community of practice (Wenger, 2006) that provides a crosswalk to connect formal music learning inside school with informal music learning outside school. It provides a window into the cultural history of the past, records the cultural history of the present and sets the foundation for a cultural history of the future. Most important, music education adds value to student's lives.

Music education students, like all students, are what I call "bi-musical." They lead a duel musical life. One part includes the music they encounter in their formal studies in college. The other is the music they listen to and enjoy on their own outside school. Future music teachers will be successful when they can integrate the two and recognize that their students will come to music classes with a wealth of musical knowledge gleaned on their own, without the aid of a music teacher. Those who teach music education courses must model strategies in music education classes for their pre-service teachers that show ways this integration might happen. A model for lesson planning is presented later in this chapter.

Much of a student's musical life is outside the school music program. The research on informal music learning and popular music pedagogies is plentiful. Lucy Green's *How popular musicians learn* (Green, 2002) and *Music, informal learning and school: A new classroom pedagogy* (Green, 2008) are seminal texts in the field. Ruth Wright (2008) explained that many students relate to popular musical icons, and because those idols did not have formal musical training in school, students don't see the need to take school music seriously. Heidi Westerlund and her colleagues at the Sibelius Academy in

Finland have contributed to changing the way music educators think about popular music in the classroom. Westerlund wrote, "The role of music education could be seen as inviting individuals and groups into such musical practices where learning is an integral constituent, and where students are participants of musical practices instead of the end points of carefully planned instructional inputs on their way to a possible real life expertise in the future" (2006, p. 122).

Designing a Relevant Pre-service Music Educator Curriculum

Music in schools is often thought of as a subject and students as objects. That is contrary to the way people engage with music in most parts of the world, including the United States. Surely, music is something we can learn "about," but we learn about music because it is a natural part of our lives. Our musical likes and dislikes are part of who we are. As preschool children, we first encounter music informally. We hear it, we sing it, and we react to it by moving. That continues throughout life. While as we grow older we recognize the cognitive properties that engagements with music may have, we focus on the affective. How does music make us feel? Why do we choose to listen to the music of others or create music of our own? We all know adults who will say, "I know nothing about music." Yet, those same adults have iPods and smartphones and listen to music that they have personally chosen based on deliberate or nondeliberate criteria, which most often they cannot articulate. Is that a bad thing? In *Case studies in music education* (Abrahams & Head, 2005), Paul Head and I wrote that music, when conceived as a program or subject, survives in schools insomuch as the school music program connects to the global goals of schooling and the mission of the individual district where it resides. But the responsibility of music education to children in schools goes beyond that. Future music teachers must embrace the idea that music is not a subject to be mastered in a school music curriculum or a compendium of facts to be recalled on an examination. It is a condition of one's being, and as such, students, with their teachers, should engage in musical encounters that are purposeful, meaningful, add value to their lives, and connect deliberately and directly to who they are and who they can become.

Music teacher preparation programs should include curricula designed to add value to the ways students engage with music outside of schools in their personal and often very private lives. Curriculum should result from the interaction of teachers and students in authentic and meaningful experiences, which are acknowledged as important to both of them. Its purpose should be to enrich and change the knowings, understandings, and perceptions that students and teachers have as individuals and as members of a specialized community of practice. When that happens, curriculum results in an enlightened vision of what is important and what adds value to the world within the context of each person's place inside and outside that reality. Curriculum is content, which becomes significant when situated in a context rich in social capital. Accrediting agencies such as the National Association of Schools of Music (NASM) prescribe percentages of coursework that include general education, music history, written and aural music theory, ensembles, and the like (NASM, 2013). The curriculum for the music education cohort should focus on behaviors, enduring understandings, experiences, and the development of habits of mind that foster a critical consciousness. Finally, the program should produce music teachers who are able to deliver instruction in ways that deliberately foster musical literacy among the future children that they will teach.

BEHAVIORS

What should a pre-service music teacher be able to do? While there are many skills for pre-service music teachers to master and methodologies that prescribe how they might be taught to children, writing a lesson plan is "one of the important markers to becoming a professional teacher" (Kizlik, 2011, para. 2). There are many ways to write lesson plans. In music education, teachers who subscribe to various music methodologies such as Kodály, Orff, Dalcroze, Suzuki, or Gordon have ways to script music lessons (Choksy et al., 2000). Regelski (2004) has one in his method book, and NAfME has a planning model on its website as well.

Danielson (2013) suggests that teachers communicate to students (1) expectations for learning, (2) directions for activities, and (3) expectations of content, and that teachers communicate with students using "vivid language and imaginative analogies and metaphors, connecting explanations to students' interests and lives beyond school" (p. 59). Distinguished teachers, she contends, link "the instructional purpose of the lesson to the larger curriculum" (p. 61). For music education, those connections are made when children create, perform, present, produce, respond, and connect (NCCAS, 2012).

I advocate a planning model that has four sections. They are: partner, present, personalize, and perform. Each section is rich with music listening and music making. The excerpts for listening are from varied periods, genres, and styles, including popular and contemporary musics. Composing and improvising provide students with opportunities to initiate, develop, express, and share their own original musical thoughts— an activity key to the acquisition of a critical consciousness. In total, the plan provides opportunities for students to master musical concepts and processes and learn to make musical decisions that may enrich and add meaning to their lives.

Partner

Teachers honor their students' worlds by beginning the lesson with an experience the students bring to the classroom. That is, start the lesson in "their" world. The Partnership for 21st Century Skills ("Framework for 21st Century Learning," 2011) suggests that teachers engage students in inductive and deductive types of reasoning and apply principles of systems thinking, whereby students analyze how parts of the whole interact with each other to produce overall outcomes. When appropriate, teachers should engage with students in arguments and debates. Collaborate with the students and facilitate the abilities of students to collaborate with each other to generate conclusions. Beginning a lesson in a way that shows students that the teacher accepts and values them is a crucial step. It acknowledges that the students come to the class not as empty vessels but as students who have significant and meaningful, albeit to them, experiences with music outside the school classroom. Teachers collaborating with students and using their knowledge as the bridge to new knowledge is an appropriate beginning to any school music learning engagement:

> Teachers and students must participate fully and jointly in activities where they can exercise the creative practices of imagine, investigate, construct, and reflect as unique beings committed to giving meaning to their experiences. In our increasingly multi-media age, where information is communicated less through numeracy and the written word, these meta-cognitive activities are critical to student learning and achievement across the arts and other academic disciplines. (NCCAS, 2012, p. 15)

Issues of musical understanding, social justice, gender, multiculturalism, media epistemologies, and globalization could inform such a discussion. Clearly, each one of these could be a chapter of its own. Suffice it to say that they are topics and issues current in music education and should be woven into the fabric of music teacher preparation programs.

Present

Present is the place in the lesson where teachers present the information they wish students to learn. McCarthy (1987, 2000) suggested that this is a significant place in the learning cycle, as it represented a shift from the students' world outside the classroom to the world inside the classroom. Sometimes, this is misunderstood to mean a shift from the students' world, rich with informal music learning experiences, to the teachers' world, imbued with formal music learning experiences. The issue is that there is a hidden understanding that the world inside the classroom, the teachers' world, is better and more valued than the students' world outside the classroom. This is unfortunate. One way to counter this misconception is to have a transition from the opening lesson experience (partner) to the presentation of the learning concept, activity, or task. Teachers do this by using the experience at the opening as a crosswalk from the students' world to the world of the school music classroom. McCarthy (1987, 2000) suggested using a different art form such as poetry, drama, or dance to facilitate this transition. Thus, this is the place in the lesson to address more of the twenty-first-century skills such as critical thinking and creativity. Students should be encouraged to ask significant questions that clarify various viewpoints and seek multiple solutions to problems. Teachers need to remember that teaching is a partnership—teacher with students and students with teacher. Opportunities for discussion, experimentation, and exploration are plentiful when applied to music teaching and music learning.

A lesson on Beethoven provides an example. Consider the final movement of Symphony No. 9, "An die Freude" (Ode to Joy). Most basal music series include a lesson on that movement. In some instances, children play the theme on recorders in the fourth or fifth grade. Children learn the melody as a hymn in church. They learn that Beethoven was deaf at the time of the premier. A middle school general music teacher might consider the form. High school choirs may sing the final movement in a festival chorus with orchestra.

The subject is introduced in the lower strings. Then the string instruments play it, and then the full orchestra plays it together. The listener hears it several times. Next, there is call and response from the bass soloist that beckons the audience to listen. He then sings the theme and the choir echoes a response. Before the movement is over, there are countermelodies for a solo quartet and the interpolation of a Turkish military march for tenor solo, drum, and bassoon. The choir sings the melody, which was originally in 4/4 meter, in 6/8 meter and in a fugue. Then there is cadenza-like material for the quartet and a coda of new material as the piece ends. In a general music class, the teacher might suggest to the students that perhaps Beethoven had the sections ordered incorrectly and that ending the symphony with the fugue would have made for a stronger finale. Using technology, students could easily reorder the sections and debate other options. They could experiment with multiple options and come to conclusions. Perhaps they will find that Beethoven did make the best decision as to the sequence of the sections. Perhaps they might find otherwise. The process however, engages all forms of critical thinking, and provides opportunity for constructivist strategies, differentiated instruction, and reciprocal teaching.

Personalize

For learning to be long-lasting, students need the opportunity to make it personal. D. Abrahams (Abrahams & Abrahams, 2010, 2012) called this "connecting." We all know of instances where we have watched someone do something many times, but it was not until we did it ourselves that we could claim that we had learned it. Lysne and Tvedte (n.d.) wrote, "learning is no direct consequence of teaching" (p. 2). When teachers merely present information, treating students as empty vessels to be filled, Freire (1970) claims the teachers are "banking." In this model, the material stayed with the student only long enough for it to be recited back on a test. Providing opportunities for students to personalize opens windows of creativity and innovation, the third of the twenty-first-century skills. It brings the content back into the student's world. As emerging musicians, and in the process of empowering musicianship, students need the opportunity to use what they have learned in new and creative ways. If the goal remains to form habits of mind and nurture a critical consciousness, students require opportunities to make musical meaning and explore their own musical ideas. They should compose and improvise.

Elementary teachers using the Orff process can attest to the power of improvisation. Hickey (2003), Kratus (1990), Stauffer (2002), Webster (2011), and Wiggins (2009), among others, have published research on the power of musical composition to unlock the creative mind. While all music lessons need not include opportunity for composition and improvisation, all music lessons should provide the opportunity for children to engage their musical intelligence and to use their musical imagination and musical intellect in creative and authentic ways.

Consider a listening lesson for children in third or fourth grade that focuses on the *Toy Symphony* by Haydn. In the *personalize* section of the lesson, students bring their favorite toy to the lesson and create a dance to do with their toys as Haydn's music plays. Then, using classroom instruments, the students work individually or as a group to compose a tune for that favorite toy, were that toy to be a member of Haydn's orchestra. Everyone shares the class creation, "Toy Story Symphony." They listen to each other's compositions and offer suggestions in the form of critique.

A drum circle provides many opportunities for students to express themselves creatively. The drum circle affords ensemble opportunities for children in general music classes and gives each student in the circle an opportunity to speak in their own musical voice. The drum circle facilitates collaboration, again reinforcing one of the twenty-first-century skills.

Lucy Green (2008) and others (Abrahams et al., 2009; Lostetter, 2009; Mak, 2006; Westerlund, 2006) advocate informal music learning. In an example of informal music learning, the teacher assigns students to copy or create an original arrangement from a recording. In essence, they do a remix of a recorded song. In Green's model, middle and high school students work autonomously in cooperative learning groups without formal input, direction, or guidance from the music teacher. Informal learning may be integrated into a formal learning experience. The teacher explicates a musical concept in the present portion of the lesson and then students continue informally.

Perform

Students need some way to demonstrate their learning. Performing also relates to communication, the last of the twenty-first-century skills (Partnership for 21st Century Skills, 2011). The plan discussed here does not suggest that performance necessarily needs to be public. It can be an in-class performance. In elementary school, it can be a performance for the classroom teacher when the students' regular teacher comes to escort the children back to their classroom at the end of the music lesson. In middle school, performance could be at a school assembly or an evening program for parents. Performances might be recorded in class and posted on a class website or on YouTube. An evening of student compositions is a wonderful way to honor the creative work of the students. Sometimes the performance can be by someone else. Whatever the venue, in class, in the concert hall, at a program for parents or a school assembly, performance is an important part of the lesson plan. If lessons are not time bound, a performance at the end of a unit of instruction is a wonderful way to provide closure.

Figure 3.1 shows the planning model complete with focusing/essential question, lesson objectives, materials, and assessments.

ENDURING UNDERSTANDINGS

Wiggins and McTighe (2005) suggest six verbs that demonstrate understanding. They are: explain, interpret, apply, empathize, have perspective, and have self-knowledge. The last two are characteristics of one who has a critical consciousness. Pre-service music teachers might best develop these understandings with their teachers. Together they might debate, problematize, and discuss the ethical implications of issues with themes of social justice, hegemony, and marginalization. Specific examples of enduring understandings may differ from program to program and may be influenced by culture and context. Enduring understandings for students preparing to teach music in urban schools might sensitize pre-service teachers to *empathize* with the challenges of the inner city as described in the elements of hip-hop. Students preparing to teach in parochial schools might *have perspective* on the relationship between music and spirituality. Those who want to teach the high school choir might learn to *apply* the principles of solo vocal technique to groups. Teaching middle school students to play jazz might require pre-service music teachers to *interpret* various styles of improvisation.

Teacher's Name: _____   Date: _____

Grade: _____   Title of Lesson: _____

Plan: *what learners will* ○ *be able to do* (behavioral objective) ○ *understand* (cognitive objective) ○ *encounter* (experiential objective) ○ *perceive differently* (critical objective)	**Partner:** *(Honor THEIR world by beginning with an experience students bring to the classroom. Include time for collaboration through sharing and dialogue.)*
	Present: *(Sequence of the lesson steps. Take the learning from THEIR world to the world of the classroom. Present the information and allow time for students to practice. Engage critical thinking, problem posing and problem solving.)*
Focusing Question: *In what ways will students (complete the sentence)*	**Personalize:** *(Make the learning personal to the student. Provide opportunities for creativity and for students to be musicians. Encourage creativity and innovation.)*

Assessment:
   Formative
   Summative	

Materials:	**Perform:** *(Communicate and share the new learning through performance, demonstration or exhibition.)*

Process: *(After the lesson, take time to reflect.)*

© Frank Abrahams, 2011

FIGURE 3.1 **Lesson Planning Format (Revised 2011)**

Designing understandings for students to pass the high school advanced placement test in music theory would involve providing *self-knowledge* and the ability of pre-service teachers to *explain* fundamental concepts of tonal harmony to their future students.

EXPERIENCES

There should be opportunities within the pre-service music curriculum for future music teachers to develop their own musicianship and hone their performance skills. These might include the usual courses in musicianship, private study in applied lessons, and participation in college ensembles. Aligning to the frameworks of the National Coalition for Core Arts (2012) there should be experiences that provide opportunity to create, perform, present, produce, respond to music, and connect music in ways that are meaningful and that contribute value to each pre-service teacher's life. In addition, experiences for pre-service music teachers should include opportunities for community service and individualized ongoing professional development. At my own institution, we require music education majors to propose and complete fifteen hours of personal professional development each semester, except during student teaching. Students attend conferences and meetings of the professional organizations, become active in the student chapter of NAfME, return to their home districts and assist the music teacher, and so forth. In addition, experiences should include as much time as is practical off campus, teaching in classrooms. This should begin in the freshman year, where students may be observing and assisting as appropriate, and culminate with student teaching in the senior year. Such off-campus practica should be varied and part of every music education course that students are required to complete. Finding appropriate placements for students is often challenging, and sometimes the music programs at such placements are not in consonance with the philosophy and preparation of the pre-service teachers. Therefore, it is important that the student teaching experience should happen in a semester other than the final one so that there is time to process and deprogram students if necessary. In the ideal, the ongoing off-campus experiences would replace the formal and traditional student teaching semester, enabling the student to formally connect theory, method, and practice at every step of the pre-service preparation experience.

ACQUISITION OF A CRITICAL CONSCIOUSNESS

In general, education at all levels should foster the acquisition of a critical consciousness, a Freirian term that comes from the Marxist literature on critical theory. Critical consciousness focuses on achieving an in-depth understanding of the world, allowing for the perception and exposure of social and political contradictions. Critical consciousness also includes taking action against the oppressive elements in one's life that are illuminated by that understanding (Freire, 2005) and facilitating the ability of students to read and write the world. Such abilities are crucial for future music teachers as they expose and resist the injustices imposed on children in schools by administrators, legislation, and policy that does not privilege the arts or arts students. Curiously, the perspective is quite similar to Dewey (1897), who often described education as a mechanism for social change, explaining that "education is a regulation of the process of coming to share in the social consciousness; and that the adjustment of individual activity on the basis of this social consciousness is the only sure method of social reconstruction" (article 5, para. 3).

To teach for critical consciousness, the teacher must know who the students are. Such knowing goes beyond knowing what students previously learned in music class, though that is also useful information. It includes what they like to listen to when they choose music for their own enjoyment. It involves knowing the dances they enjoy, the television shows and movies they watch, the video games they play, and the kinds of activities they enjoy with their friends. It considers the kinds of music making they participate in: playing musical instruments, composing original songs, performing in garage bands, or singing in church choirs. Eunice Boardman (1988–1989) and Jerome Bruner (1974, 1992) advocated beginning with the known and moving through the unknown, which becomes the new known. They said that this generative teaching model promoted long-lasting learning. In Freirian terms, the acquisition of a critical consciousness is a process that begins with the identification of "generative themes" that impact the lives of the learner in powerful and emotional ways (Freire, 2005).

Reflection is also a component of a critical consciousness. Reflection should be integrated into every course. A blog that begins in the freshman year and continues through graduation chronicles a student's journey toward critical consciousness. It also documents the acquisition of habits of mind and teaching dispositions as they emerge throughout undergraduate pre-service teacher preparation. Such dispositions and habits of mind question and challenge the status quo, and think critically about the political aspects of schooling that include hegemony, marginalization, and other inequities.

Musical Literacy

At the core of a new sociology for music education is a new notion of musical literacy. Members of the National Coalition for Core Arts Standards (2012), working on the creation of new national standards for arts education, define literacy in the arts as the ability of students to engage in the creation of artistic forms in various ways, but always with the goal of making meaning. They further suggest that the abilities to create, perform, present, produce, respond, and connect in meaningful ways are indicators of such musical literacies. Their framework states:

> While individuals can learn about dance, media, music, theatre, and visual arts through reading print texts, artistic literacy requires that they engage in artistic creation processes directly through the use of materials (such as charcoal or paint or clay, musical instruments and scores, digital and mechanical apparatuses, light boards, and the actual human body) and in specific spaces (concert halls, stages, dance rehearsal spaces, arts studios and computer labs). (NCCAS, 2012, p. 15)

The late Steve Jobs, founder and CEO of Apple Inc., changed the way we conceptualize musical literacy when he introduced the iPod. This device stores vast amounts of music and enables folks to listen to that music privately through earbuds. What is significant about the iPod and other MP3 players is that they do not come preloaded with music. The owners must decide for themselves what they wish to download and more important, how they wish to classify the selections. In other words, people must make sophisticated musical decisions as to how they organize their playlists. Eric, at eight years old is making such decisions as he searches for just the right beat for his rap.

Are eight-year-old Eric and students who engage in music making like his musically literate? I contend that, although Eric may not know the key signatures of the tunes he downloads and enjoys, or may not be able to articulate the meter or the form, he is musically literate. For Eric, musical literacy is not practicing exercises to keep a steady beat or learning songs about people, foods, and places that have no meaning for him. In writing the Thanksgiving rap, he is demonstrating an understanding of style, genre, and culture. By performing the rap, he is demonstrating the ability to keep a steady beat and to move appropriately to and with the beat in ways that are consistent with the style, genre, and culture of hip hop. In selecting an accompanying beat, he shows the ability to audiate, to compare and contrast, and to differentiate between appropriate and inappropriate. He does this according to criteria he has picked up through his own experience listening to raps outside of school. Some of these are exemplars and some perhaps not, but he is mastering the style nonetheless. Can he use appropriate vocabulary to describe his musicking? For his age, the answer is yes.

Conclusions

Ashante, our student teacher, and Joel, our junior music education student, are on the right track. Ashante is building habits of mind by encouraging her band students to solve their own problems and find answers independently. Joel is bringing the musical engagements his singers have outside school inside his rehearsal. Both are honoring who their students are and moving them from where they are to where they might be. Eric, our young rapper, is finding ways to make music outside the confines of and despite a school music program that is not meeting his needs. Even at eight years old, he will not allow his music to be marginalized or on the fringe. Most important, he will not tolerate those who try to silence his musical voice. True to Freirian teaching (Freire, 1970), he is determined to "read the world" from the inside and through his own music making.

Eric's hope lies in pre-service music teacher preparation programs that consider the ways children engage with music informally and outside school. Hopefully, Ashante will continue to resist the hegemony rampant in schools and to engage students in problem posing, problem solving, and dialogue. For Joel, the challenge is to find, in his pre-service teacher preparation, that perfect balance of philosophy, psychology, or learning theory and praxis to ensure that he is prepared to foster musical potentials, hone new literacy skills, and facilitate musical understanding in ways that add value to the lives of the students he will teach. The new sociology requires music teachers who know and honor who their students are, and who understand the importance of an individual's place in society. They need to encourage students, like Eric, to find and speak their musical voice. Everyone—teachers and their students—must accept responsibility for repairing the world by being agents of change. This begins with music teacher education curricula that support and encourage pre-service music teachers who will charge forward despite the forces of power and intimidation used by those who maintain a status quo of mediocrity.

Notes

1. The "Harlem Shake" is an Internet meme (an idea that spreads from person to person via the Internet), in the form of a video in which a group of people perform a comedy sketch accompanied by a short excerpt from the song "Harlem Shake." As a meme, many people, using the same concept, replicated the video and this rapidly led to it becoming viral in early February 2013, with thousands of "Harlem Shake" videos being made and uploaded to YouTube every day at the height of its popularity (Allocca, 2013).

References

Abrahams, F. (2005). The application of critical pedagogy to music teaching and learning. *Visions of Research in Music Education,* 6. Retrieved from http://www.rider.edu/~vrme.

Abrahams, F., & Abrahams, D. (2010). The impact of reciprocal teaching on the development of musical understanding in high school student members of performing ensembles: An action research. *Visions of Research in Music Education,* 15. Retrieved from http://www-usr.rider.edu/~vrme/v15n1/visions/Impact%20of%20Reciprocal%20Teaching%20on%20Musical%20Understanding.%20Abrahams%20and%20Abrahams.pdf.

Abrahams, F., & Abrahams, D. (2012). The impact of reciprocal teaching on the development of musical understanding in high school student members of performing ensembles: An action research. In K. Swanwick (Ed.), *Music education: Major themes in education* (Vol. 3, pp. 239–259). New York: Routledge.

Abrahams, F., Abrahams, D., Rafaniello, A., Vodicka, J., Westawski, D., & Wilson, J. (2009). Going green: The application of informal music learning strategies in high school choral and instrumental ensembles. Princeton, NJ: Westminster Center for Critical Pedagogy. Retrieved from http://www.rider.edu/sites/default/files/docs/wcc_wccp_abrahams_goinggreen.pdf.

Abrahams, F., & Head, P. D. (2005). *Case studies in music education* (2nd ed.). Chicago, IL: GIA.

Allocca, K. (2013, February 12). *The Harlem Shake has exploded.* Retrieved from http://youtube-trends.blogspot.com/2013/02/the-harlem-shake-has-exploded.html.

Boardman, E. (1988–1989). The generative theory of music learning. *General Music Today,* 2(1–3). Retrieved from http://www-usr.rider.edu/~vrme/v11n1/vision/Boardman%20Generative%20Theory.pdf.

Bruner, J. (1974). *Toward a theory of instruction.* Cambridge, MA: Belknap.

Bruner, J. (1992). *Acts of meaning.* Cambridge, MA: Harvard University Press.

Choksy, L., Abramson, R. M., Gillespie, A. E., Woods, D., & York, F. (2000). *Teaching music in the twenty-first century* (2nd ed.). Upper Saddle River, NJ: Prentice-Hall.

Consortium of National Arts Education Associations. (1994). *National standards for arts education: What every young American should know and be able to do in the arts.* Reston, VA: Music Educators National Conference.

Danielson, C. (2013). *The framework for teaching evaluation instrument.* Princeton, NJ: Danielson Group.

Dewey, J. (1897). My pedagogic creed. *School Journal,* 54, 77–80.

Freire, P. (1970). *Pedagogy of the oppressed.* New York: Continuum.

Freire, P. (2005). *Education for critical consciousness.* New York: Continuum.

Gardner, H. (1983). *Frames of mind: The theory of multiple intelligences.* New York: Basic Books.

Green, L. (2002). *How popular musicians learn: A way ahead for music education.* Burlington, VT, and Aldershot, UK: Ashgate.

Green, L. (2008). *Music, informal learning and the school: A new classroom pedagogy.* Burlington, VT, and Aldershot, UK: Ashgate.

Hickey, M. (2003). *Why and how to teach music composition: A new horizon for music education.* Lanham, MD: Rowman & Littlefield.

Kizlik, B. (2011). Lesson planning, lesson plan formats and lesson plan ideas. *Education Information for New and Future Teachers.* Retrieved from http://www.adprima.com/lesson.htm.

Kratus, J. (1990). Structuring the music curriculum for creative learning. *Music Educators Journal,* 76(9), 33–37.

Lostetter, K. (2009). *The application of informal learning principles in an eighth-grade saxophone sectional: A case study.* Unpublished master's thesis, Westminster Choir College of Rider University, Princeton, NJ.

Lysne, S. O., & Tvedte, J. (n.d.). Learning without teaching: Use of ICT-based models in teacher training. Retrieved from www.icte.org/T01_Library/T01_134.PDF.

Mak, P. (2006). Learning music in formal, non-formal and informal contexts. *Lectoraat Lifelong Learning in Music,* 1–7. Retrieved from http://www.emc-imc.org/fileadmin/EFMET/article_Mak.pdf.

McCarthy, B. (1987). *The 4MAT system: Teaching to learning styles with right/left mode techniques.* Barrington, IL: EXCEL.

McCarthy, B. (2000). *About teaching: 4MAT in the classroom.* Waucaonda, IL: About Learning.

National Association of Schools of Music (NASM). (2013). *Handbook 2012–2013.* Retrived from http://nasm.arts-accredit.org/index.jsp?page=Standards-Handbook.

National Coalition for Core Arts Standards (NCCAS). (2012). *National core arts standards: A conceptual framework for arts learning.* Retrieved from http://nccas.wikispaces.com/.

Partnership for 21st Century Skills. (2011). *P21 framework definitions.* Retrieved from http://www.p21.org/storage/documents/P21_Framework_Definitions.pdf.

Regelski, T. A. (2004). *Teaching general music in grades 4–12: A musicianship approach.* New York: Oxford University Press.

Stauffer, S. L. (2002). Connections between the musical and life experiences of young composers and their compositions. *Journal of Research in Music Education, 50,* 301–322.

Webster, P. (2011). Children as creative thinkers in music: Focus on composition. In S. Hallam, I. Cross, & M. Thault (Eds.), *Oxford Handbook of Music Psychology* (pp. 421–427). New York: Oxford University Press.

Wenger, E. (2006). *Communities of practice: Learning, meaning, and identity* (2nd ed.). New York: Cambridge University Press.

Westerlund, H. (2006). Garage rock bands: A future model for developing musical expertise. *International Journal of Music Education,* 24(2), 119–125.

Wiggins, G., & McTighe, J. (2005). *Understanding by design* (2nd ed.). Upper Saddle River, NJ: Prentice Hall.

Wiggins, J. (2009). *Teaching for musical understanding* (2nd ed.). Rochester, MI: Center for Applied Research in Musical Understanding.

Wright, R. (2008). Kicking the habitus: Power, culture and pedagogy in the secondary school music curriculum. *Music Educators Research,* 10(3). Retrieved from http://eds.b.ebscohost.com/ehost/pdfviewer/pdfviewer?vid=3&sid=7bb787d4-c3be-485a-82cc-8bcf65cdb03e%40sessionmgr110&hid=109.

4 }

Entrepreneurial Music Education
Janice Smith

What will work as a musician and educator look like in twenty years? Or even in ten? Are colleges preparing students to assume the various roles of musicians in a society where rapid change has become normal? Are we training music teachers or educating music students to adapt to the rapid changes they will encounter not only as they enter the job market, but throughout their lives?

In this chapter I explore what it means to be an educated music teacher and the role of music teacher in the twenty-first century. I will consider the spaces where music may be learned and taught and how prospective educators can best prepare themselves to work in environments quite different from those where they began their own musical lives. Where, in addition to schools, can one be a music educator? Where does a student acquire the skills of entrepreneurship and marketing to create a life as a musician and music educator? These and other questions will be briefly addressed.

What Does It Mean to Be an Educated Music Teacher?

All certified teachers go through some type of teacher education program. However, these programs usually have very prescribed lists of courses and requirements (which expand periodically to accommodate some supposed newly perceived lack in teacher preparation; it seems no one ever takes away a certification requirement). Being certified means that the teacher has met some set of state-specified requirements.

Sometimes a "provisional" certificate is offered to those who do not completely meet the specifications, but are deemed qualified enough to be placed in a classroom while they complete the missing requirements. These provisional certificate programs include teachers from teacher education programs that provide prospective teachers with a few weeks of courses in a summer and then place them in a classroom in an urban school to sink or swim while meeting the additional requirements. (See www.teachforamerica.org.)

The new, provisional teachers agree to work in underserved areas for a specific length of time in return for employment and free additional education. Many of these people seek employment elsewhere as soon as their commitment to the program (usually as little as two years) is completed. Often these programs prove less successful than was expected when they were implemented. It could be that subject-specific content knowledge is not all that is needed for teaching success (Darling-Hammond et al., 2005).

TEACHER-PROOFING EDUCATION

Much of the emphasis of the so-called education reforms instituted in the early twenty-first century was directed toward making schools teacher-proof. It was assumed that if the teacher simply followed the scripts provided, collected enough data, gave enough tests, and so on, that the children would learn. It frequently seemed that all the emphasis was on the teachers and what they did, with very little emphasis being placed on the other variable in this setting: the children.

Somehow in all the testing and standardization, the experts did not consider the unique capacities and needs of the children themselves. Who is available to "lead through" (from the Latin word for "educate") these children into a life filled with possibility and promise? No teaching script or test inspires a child to learn, but often a good teacher can. Notice the word inspire—to give breath to. It is not just about motivation, but also about creating a spirit that seeks to know more on its own long after all the tests have been taken.

To be an educated teacher implies that the teacher has a lively intellect and a passion for her students that is equal to or greater than her passion for the subject matter. Educating implies that something is added to the fullness of life that makes it more satisfying. The "leading through" that a teacher does cannot be quantified or reported as data. Yet many adults can recall those inspiring teachers who made a difference in their thinking and their lives. Education is more than facts and reasoning. Good teachers provide social skills and values as well inspiration and motivation. Where are these dimensions in today's data-driven classrooms?

The older term "teacher training" is frequently more appropriate to the current state of teacher preparation than "teacher education." Most often we are training college students to train other students. Musical replication is the goal rather musical creation or invention. Training is "the action of teaching a particular skill or type of behavior through practice and instruction over a period of time" (Apple online dictionary, ver. 2.1.1). Currently universities are under pressure from various political entities to teach only that which leads directly to job preparation and to do so in not more than four years, regardless of the student's initial level of preparation. Outside agencies demand data on graduation rates, job placement success, and a host of other information that can then be used to determine funding for programs of all sorts—and by extension what types of classes can be offered.

It is a common perception that good teaching can be accomplished through training. However, again, such training often omits the variable of the students. It is formulaic: do X and the students will learn Y. Rarely does that work. Human beings are simply not that predictable. Conversely, teachers can also be part of this challenge when they are unwilling to adopt new curricular offerings that might be inspiring for some students and instead teach their favorite timeworn content.

MUSIC EDUCATORS AS PART OF THE PROBLEM

Many currently practicing music teachers are interested only in preserving music programs as they are currently constituted. Band, orchestra, and choral (BOC) directors are usually very skeptical of curricular re-visions that include the types of programming advocated elsewhere in this book. They usually feel their programs would be threatened by such new offerings, even though new curricular areas specifically target students not currently in performing ensembles. They blithely ignore the fact that fewer than a quarter of high school students participate in their ensemble classes (Elpus & Abril, 2011). This statistic is nothing new, but those students who do not participate in BOC ensembles do grow up and can vote on school budgets that sometimes cut those BOC music programs. Could it be that these voters do not have a direct personal connection to music education because their own formal music education ended in fifth grade?

The argument could be made that these BOC directors are preserving standards. However, society determines what is of lasting value and people vote for those values with their time and money. When education in a subject no longer seems relevant and of value to many of the students in schools and to their parents, that subject can more easily lose funding and a place in the school day schedule. How ironic is it that something as ubiquitous as music is being eliminated from formal education possibly because its teachers insist on preserving the past as the *only* form of secondary music education! Others in this book have argued for change in teacher education programs; these changes may well be a matter of the survival of school music programs. However, these changes may occur in higher education too little and too late.

JUST TEACH ME WHAT I NEED TO KNOW TO GET A JOB

When today's education is all about data and increasing test scores, it is no wonder that prospective music teachers are very focused on acquiring the skills that will allow them to compete with each other in an ever-shrinking music teacher job market. While some college students enjoy the intellectual stimulation of a broad liberal education, most are focused on the goal of getting and keeping a teaching position in a school. Music education students are concerned that they will not have the skills to survive in schools even if they are fortunate enough to be hired for a teaching position. Our students expect us to teach them how to survive in this job market.

Unfortunately, this is not really about the survival of the fittest. Very intellectually capable and pedagogically experienced teachers are losing their positions every year in schools near the campuses where our students are taking classes. Even the best teachers can lose their jobs because the funding is cut or test scores do not rise fast enough. Looking one step further in this discouraging job market, if new teachers are not able to find positions, what will become of music education faculties in university schools of music when there are no students applying for programs because there are no jobs waiting for them at the end of four years?

Teaching job survival skills in music—in the face of the emphasis on science, technology, engineering, and mathematics (STEM) subjects and the attempts to make education serve the needs of corporate America—is probably not even possible, let alone desirable. As higher education is pushed to become more "accountable" and colleges have to prove their graduates get jobs at the end of four years, it becomes ever more clear that music teaching is not a "successful" position in the eyes of our political and corporate leaders. They want workers who are ready to assume the life of work, not workers who pursue the life of the mind, let alone workers who deal in the "feelingful" work of music making and enjoyment.

Is this really all a college education in music should be—a preparation for a job that may not exist in the future? What if we were preparing our students for a profession in music education that was much more broadly conceived and implemented? Music has existed for thousands of years and is alive and vibrant in American society today. Just because our current education system privileges older styles, genres and performance practices does not mean that music in the broader society is in any danger of disappearing.

Access to music is greater than at any time in history. Everyone can hear music anywhere they wish. What is it that is missing in music education that causes music teachers to be of so little value in schools when music in society is so available? It could be argued that it is the narrowness of what so many music teachers define as music that has led to the decline in school music programs. If that should prove to be the case, where will music educators of the future find employment?

Can Music Educators Be Replaced?

There are some aspects of music making and enjoyment that are in no danger of disappearing. It is exceedingly rare to find people who say they never listen to music. It is very common to find adults who say they wish they could play guitar or keyboard or a variety of other instruments. These adults often say they wished someone had made them take lessons as a child, yet they seem reluctant to pursue music instruction as adults.

Has music education possibly been ignoring a needy population? What if we started advertising that anyone who was willing to put in the hours needed to develop basic skill on an instrument could learn to play? Instead, the focus is often on those who are young and with natural talent and who can excel quickly. But if talent is normally distributed in the population, then there should be many people out there with enough natural ability to play for their own satisfaction, even if they will never be of professional caliber. They represent a somewhat untapped population of learners.

The question then becomes: can they learn to perform from a machine (computer, video, etc)? In his book *The lights in the tunnel: Automation, accelerating technology and the economy of the future* (2009), Martin Ford suggests that technology or outsourcing can replace any worker whose task is repetitive or to whose work there is a routine. If something is algorithmic, eventually the technology can be designed to replace the person.

On the other hand, work requiring small motor skills and human thinking are less susceptible to replacement. Ford suggests that waiters, auto mechanics and nurses are examples of workers who can find their jobs enhanced by technology, but are unlikely to be replaced. So what about music teachers? Ford suggests they will continue to have jobs. "In the future, we will continue to need social workers, community activists, healthcare workers, and people who specialize in working with children. By [having a society focused on] emphasizing education, we will likely we create many traditional jobs for teachers at all levels" (Ford, 2009, p. 175).

As massive open online courses (MOOCs) have shown, some aspects of music teaching can be replaced by distant expert teachers. These classes tend to be the kinds of musical learning that are factual—the "knowing about" music type of instruction. Music theory and music listening might be prime examples of this type of instruction. It could be that the "knowing how" type of instruction is still better accomplished by interaction with a teacher. MOOCs have not shown themselves to be particularly useful at refining physical skills.

It may be that in-person educational experiences will at some point become more like private lessons or small group tutorials. These are the areas where MOOCs and other kinds of distance learning seem least effective. Anything skills-based usually requires some level of one-on-one attention in order for students to progress. While this can be done over the Internet through videoconferencing software, it still seems preferable to be in the same location when possible.

Musical creation and performance require skill, especially if the result is to be evocative and expressive. While laptop, smartphone, and other kinds of electronically modified ensembles are making music, they so far require human participants. Ensembles with interesting music often require musicians to provide musical intention, feelingful expression, and artistic craftsmanship as they organize their sounds into music (Kaschub & Smith, 2009). Each of those creative capacities can be refined by the instruction of a compassionate, careful, creative teacher.

So it seems almost certain that some aspects of music will always need human intercession. But will those providing this human involvement be trained music educators? Or will any musician—or for that matter anyone with musical ability—be all that is required? In some cultures and societies there is no concept of music teacher separate from musician. Will there continue to be a role for music educators in the United States? The answer may depend in part on what skills those music educators possess and where they are willing to use them.

Teaching as a Profession, Not as a Place

The assault on publicly funded education from the radical conservatives in the United States may well continue, and there is no guarantee of the outcome of this battle. As more of our national income becomes concentrated in fewer people, the economic and political power of everyone else appears to decrease. Those who wish to concentrate power and wealth under their own control do not value an educated public. It is discouraging to read the propaganda of those who feel education should be privatized, who want all children to have only a very basic education, and who believe the wealthy are the only ones who deserve to attend high-quality schools.

In some parts of the United States, this division is already painfully obvious. Those with the financial means send their children to private schools and resist paying taxes to fund education for the children of people who have not inherited their place of privilege. If these wealthy conservative voices prevail and public education becomes a pared-down institution for those without other options, music is not likely to have a place in schools for much longer.

However, music as an art form is not going to go away. The children of poverty will find a way to make their own music. Children who attend more wealthy schools will continue to take music as a subject in those schools—providing music can demonstrate its worth in the marketplace.

MUSIC EDUCATION AND PUBLIC SCHOOLS

On the other hand, perhaps the voices of the wealthy will not be the only ones to be heard, and perhaps there will be hope for public education. Similarly, perhaps music education in the remaining public schools will take a broader approach and include secondary music education offerings beyond the traditional band, orchestra, and chorus. When directors feel threatened by offerings such as guitar, recording technology, and songwriting, they need to think deeply about why this is so. Is it because their performing ensembles are not relevant to their students? Or is it because they lack the skills and knowledge to teach such courses? Some secondary teachers accuse those who advocate broadening course offerings of dumbing down the curriculum (Gena Greher, personal communication, 2013). This accusation smacks of elitism, but also reveals a lack of understanding of what skills and knowledge are required write an effective song or create a well-produced recording.

How many of those same ensemble directors have written works for their groups? How many have helped members of their ensembles to compose something to play themselves or for their classmates to play? Some would tell you they do not have the time to teach such things. Yet they do not want there to be a separate class available to provide that instruction. Others feel that a secondary level theory class is the proper venue for such instruction. That kind of reasoning is like saying that a computer keyboarding class should teach students how to write an essay. The tools of instruction and knowledge about the subject matter do not necessarily enable creative production in that subject area. Teachers who have never composed anything themselves outside of their college-level theory classes are not likely to enable others to do so.

Similarly, those who perform only what is written on a printed page or computer screen are not likely to organize informal musical performances where everyone involved plays along by figuring things out as they listen. Where are the skills of informal music making in school music programs? Where is the sense of egalitarian community that such practices can enable? Notation is merely one way of preserving sound. Much music is created without the use of this tool and without the assistance of a conductor. Where in music education do students have the chance to experience this? Where might they enjoy attempting it?

PREPARING FOR A FUTURE AS A MUSICIAN AND EDUCATOR

Preparing for a future as a musician is not the same as preparing for a future as a performer. Musical skill can include a wide variety of roles including that of composer, theorist, sound creator, recording engineer, sound designer, and teacher. Hannon (2003) described 150 different jobs involving music. More are probably now available. The more broadly based a person's exposure is to the ways humans can be musical, the more avenues for being musically expressive become available to that person.

By the time students reach the university level they have already spent countless hours learning to perform. Their many hours in ensembles (unless perhaps piano or classical guitar was their instrument) have taught them skills that would be useful in many professions that have nothing to do with music. Here are some examples. They should be able to concentrate amidst distraction. They know the value of working toward long-range goals in incremental steps. They can organize their time to accomplish what is needed. They should have mastered nerves and anxiety attacks. They know how to find others with similar interests and diverse skills to put together an organization. They can communicate with colleagues and superiors with tact and skill. This is an incomplete list, but does point out some of the nonmusical advantages of music study.

MUSIC EDUCATION AS A WAY OF LIFE

Being a music educator is never simply a job, but rather it is a way of life. Music educators have always had to have a portfolio of skills at their disposal. They need as much experience as they can garner with a variety of musical roles. There has always been very little job security in many school music education positions because the program can be eliminated, the students can quit or the teacher herself can lose her passion for teaching and resort to merely putting in her time in the classroom.

Yet many music teachers find their jobs so satisfying that they cannot imagine pursuing any other line of work. Even though schools and education change, those teachers with the passion for young people and for all the art of music can bring to life will continue to find ways to practice their art and their pedagogy. However, the next generation of music educators may need to seek other venues and become entrepreneurial about finding students.

Their lives may become similar to that of private music teachers, except that they may be teaching classes. They will need to be technologically savvy, and to seek new arenas for teaching and for engaging with students. In the very near future making a living as a music educator may not be defined by teaching in a public school. This would mean that students would need to redefine what it means to be a music educator and where one can be a music educator. It may mean becoming proficient at grant writing and obtaining funding for nontraditional teaching venues. Music teachers in urban schools already know that grant writing is a fact of life.

As fewer and fewer school music programs are available, community-based programs funded by grants may become more the norm. The security of a continuing contract, public school teaching position with health insurance and nearly automatic salary raises may soon become a thing of the past in many locations. However, that does not mean that there will not be opportunities to teach. This is why music educators will need to be trained to be entrepreneurs—those who undertake something new.

MUSIC EDUCATORS OR TEACHING ARTISTS

For many years we have been told there is a coming teacher shortage. As the teachers who are from the baby boomer generation retired, there was supposed to be a shortage of teachers at every level. If teaching were still a desirable and sensibly funded occupation where the practitioners were respected members of the community and valued for their knowledge and insight of children, this would probably still be true. However, with the scapegoating of teachers, the scripting of lessons, the incessant testing, and the feeling of being overwhelmed while trying to meet the needs of their students, it would be surprising if many people now chose to enter the profession. It would be even more surprising if they chose to stay.

Yet it is the veteran teachers—at least, those who have supportive and understanding communities and administrators—who make a difference in the lives of their students. How sad it will be for education if only new and enthusiastic teachers are the ones who take jobs in schools, and then become disillusioned and choose some other line of work. Even sadder, if they choose to stay and become discouraged, burned out, and ineffective. Skilled veteran teachers do make a difference in the lives of their students—and in their test scores (Darling-Hammond et al., 2005). Still, if the place of music in schools continues to decline, where will music educators find places to be musicians and teachers?

Music educators need to develop skills similar to those of teaching artists and private teachers. In fact, the lines between these three professions may become increasingly blurred. Most teaching artists benefit from some training in education and those with this background are usually in greater demand. The requirement that they be able to work effectively in many settings may well be a future requirement for music educators as well. Obviously, these artist residencies are not the same as a balanced, comprehensive, sequential program of instruction in music. However, if one can build a long-term relationship in a particular setting, it is possible over time to create that type of educational experience.

Sequential, long-term curricula are another thing that is being lost when music programs are removed from schools. Musical skills are developed over time and with consistent practice. Teachers teaching in settings other than schools will have to be able to recruit and retain students in much the same manner as performance ensembles in schools have done in the past. The problem with the teaching-artist model is that the interactions are often merely exposures to music, or music is presented as entertainment, or merely an isolated experience. Teaching artists usually do not represent the best aspects of what music education can be, but rather serve as a stopgap measure in schools or other settings where there is no regular, ongoing program of instruction in music.

Ideally, teaching artists would work with on-site music teachers to enrich what was already a comprehensive curriculum in music. Unfortunately, this is often not true in urban schools. The teaching artists are viewed as a less expensive substitute for hiring a full-time music educator and funding a comprehensive music program. It remains to be seen whether music education can make the case to the greater public that the profession is about more than exposure, experiences, or entertainment.

Personal Qualities of Entrepreneurial Music Educators

The idea of entrepreneurial teaching is not new (see *New York Times*, May 21, 1995). Private teachers have always been entrepreneurial. The difference is that more teachers may have to become entrepreneurs if and when schools no longer house music programs. Other professionals with equivalent educations—architects, lawyers, nurses, and so on—have often had options as to where to practice their professions. For teachers, the spaces have been limited to public or private schools, or religious institutions and private teaching. While entrepreneurial teaching lacks the job security and built-in benefits of teaching in a school, it could have appeal for people who like working independently, or who have personally designed ways of teaching, or who do not want to work full time. Additionally, in some forms of entrepreneurial teaching what is being taught can be tailored specifically to the student and what the student wants to learn or needs to learn next. There is a great deal more flexibility in entrepreneurial teaching than there is in a school setting. It takes work to make entrepreneurial teaching a financial success, but private-lessons teachers have made this work for many years.

To be successful entrepreneurial teachers, people will have to be not only good musicians, but also demonstrate personal responsibility and be easy for others to work with. They will need to know how to attract students and manage the administrative aspects of teaching, while maintaining their creativity and the authenticity of the art form. Adaptability and flexibility are key to success in any field, but absolutely necessary in entrepreneurial teaching. Finally, there needs to be something about these teachers that will set them apart from everyone else applying for a position or seeking the same students. While this has always been true, it will be even more necessary for people who build careers that are not based in school settings.

Entrepreneurial teachers are good musicians who constantly expand their repertoire and skills. If one wishes to reach students in nontraditional settings, with nontraditional backgrounds, and of nontraditional ages, it helps to have a breadth of knowledge and skill with which one can market oneself. Often schools of music focus solely on the canon of Western classical art music, but this is a disservice to music educators who will have to deal with students from many different backgrounds and preferences. While having a background in classical music is definitely one aspect of training, a working knowledge of pop music and at least one non-Western tradition will better prepare music educators to be accepting of, and work within, other music cultures. Entrepreneurial music educators should study music beyond the traditional standard repertoire in order to make themselves more marketable.

Entrepreneurial teachers are responsible and easy to collaborate with; they take care of administrative details. When there are choices about whom to hire and why someone should be hired, the person who has a track record of completing work on time and with little assistance will have an advantage. People who neglect to submit requested paperwork or who fail to document progress and achievement will not be rehired. Attention to details and documenting progress are important in most educational settings, but the entrepreneurial teacher who keeps clear records will not only help herself be rehired and gather new sources of students, but also be able to provide prospective employers with specific details of her accomplishments.

Entrepreneurial teachers have the ability to communicate with and work with others who may not share their background or personal style. Teaching has always required outstanding written and oral communication skills. Because of the need to promote oneself in social media as well as in the classroom, music teachers need a wider variety of communication skills than were needed in the past. This becomes even more important in settings where there is a diverse audience. The ability to communicate effectively and work with others—who may not share the teacher's cultural background or who conflict with the teacher's preferred working style—is a skill entrepreneurial music educators must develop and actively work to improve. Additionally, students who are fluent in a second language will likely have more teaching opportunities both inside and outside of schools.

A music teacher needs practice to be able to communicate confidently and clearly. Those skills are refined only when prospective music teachers have the opportunity to practice them in authentic settings. Music educators need experience in communicating with many people with differing perspectives on music education. They need to be used to speaking in classes, at recitals, to younger and older students, and to many types of stakeholders in the education process. That includes speaking with parents, principals, administrative assistants, custodians, and politicians. Entrepreneurial teachers must have very polished communication skills to create opportunities for themselves.

In a similar vein, entrepreneurial music educators benefit from having experience with a variety of special populations. This might include preschools, prisons, people with special needs, nonverbal people, non-native English speakers, and people on the autism spectrum. Experience teaching in adult settings is also desirable. The growth of adult communities for aging people provides another venue for music educators to practice their pedagogy and musicianship.

Entrepreneurial teachers recruit students and venues. It is no longer sufficient to limit one's teaching to schools. There are community ensembles, music storefronts, online spaces, remote access video sessions, as well as the traditional private studio to consider. Teaching can go on wherever someone can be found who wants to learn something from someone who knows how to do the task or where to find the information. Teachers of skill-based actions become coaches to whomever is learning.

One way some colleagues of mine approach this is through video assessment using tools such as *Coach's Eye* by TechSmith Corporation. This allows the "coach" to speak over a video submitted by the student and draw on the video to annotate areas of excellence or those needing improvement. While this tool was developed for athletic coaches, it works very well for other kinds of skill-based instruction, such as conducting and teaching instrumental music. Students submit videos of their work and the teacher views and responds. This can be done anywhere both parties have access to video equipment and computers. It need not be limited to the traditional classroom, but also works well there to augment and individualize instruction.

Entrepreneurial music teachers can become agents of social change. One more opportunity often presents itself to entrepreneurial teachers: they may be uniquely positioned to use music as a force for social change. Xiomara is a young general music teacher in a K–5 school in an urban setting. She has just completed her third year at her school. She is an accomplished dancer as well as a singer and conductor, and brings a cultural background from her native Columbia to her work. She has always been interested in using music to improve the lives of her students, and works with several after-school and community organizations to increase the musical offerings to her community. She is currently seeking a master's degree in community education. Here is what she says about her work beyond her classroom.

> Parallel to all this work, I expanded my involvement with out-of-classroom education by conducting the WHIN Children's Chorus (created by David Gracia), collaborating as a resident teacher with the Young People's Chorus of New York—Washington Heights, and I also started a drama club on Fridays with two parents where we staged the scarecrow scene of *The Wiz* with fourteen third graders. All this work with the community reaffirmed my conviction that education that is confined to the institution of school is incomplete (especially now that the Common Core and high test scores are priority) and that only by including the community can we nurture children to develop into compassionate, responsible, creative human beings.... I am curious to find

out how the school can function as a liaison between different entities in the community and be used to its fullest potential to also teach adults (our parents are not very involved in our kids' education; most of them are not Internet literate). School can also serve as a space for after-school programs to take residence, especially now that the arts are being cut out of the school budgets. (personal communication, June 11, 2013)

Being involved in the community means spending significant amounts of time there. Recruiting students and involving their parents takes consistent effort. This is often easier in smaller communities where musicians are often known by potential students simply by virtue of where they live. However, these same types of relationship can be developed in larger communities based on neighborhood groupings. It may take longer, but there are more potential students than there are in locations with smaller populations.

So, given all of these possibilities for entrepreneurial music teaching, can talented musicians simply go out and develop careers on their own? The answer clearly seems to be yes, and private teachers already do so. So then the question becomes: Is there a role for a college education in developing these necessary skills? Moreover, given the cost of a college education, can we justify that expense in terms of value added to entrepreneurial teachers' future careers?

The Place of College in Entrepreneurial Teacher Education

Preparing music teachers for the world of work in the twenty-first century means preparing them to teach in a variety of settings beyond those of the traditional school. It means preparing them for a life that may have many different teaching positions as well as music positions. They will need to create their own opportunities and career paths.

MUSICAL PREPARATION

Teacher education programs have always emphasized professionalism and musical preparation. Perkins (2012) advocates developing a flexible identity as a musician. "A flexible identity involves incorporating a wide range of skills, taking the initiative and gathering professional know-how, as well as allowing space for redefinition of goals" (p. 15). Many musicians have found while pursuing undergraduate degrees that music education does not seem like the best choice for them. On the other hand, performance majors occasionally fall in love with teaching as part of their undergraduate experience. The college music experience can help define who one is as a musician. Admittedly, other experiences can have a similar effect; but in college classes, where musicians of various interests are constantly interacting, it would seem more likely for possible alternative identities to arise.

While it is possible to study privately with fine teachers, most postsecondary musicians who aspire to be teachers study with university-based professional teachers. In the pop music industry it is most often true that musicians do not study at the university level. Performance skills can be developed in many settings, but for traditional wind band, orchestra, and keyboard instruments, university training remains the primary means through which young musicians polish their skills. These skills seem to be one of those areas where individually tailored instruction produces the fastest gains and most enduring results. At least for the time being, it would seem that there will be a need for tertiary-level performance training.

Moreover, the college classroom is really the only place where the history of Western music and the theory of Western classical practice can be studied. While this may be a narrow field of endeavor, it is one of the bases of the popular music that evolved in the twentieth century. At present, university music programs are the only places where this type of training can be obtained. It remains to be seen if this continues to be the case or if online education will gradually replace the college classroom and make access to music theory and history classes available to everyone with an interest in studying those topics. Nonetheless, if performance skills and musicianship allow one to reach a wider variety of students, connect with a wider variety of venues, and lead more interesting and productive lives, it is harder to argue against the need for college education in music.

ADMINISTRATIVE SKILL DEVELOPMENT

College-level programs are also good places to learn administrative skills. Students can acquire the skills of booking a hall, arranging for performers, obtaining instruments and other necessary equipment, advertising a concert, creating programs, and all the other things that go into organizing public musical performance. They can do this by assisting other performers as they present recitals and by presenting recitals and concerts themselves. When all of these details are handled by administrative staff at the college, or by the conductors of the ensembles, students are deprived of an opportunity to acquire skills that have value beyond the college setting and that can serve them well in the future.

Music education programs often emphasize the need for professionalism in dealing with others in the educational world and with parents and students. It might be wise to expand this to include dealing with outside presenters, arts organizations, and other music business professionals. Entrepreneurial teachers need to develop those professional skills and professional contacts while they are engaged in preprofessional training.

COMMUNICATION SKILLS

Primary among the needed skills is the outstanding ability to communicate. Again the college classroom can provide an excellent setting for developing and refining a wide variety of communication skills. In her chapter in *Life in the Real World*, Weller (2012) suggests a list of communication skills all musicians need to possess. Her list includes:

- The ability to write biographies and program notes for student recitals,
- The ability to correspond professionally and respectfully by email,
- The experience of giving oral presentations in class and in performance,
- The ability to deal promptly with phone calls, emails, and other correspondence,
- The ability to use social media professionally.

She says, "Learning to balance the challenges of musical and administrative preparation and planning is essential for the day-to-day real world" (p. 57). Again, this is always been true for music educators, but it has become even more important for entrepreneurial music teachers.

GAINING WORK EXPERIENCE

Another opportunity that can be provided as preprofessional training involves those schools of music that have preparatory divisions. These pre-college programs are usually administered by the school of music, but often use additional outside faculty. Students can gain valuable experience by volunteering time to work in these programs. They can observe and assist the teachers, and deal with many of the administrative aspects of running such programs under the supervision of the faculty and staff. Another area they might be of use in is recruiting students for the program. Raising money for scholarships, advertising the program, helping to retain students already involved in the program are all things that could be done by college-level student music educators. This record of service would have value for them as they search for employment after graduation.

RESPECT AND APPRECIATION FOR DIVERSITY

Another area for growth that college experience can facilitate is the development of tolerance and respect for "differing personal, cultural, and social constructions" (Webster & Campbell, 2010). College classes and other collegiate experiences inherently expose future music educators to people from diverse backgrounds and viewpoints. This can allow future entrepreneurial music educators to hone their collaborative skills and to develop partnerships that may continue as they begin their post-college careers. By definition, entrepreneurial music teaching requires working effectively with others. Group learning experiences, service learning projects, and community-based internships facilitated by college programs are valuable, group-based professional training. While all of these can be made available outside the college setting, it seems reasonable that undertaking them as part of an educational program is not only beneficial, but also convenient.

Hope for the Future of College Music Programs

Carruthers (2012) states:

> One thing is for certain: for the foreseeable future, professional musicians will be galvanized and communities will be animated not by entrenchment, specialization, isolation and privilege, but by adaptability, all roundness, reciprocity and democracy. These characteristics form the basis of enlightened curriculum reform that will serve the interests of today's students tomorrow (p. 94).

Study in the liberal arts should be undertaken by undergraduates for joy and pleasure, not simply to meet a requirement. What interests the student is what should be studied first, but a broad education outside of music should not stop with what one already enjoys. An educated teacher needs to know far more of the world than the specific culture and social milieu in which he or she grew up. An openness and broadening of thinking should be cultivated. Students will continue to need to learn to gather, interpret and assess data and knowledge. Entrepreneurial teachers need to be able to produce well-reasoned arguments based on evidence and not just their opinions. Well-taught liberal arts classes develop the skills of identifying basic concepts and methods used in disciplines other than music. These concepts and methods should then provide additional ways of thinking about the concepts and methods music teaching involves, and may provide other avenues for music education entrepreneurship.

In undergraduate programs, there should be an emphasis on learning how to learn within the various roles musicians have in society (Reimer, 2002). Hannon (2012) goes even further and suggests that professional musicians will undertake a variety of musical roles over the course of their careers both out of necessity and by choice. He states:

> Whilst most professional musicians undertake a broad range of activities in order to survive, these activities are not driven solely by survival.

It is exciting to be involved in the many facets of being a musician through performing, composing, arranging, producing, organizing, directing, teaching, researching, critiquing, philosophizing, promoting, advocating and facilitating. There are many ways for musicians to utilize the skills they have acquired through their education and experience, and most musicians feel honored and satisfied to be participating in these ways (p. 140).

It is very likely that there needs to be less emphasis on specific content and more emphasis on the ways musicians learn in postsecondary training. Education now should be less about acquiring specific factual knowledge and more about learning how to learn and the various ways to teach something to someone else. As previously mentioned, it is difficult to see what music education might be like in ten years, let alone in twenty. Knowing how to learn allows individuals to retool their skills whatever the changes in the educational landscape may be.

How else might people broaden their thinking? Well, by traveling for one thing, and many colleges facilitate those experiences for their students through summer or semester-abroad programs. Interacting with music and musicians in other parts of the world might also broaden one's outlook. This can be done independently, but how much more useful might it be if it were part of an academic program designed for that specific purpose? Video conferencing with other entrepreneurial educators and prospective educators could also expand one's vision of music education.

Universities as we know them currently may not the best model for all of this preparation for entrepreneurial teaching. However, at present, they continue to be the best option for many young music educators. It may be that colleges will evolve into something more compelling than their current structures. Entrepreneurship in music teaching will likely become a lifelong pursuit for many current music and music education students. One can hope that colleges and universities will evolve into places where new learning is enthusiastically, passionately pursued at any point in one's life. That is the type of learning that best serves entrepreneurial educators throughout their careers.

References

Applebome, P. (1995, May 31) New breed of teachers become entrepreneurs and roving innovators. *New York Times, Education Section.* Retrieved from http://www.nytimes.com/1995/05/31/us/new-breed-of-teachers-become-entrepreneurs-and-roving-innovators.html?action=click&module=Search&region=searchResults%230&version=&url=http%3A%2F%2Fquery.nytimes.com%2Fsearch%2Fsitesearch%2F%23%2Fnew%2Bbreed%2Bof%2Bteachers%2F.

Carruthers, G. (2012). Making the connection. In D. Bennett (Ed.), *Life in the real world: How to make music graduates employable* (pp. 79–97). Champaign, IL: Common Ground.

Darling-Hammond, L., Holtzman, D., Gatlin, S. J., & Heilig, J. V. (2005). Does teacher preparation matter? Evidence about teacher certification, Teach for America, and teacher effectiveness. *Education Policy Analysis Archives, 13*(42). Retrieved from http://epaa.asu.edu/ojs/article/view/147/273.

Elpus, K., & Abril, C. R. (2011). High school music ensemble students in the United States: A demographic profile. *Journal of Research in Music Education, 59*(2), 128–145.

Ford, M. (2009). *The lights in the tunnel: Automation, accelerating technology and the economy of the future.* United States: Acculant.

Hannan, M. F. (2003). Mapping the Australian music industry through careers research, *Music Forum, 9* (5) 20–22.

Hannon, M. F. (2012). Reflections on the Protean music career. In D. Bennett (ed.), *Life in the real world: How to make music graduates employable* (pp. 125–143). Champaign, IL: Common Ground Press.

Kaschub, M., & Smith, J. P. (2009). *Minds on music: Composition for creative and critical thinking.* Lanham, MD: Rowman and Littlefield Education.

Perkins, R. (2012). Identity and vision. In D. Bennett (Ed.), *Life in the real world: How to make music graduates employable* (pp. 11–26). Champaign, IL: Common Ground.

Reimer, B. (2002). *A philosophy of music education: Advancing the vision* (3rd ed.). Englewood Cliffs, NJ: Prentice-Hall.

Webster, P. R., & Campbell, M. (2010). *Tipping over: Selected literature on music teacher education redesign.* Paper presented at the Biennial Music Educators National Conference. Anaheim, CA, March 26, 2010.

Weller, J. (2012). The transition to professional life. In D. Bennett (Ed.), *Life in the real world: How to make music graduates employable* (pp. 45–62). Champaign, IL: Common Ground.

Educating Teachers for 21st-Century Challenges

THE MUSIC EDUCATOR AS A CULTURAL CITIZEN

Cathy Benedict and Patrick Schmidt

The first step in winning the future is encouraging
American innovation. None of us can predict with certainty
what the next big industry will be or where the new jobs
will come from. Thirty years ago, we couldn't know that
something called the Internet would lead to an economic
revolution. What we can do—what America does better
than anyone else—is spark the creativity and imagination
of our people.

—President Barack Obama, January 25, 2011[1]

Teachers in general and music teachers in particular find themselves in a fight against conceptions and policies that place them in a position of 'compromised citizenship' (Henderson & Forbat, 2002). We need only look at the absence of pluralist practices defining professional autonomy and accountability to understand this 'compromised' position and affirm that teachers' capacities for adaptive, unorthodox, and innovative thought and action are not fully encouraged today. Starting from this premise, we explore two pathways to rethink the formation of music teachers. First, we unpack the incongruous role creativity has played in American educational politics. Second, we argue for a rethinking of the undergraduate music curriculum, based on the idea of the music teacher as a "cultural citizen," that is, an impactful agent within the school or other learning communities, who can advocate, model, and make evident the realization of the cultural rights of school-age children and youth. To embark in this journey, then, we must start with our own story.

Throughout history, governmental leaders have called US citizens to task. Whether through a call to arms or a call to a better-educated citizenry, we have been beholden to multiple reminders of various obligations. After all, "Out of many, one."[2] More often than not, monumental calls to change are precipitated by unimaginable world events whose magnitude resounds through time in ways too dire to go uninterrogated. Multiple discourses on meritocracy, modernity (with its measurable outcomes), equity and access, moral agency, and voluntary consent, have shaped the shifting story of us. Regardless of numerous and at times conflicting positions, however, the story of educative action in the modern United States[3] has two conceptual constants: creativity and innovation.

President Truman was perhaps the first modern American leader who, confronted "by the atrocities of war" (Hutcheson, 2007, p. 108), recognized higher education as an essential tool for a complex understanding of the global borders opened up by war and technological advancement. In 1946, he appointed a Presidential Commission on Higher Education, called to inform policy. Among the many goals for higher education were those directed at creative imagination within the democratic process, namely:

> Education for a fuller realization of democracy in every phase of living.
> Education directly and explicitly for international understanding and cooperation.
> Education for the application of creative imagination and trained intelligence to the solution of social problems and to the administration of public affairs. (King, 1998; citing Commission Report, p. 2)

Interestingly enough, this first call for "creative imagination" was shaped by the notion of "creativity for the social good" (Banaji & Burn, 2007, p. 63). Ten years later, however, the national panic brought on by the Soviet launching of Sputnik refocused creativity and innovation as technological advancement, where "public education was charged with producing citizens with the knowledge and skills the nation needed to build and maintain its defense establishment and to maintain the nation's economic competitiveness" (Johanningmeier, 2010, p. 350). In the following decades creativity and innovation became associated with giftedness and talent, shifting the role of educational policy from arguing for a common "social good" to advancing creativity as an "economic imperative" (Craft & Jeffrey, 2008, p. 577). Indeed, rallying the "support of all who care about our future," *A Nation at Risk* (NCEE, 1983) deemed innovation such a fundamental element as to be essential to our identity as a people. With a language that masterfully linked "mediocre educational performance" to acts of "warfare," we were shamed into action against "a rising tide of mediocrity that threatens our very future as a Nation and a people" (pp. 7–8). In the arts, computing, or engineering, in sports or in the stock market, we lose ourselves in the performativity of innovation and creativity.

The familiarity of creativity and innovation as the story of us has indeed made our relationship with those two terms quite problematic, often drowning criticality, consciousness, and responsibility. If this is at least partially true, then we must ask ourselves how to re-engage with these terms in the twenty-first century. In what ways can we take further ownership of them? How can teachers be asked to fully explore their meaning? How do we, responsible for the education of teachers, ensure that young music teachers take on a new, complex, and personal story of educational and artistic creativity and innovation within their own classrooms? The challenge is pressing and imminent, but certainly not new nor unusual. The story of the encroachment of the state as the centralized space for accountability demonstrates that the challenges are many but the questions remain relatively straightforward: Is there no space for serious interaction between state and the teaching professional? What is the ethical responsibility higher education has in fortifying and mediating this interaction? And given that we have to start somewhere, we begin with the notions of "multi-competent graduates" (Yorke, 2006), asserting that "entry-level skills" are woefully inadequate today, as teachers will be "performing work that is less focused on routine problem solving and more focused on new social relationships and novel challenges" (McWilliam, 2009, p. 284).

In this chapter we seek to explicate a twenty-first-century vision of music education that balances and interrogates the universality of innovation and creativity as global competition and embraces an educative process that forwards creativity in respect to our own cultural rights and those of our students. We begin first by thinking through creativity and its multiple manifestations and implications, for as we have already seen, creativity, and its synonym innovation, has served to create a particular "memory" (Wood, 2008), perhaps even a collective myth around which we construct our identity. We place the challenges and problematics of creativity within the possibilities of the Common Core Standards by recognizing the potential they carry in shifting educational leadership. We then focus more closely on teacher-preparation curriculum in higher education and what it might mean to reengage with the notion of "being prepared" for a twenty-first century in which policies of creativity and innovation are closely linked to both free-market enterprises and a democratic citizenry. Finally, we outline a curriculum re-vision for a four-year program in teacher education, whose coursework is designed to stimulate "epistemological agility" (McWilliam, 2009), fulfilling the call for a critical educator that, aware of the complexities of learning and teaching, leaves behind traditional existential doubts about a divided identity (musician/teacher) and forges ahead inhabiting multiple sites of identification or subjectivity that better represent the cultural citizen the music educator must be in the twenty-first century.

Critical Creativity as the Uniform Parameter in the Formation of Teacher

Education in general and the education of teachers both face challenging realities today. As we have seen, creativity is clearly established as one concept that is at the same time essential to educational growth and simplistically yielded as a policy and political construct. Consequently, in its role serving to "fortify" educational achievement (OECD, 2005), creativity faces a conundrum. On the one hand, it must nurture individual innovation, while, on the other, fostering the development of entrepreneurship as a marker of an outcomes-based education that "delivers" efficient human capital, able and ready to serve the new "creative economies" (Florida, 2003).

It is thus imperative to think about creativity broadly and critically today. However, given the remarkable complexity surrounding the idea, the task is certainly not a simple one. Sawyer (2012) brings to our attention creativity's multiple meanings, plural research arenas, variant epistemological conceptualizations, and myriad practical manifestations. Creativity is all over the place. And, being many things and being everywhere, surely creativity must play a role in higher education and more specifically in teacher education. Where to begin then? Which *creativities* to engage with? Should we focus on teaching creatively, teaching for creativity, or on the formation of habits of mind that embrace both?

The first incarnation of the National Standards for Arts Education was published in 1994. Included in the then nine content standards was the call for both improvisation and composition. Hickey (2001) addresses the sea change of sanctioned possibilities brought on by the National Standards for Arts Education and views this moment and time as one in which music educators had "not since the 1960s . .. faced such an opportunity for curricular change" (p. 17). She also reminds us, however, that as early as 1929, Mabelle Glenn was addressing what creativity might mean for music education teaching and music curriculum. As we read Glenn it is easy to recognize the seeds of both constructivist pedagogies and the Freireian idea that we are not vessels in which to pour content. In her own words:

> America is in the midst of a vigorous change in education. Instead of subject matter to be learned and tests of achievement to be passed holding the center of the stage, at present, child interests and needs are in the spotlight. Pupil responsibility, initiative and self-expression are taking the place of the memorization of textbooks. "What the book says about it" has given place to "what I think about it" in the modern classroom. "Pouring in" environment has been replaced by "drawing out" environment. (Glenn, 1929, p. 15)

While it is rather frustrating to be reminded that we might as easily situate this quote in the twenty-first century, it is also reassuring to recognize that creative habits of mind have as much to do with thinking and mental processes as they do with the goal of "nurturing children's inherent ability to think creatively in music" (Hickey & Webster, 2001, p. 19).

Webster (1990) underscores this as he provides the argument for teacher education to focus on "creative thinking" rather than simply on creative outcomes or what creative teaching looks like. He contends that in making this shift we are then "challenged to seek answers to how the mind works with musical material to produce creative results" (p. 22). Focusing on the mental processes creates room to consider the habits of mind necessary in crafting musical encounters with creativity, but also helps us consider teachers' creative potential to generate new ideas, solutions to problems, and the "self-actualization of individuals" (Lin, 2011, p. 151). Reclaiming creativity as a social and democratic value might help us find a balanced and sustainable future in the global environment, where critical habits are indeed necessary in "challenging parts of neo-liberal and neo-conservative policies in education" (Apple, 2004, p. 13). Embracing creativity as a complex system of meanings and engagements reframes the "use" of creativity in music teacher education, linking it to a political and epistemological agility we mentioned above. This is significant in establishing teacher agency for, as Burnard and White (2008) remind us, "how teachers attempt to 'balance' requirements to meet benchmarks and improve standards while promoting and fostering creative teaching and learning remains dependent on how policy is interpreted by teachers, principals and school communities" (p. 668).

While understanding the many limitations teachers encounter, we should be prepared to accept that, to a great extent, the parameters of government and state policies such as the Common Core Standards are only as constraining as we interpret them to be. We can enter the Common Core Standards because we are forced to, but we can also choose to engage with them intently and creatively; that is, with agency. To choose the second path, however, pre-service teachers must have experienced creative pedagogies and multiple constructions of innovative engagements both within the domain of music and outside it. The question remaining is: are current music teacher programs structured to provide such experiences?

The Common Core Standards

Performativity (as accountability) is best described by Ball (2003, 2008) as "a culture or system of 'terror' . ... as a regime of accountability that employs judgments, comparison, and displays as means of control, attrition, and change" (2008, p. 49). In the United States, as we only now begin to move out from under the assessment constraints of No Child Left Behind, autonomy has been slowly dismantled and has subjugated us to high levels of surveillance. As music educators, many of us have also been held accountable and have been told we must also include literacy activities that will support the testing culture brought about by No Child Left Behind. We have been called upon to be part of the larger educational community, but what really has that meant?

For many of us our day revolves around traveling between two and sometimes three schools, pushing a cart with a portable sound system. For others there is small likelihood of joining full group planning sessions when those times specifically fall during the "specials" or after school rehearsals. For us, then, being a member of a community has resided in doing what we have traditionally been prepared to do. We are called upon to present at the very least two concerts a year, and we are tied to the desires of school board members and parents to construct (and reproduce) an identity built upon high scores in statewide adjudicated competitions (where repertoire choices are limited to sanctioned lists). In this sense the focus has not been (and rightly so, given this has not been our charge) in:

(1) fostering an environment where the expression of diversity is promoted,
(2) developing a flexible leadership style for encouraging development, or
(3) giving students themselves opportunities to exercise leadership.

However, Common Core Standards (NGA Center, 2010) have emerged in the United States[4] and in profound ways they provide an opportunity to reconceptualize leadership as something more than just leading an ensemble or coordinating and running a music department. They require a vision of leadership that would require music educators to work as school-wide leaders, who can:

(1) Impact larger curricular decisions;
(2) Interpret new mandates and policy directives, which often do not directly address music as a discipline (a challenge that we share with other disciplines);
(3) Instruct and lead toward broadening conceptions of multiple literacies and interdisciplinarity.

And while the Common Core Standards are aimed at the generalist curriculum (language arts and mathematics) most of the music education pre-service teachers we are preparing today will likely be affected by these particular standards tomorrow. Indeed, the Common Core Standards for English Language Arts call for "Shared responsibility for students' literacy development":

> The Standards insist that instruction in reading, writing, speaking, listening, and language be a shared responsibility within the school. (NGA Center, 2010, p. 4)

We can interpret "shared responsibility" to mean what we have too often taken this to mean—incorporating busy work tasks that get in the way of "real music teaching." Differently, we can choose to interpret these—and other—curricular goals as ones that can enrich our practices as well as those of the generalists in our schools. Indeed, this would be in line with the suggestions from the 2011 report from the President's Committee on the Arts and Humanities, which argues that a "reinvestment in the arts" requires a more collaborative, multidisciplinary, and complex approach to learning within schools. Similarly, at the heart of the English Language Arts Standards is a more nuanced engagement with "what it means to be a literate person in the twenty-first century" (p. 3). The standards seek to move educators toward "readings of rich texts and critical content." While decidedly not prescribing how teacher should teach, our focus should be on an informed interpretation of rich texts and multiple literacies.

What then is a rich text? Moreover, what is a text? The standards refer to video and media materials aₒ text, so a nuanced and postmodern reading of text already exists. As such, musical compositions (with and without text), including those students compose on their own, certainly can present examples of rich texts. Allsup reminds us that when choosing repertoire we must consider not only "the *why* and *how* of choosing music literature... [but also] the *where* and *when*, the *whether* and *for whom*, and the *under what circumstances* and *in what manner*" (p. 45). While this may seem sensible at the middle and high school level, this would also mean addressing these questions at the Pre-K and elementary levels. As such, layering of texts throughout a K–5 curriculum so that students engage with "increasing text complexity" (NGA Center, 2010, p. 8) balances traditional skill development with broader conceptions of literacy. And if we embrace the Common Core's "vision of what it means to be a literate person in the twenty-first century" (p. 3), what then would a literate person in "music" be? If "literate" means to have skills that are applicable in multiple settings both "inside and outside the classroom" (p. 3), in order for students to be "to prepare all students for success in our global economy and society" (http://www.corestandards.org/read-the-standards/), what implications does that have for a curriculum built solely upon sequencing Western classical note reading and writing?

We suggest that the Common Core allows us to move beyond the stricture of the traditional functional literacies of music education toward critical literacy, so that a literate person in music would be someone who can "approach knowledge critically and skeptically, see relationships between ideas, look for underlying explanations for phenomena, and question whose interests are served and who benefits" (Gutstein, 2006, p. 5). Moving away from book reports on composers, that seem only to demonstrate an "alphabetic literacy" (as cited in Tierney, Bond & Bresler, 2006) and that lead, as Christensen (2006) suggests, toward the equivalent of "fake papers that no one wants to write and not one wants to read" (p. 393), toward attending to "what if" questions (Craft, 2012; Cremin et al., 2006) may, in essence, help pre- and in-service music teachers see themselves as educators who can both teach for critical and creative engagements and teach creatively. Critical literacy would allow us to address the false dichotomy of global initiatives that speak to the substantiality of our world and the call for free-market engagements in which "the individual is conceived as an autonomous entrepreneur who can always take care of his or her own needs" (Hursh, 2007, p. 496). Critical literacy would embrace both mindful and reflexive habits of musicking as well as habits of mind that encourage us to challenge literacies that maintain "the dominant interests in society" (Gutstein, 2006, p. 5). Surely these are engagements that reflect the sentiment of the Common Core Standards, in which literate persons are those who:

> actively seek the wide, deep, and thoughtful engagement with high-quality literary and informational texts that builds knowledge, enlarges experience, and broadens worldviews. They reflexively demonstrate the cogent reasoning and use of evidence that is essential to both private deliberation and responsible citizenship in a democratic republic. (p. 3)

The Formation of Teachers and the Undergraduate Curriculum

Keith Jenkins (1999) reminds us that "history is always for someone" (p. 2). We highlight the following events in order to present a historical narrative that reminds us of the recurring nature of both our infallibility and the ethical imperative of attending to the educative paths of others, so that "responsible citizenship in a democratic republic" (NGA Center, 2010, p. 3) guides and shapes policy formation. Reading past events encourages us to attend to language and concepts so that we are able to fend off what Debord (1988) refers to as a "rapid invasion" of polices which we experience "rather like some inexplicable change in the climate" rather than as informed agents.

In 1988 Charles Leonhard charged that the music education curriculum was a "hybrid" (which in his words appears as an "overgrown thicket") that was both ineffective and, given the history of compromises related to its constitution, unbalanced and pleasing to no one. In 2000, Paul Lehman stated that music programs that were acceptable in the twentieth century would no longer be acceptable in the twenty-first century. In 2002, Tim Brophy began his analysis of the challenges of music teacher education citing a 1972 national report in which the two key issues were: (1) "course work for potential teachers is often inadequate and lacks relevance to the specific task of preparing students for the realities of teaching," and (2) "teaching candidates are too quickly immersed into full teaching responsibilities and lack the opportunity to gradually gain competence in their new professional role" (p. 21). And finally, in a more recent 2000 editorial addressing the growing variability of possible musical contents available to both teachers and students, Ed Asmus also calls for the clear delineation of "competencies that all principals, district supervisors, personnel directors, and fellow music educators can be assured of in graduates of our music teaching programs" (Asmus, 2000, p. 5).

While we don't consider it prudent to determine specific competencies in a growingly diverse world, we do agree that addressing curricular issues is, as Asmus places it, "a moral requirement for those of us in music teacher training" (2000, p. 5). What we present here is consequently in tandem with Asmus's three implications. First, a variable environment requires adaptability, and thus an undergraduate degree must first and foremost seek "to establish within each future teacher the skills, knowledge, and attitudes to be an on-going learner." Second, variability and a complex set of educational realities require a framing capacity where a " 'tricks that click' approach will not fit," and "only a solid theoretical base will provide our future music teachers with the basis to grow and meet the needs of their specific teaching duties." His last implication is directed at the raising of entrance credentials and here our thinking diverges, focusing on the need for a more comprehensive, attuned, and cohesive educational experience that accepts the music educator as "distinctive" within the school of music (or college of education) milieu, requiring not acute specialized skill, but a comprehensive interest and an adaptive disposition.

It is clear to us that we have a pragmatic and conceptual challenge when music teacher education programs remain resistant to the fact that teaching is a *sui generis* enterprise that requires the development of *teachership* as much as *musicianship*. The incremental practical engagement with teaching needs to start in the first year of teaching—easing the burden currently placed on student teaching—and a strong conceptual formation of teachership must also gradually follow students throughout the four years of their education. This has traditionally been the parameter through which *musicianship* is conceived in a bachelor degree, but somehow we remain acceptant that a similar framework for *teachership* is either not viable or unnecessary. The pervasive common assumption widely expressed in today's general parlance is that "teachership" and musicianship are, equally, a vocation and a "talent." The trouble is that they are simply not given the same value, space or consideration in our curricular maps.

Music Educators Rather than Micro-Specialists

The *NASM Handbook* articulates that music education candidates should have the "ability and desire to remain current with the developments in the art of music and in teaching, to make independent, in-depth evaluation of their relevance, and to use the results to improve musicianship and teaching skills" (p. 118). In what could be seen as divergent from the ideals articulated above, Brophy (2002) shows that young music teachers, with less than fifteen years of teaching experience, were more inclined to say that "methods classes" (alongside student teaching) were most helpful in "preparing" them to teach. We hope, however, that this may alternatively be representative of an interactive, micro-level change we have begun to see in music education in the last decade or so. As music programs have developed myriad ways to approximate conceptualization and practice, "methods" courses have become more dynamic and focused more intently and directly on creative practices and problem solving; data shows syllabi content only and practice can be accounted for merely anecdotally. The challenge, then, is how to capitalize on and optimize this interactive or micro-level trend into a more pervasive and structural change. A first step might be to look at our counterparts in other subjects. At the rhetorical level, math educators are using the Common Core to articulate this same argument in a tangential manner—something we should emulate. They argue: "what and how students are taught should reflect not only the topics that fall within a certain academic discipline, but also the key ideas that determine how knowledge is organized and generated within that discipline" (Schmidt, Houang & Cogan, 2002, pp. 3–4). Standards endeavors therefore should follow this notion, "not only by stressing conceptual understanding of key ideas, but also by continually returning to organizing principles" (pp. 3–4).

It is imperative, then, that at the forefront of a strategic rethinking in the next decade should be time, resources, and a curricular realignment between the professional and labor complexities required within the teaching profession and the nature and structure of teacher education programs. Indeed, at the time of the writing of this chapter, the College Music Society (CMS) is embarking on such a task, asking that all of us working within schools of music consider how to redefine the nature of professional work in music and its twenty-first-century realities and needs. The National Association for Music Education (NAfME) too has currently revised the national arts standards,[5] while the vast majority of states are engaged in examining how the Common Core and its principals would be implemented and how they will impact or shape certification requirements.

Of course, part of the issue is a shift in language, from how to "prepare" pre-service teachers to how to develop a *framing capacity* in each music education student, that is, the ability to articulate to herself and others the complex environ of an education in and through music. The challenge is to develop a new labor force. The opportunity is to foster a highly participative professional identity. While many would answer that it is unreasonable to ask this of novice teachers, what seems to be more unreasonable, and indeed unethical, is to launch "fully certified" teachers without the complex wherewithal necessary to withstand a teaching career. We know that nearly 40 percent of the teaching population leaves teaching within the first five years. Do we not believe that a significant part of this turnaround has to do with professional immaturity, which is at least in part due to a structure that offers high qualification in performance and musicianship but often near marginal understanding of the political, curricular, pedagogical, sociological, and cultural demands of schooling? Teachership as an aim, matched by a curricular restructuring that is significant, must be at the core of our strategic thinking in the next ten years.

In a presentation at the 2012 NASM meeting, Sandra Stauffer (2009) introduced the changes in Arizona State University's undergraduate music education program by denying the "myths" that NASM or state requirements prevent curricular innovation in music teacher preparation. Indeed, she cites "Section M" of the *NASM handbook*, on flexibility and innovation, where it is clearly stated: "NASM standards constitute a framework of basic commonalities that provides *wide latitude for the creativity* of faculty, students and institutions" (her emphasis). Even if the NASM "guidelines" were indeed arbitrary and enclosing, we would still expect action from what Stanley Fish calls the "interpretive community" (p. 14). A central policy question for our field is indeed why all those engaged in music teacher education, who can agree upon or dispute parameters for practice, have failed to foster interpretive variance that would offer pragmatic advantages or ideological uniqueness, or that would simply match the contextual needs of different institutions? If schools of music have been slow to act as an interpretive community, we might begin to see a push from another external constituency, those hiring music teachers. Addressing this complex reality, Stauffer cites an administrator in her vicinity who articulates this same view point, saying, "as a district-level fine arts administrator, I wish I had more candidates who were music educators, rather than micro-specialists… someone who would step away from existing structures and labels (band director, choir director, general music teacher, etc)." While the evidence is anecdotal, it certainly points to a concern and disposition that are clearly present and are likely to increase in the next ten years.

On the other side of the this process, we face a challenge nearly as daunting, expressed in the recognition that, as Lamont and Maton (2010) have demonstrated, young people show a much greater commitment to music outside school than in school. Lamont et al. (2003) have argued convincingly that "the challenge for school music is to maximize the experience of *all* pupils," while also helping "those who show an additional interest in music" (p. 240). The learning experiences of young music educators then must focus on how, why, where, and for whom to develop "valuable social, cultural, and primarily musical experiences." We would argue that considering *where, why*, and *for whom*, over the current emphasis on *how to* engage in an education in and through music, might be a helpful guideline for the strategic rethinking we are suggesting. Indeed, Sloboda (2001) points out the need for curricula that consider where, why, and for whom (alongside how), as he articulates that "classroom music, as currently conceptualized and organized, may be an inappropriate vehicle for mass music education in the 21st century" (p. 243). He justifies his viewpoint by highlighting several trends, namely youth culture, feminism, secularism, niche cultures, electronic communication, multiculturalism, and postmodernism. The challenges of becoming adaptable, attending to diversity of background and learning disposition, seeing culture as mobile, among others, are all embedded in the trends Sloboda identified over a decade ago, and they will remain pertinent over the next decade.

Given this complexity, the notion of the music teacher as a cultural citizen is a proposal that can be made manifest only by a more complex and aligned undergraduate curricular experience that has at its core the understanding that "culture exists to be contested" and that we are unlikely to see "a moratorium in the struggle for legitimacy" (Finney, 2009, p. 19). As they enter student teaching, many pre-service teachers see music as a constituency of one, that is, that of the teacher. As they experience life within schools, however, the constituency of music education gradually expands, first (one hopes) to incorporate students, then the school community (administration, peers, and parents), and finally to involve policy and political life, be it articulated by professional organizations, district policy, or federal mandate. Of course, as Finney argues, there are still other constituencies, such as media, music industry, local and nonlocal subcultures, as well as those connected to unions and legislators. While we cannot expect pre-service teachers to become fully fluent in all the discourses outlined above, we must find ways, structural as well as interactive, so that the contested cultures surrounding schooling can be better understood by young teachers.

To *name*, Paulo Freire suggests, is the first step toward consciousness and agency, and we in music teacher education need to name the complexity of the enterprise we foster, calling for a redesign of its characteristics, aims, and desired outcomes. To become a cultural citizen of the complex life of schooling is an important responsibility for all music teachers. Said citizenship becomes an unduly heavy burden, however—one that can lead to disengagement, retrenchment, or simply abandonment of the profession—if not eased by teacher education experiences. And that, we offer, is the key challenge for music teacher education programs today.

A Rhizomatic Model for Music Teacher Education

A conscious effort to impact how we educate in and through music requires that we challenge what Rietzschel, Nijstad, and Stroebe (2007) call *unoriginal ideas*, that is, those "mentioned very often, well-known complaints about teaching, ideas that concern measures that have already been taken, or ideas that involve only a minor change of the existing situation" (p. 935). In the coming years, curricular aims of music education programs (regardless of the relatively narrow format that continues to outline, either by inertia or consensus, what the national paradigmatic vision is) will bump up against societal changes in ways that should become quite impactful. Stauffer's scholarly insight gives us much to consider. She grounds her discussion of the "placeness" of curriculum around the notion that educational acts in and through music should be "fluid, dynamic, and contextual... and recognize the need for continual examination of the intersections of people, place, and practice" (p. 183). However, and unfortunately, we continue to experience a deficient or disempowered examination of these guidelines within the curricular borders of the average undergraduate music education curriculum.

The challenges for a music education undergraduate program could be framed from several standpoints, as conditions do vary at times quite significantly among institutions. Consequently, we suggest the following elements as a macro stance that can function as guiding posts for specific and situated action. We contend any curricular reform today requires: (1) a greater balance between innovation and tradition to become the new norm; (2) synergy and integration between performance, composition, and improvisation to become foundational structures for learning (in the case of music education, the integration should reach musicianship/skill classes and teaching/pedagogical classes); (3) a guiding understanding that schools present varied experiences (urban, suburban, for example) and that they are only one of the available realms for musical teaching and learning (community, NGOs, nonprofits); (4) an understanding of the impact of media and technology in the creation and exchange of music in today's society; (5) an understanding of musical variability in terms of genre, use, formal and informal practices, as well as artistic and cultural conception; (6) a closer balance between aural, oral, and notational (visual) musical literacies and understandings; (7) clear representation of music as a political phenomenon that is impactful in social and individual life with educational, artistic, and economic outcomes.

While we offer a concrete plan of action below via a linear structure of curricular course work, we find it necessary to place such a curriculum as nothing more than one exemplification and nothing beyond a first skeletal and structural step—out of myriad possible permutations and models—of a more complex and nonlinear set of dispositions that must accompany said structure. In order to think about disposition then, we find it helpful to organize it visually through the metaphor of the rhizome. A rhizome has "neither beginning nor end, but always a middle (milieu) from which it grows and which it overspills" (Deleuze & Guattari, 1987, p. 21). Similarly "in the middle," a music educator is asked to focus on the variable intersection of professional, conceptual, emotional, personal, pedagogical, musical, artistic, economic, and cultural continua, to name just a few. If we acknowledge this plurality, a key challenge in the formation of the individual and her professional growth is how to optimize and extend how she is able to imagine, capture, actualize, and creatively generate ideas and practices while taking these intersecting continua in consideration. While this seems complicated and abstract, the shift can be explained with an image. Consider that the traditional way of looking at the formation of music teachers asks then to image a content, material, or repertoire, and deliver a way to transmit to the student this piece of information, do it well and compellingly. Now, consider that a rhizomatic stance asks the teacher the following: Imagine a group of individuals, their context, and their already manifested capacities and deliver multiple ways to expand and challenge their known contexts and known abilities. This critical task, which obviously involves content delivery, should be the focus of teacher preparation in the twenty-first century.

The rhizomatic model below then places the music teacher as a cultural citizen, capable of serving as a voice box for their own cultural rights as well as those of children and youth under their care. Indeed, the model links music educators to Deleuze's interest in art as an active cultural force, as something that invents "new possibilities of life" (Deleuze & Guattari, 1987, p. 103). Music teaching based on the complex rhizomatic idea presented below emerges as the representation of cultural rights (Weintraub & Yung, 2009) or a set of entanglements that teachers must embody, so that by modeling these ideals they can invite student participation in the formation of communities, establishing stewardship, demonstrating hybridity, and encouraging creative reimagining.

But in order for that to take place, two essential changes must take place. First, engagements with learning must break set with center-periphery assumptions embedded in current teacher preparation thinking, which Wenger (1998, p. 100) has called "legitimate peripheral participation," where neophytes are assimilated into a preexisting culture (of teaching in our case) often via a simplified and selective experience of "consensual" practices. Second, as teachers we must challenge our engagements with "locally negotiated regimes of competence" (Wenger, 1998, p. 137), facilitating more critically local needs and expertise that certain places already possess toward specific kinds of musicking (be it Conjunto, band, technology-based exploration, or any other) or delineated pedagogy (addressing, for example, the fact that urban and suburban music education are different and require different educational frames).

The model below (Figure 5.1) shows, in a limited manner, the lifeworld of a twenty-first-century music educator, with what we assert to be key realms of action.

Engendering curricular variability is then necessary to ensure experimentation and innovation. A universalistic approach to program structures might

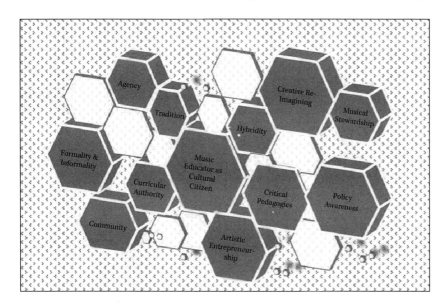

FIGURE 5.1 **Rhizomatic model**

be at the center of current difficulties faced by efforts toward critical leadership within music teacher education. As an example, Jones (2008) argued for variability at the graduate level, but as Webster and Rutkowski (2011) show, convergence and similarity still mark our graduate program designs. At the undergraduate level, regardless of recent developments, greater traction toward variability is needed. Such a disposition, triggered by the complex set of needs articulated by our rhizomatic model, can lead to a movement to champion *program activism*, where design variance would reduce the dependence upon tried scripts and help the profession to invest in and investigate new models. The key and exciting possibility would be for us in higher education to act as we are asking our students to act, with the courage to start from "ill-defined" problems or challenges, allowing creative practice to emerge out of the process of "failing often" (Amin & Roberts, 2008). This follows the notion of animation and entrepreneurship articulated by Bresler (2009), where collaboration allows for the formation of more complex, sustainable, and innovative action—be it in the classroom or in the curricular milieu. The question remains: Do we dare?

Generative Curricular Structure

The aim of the curricular map below is twofold: first, to outline key conceptual and practical needs for the formation of teachers as cultural citizens, and second to demonstrate a structure (near the traditional format) that would help educate young music teachers into developing a *framing capacity*, that is, a disposition to see themselves as professionals capable of fully participating in the lives of schools and their communities.

According to the framework ideas we establish above we offer a list of twelve courses (see Table 5.1) that would be a starting point for curricular investigation at the programmatic level. In our view they would offer an outline that more aptly matches the needs of a twenty-first-century music educator.[6] Additional to student teaching, these would establish a forty-two-credit music education segment of a Bachelor of Music education degree, thus instituting a greater balance (one-third of the traditional 128 credits many music education degrees present) between professional area, content area (music), and general arts and science and educational core.

It is important to note that concepts and dispositions developed in the first year would be extended and strengthened in subsequent years. This could be done via syllabus coordination, where key elements are reintroduced in subsequent courses, for instance linking critical media literacy basics into advanced projects developed in Critical Music Experiences (CME) at the elementary and secondary levels. Another noteworthy element would be the notion of flexible workloads, where faculty would contribute to or share the same course, divesting the notion of ownership of material and encouraging a collaborative disposition. The formation of key projects outlined as program requirements (just as portfolio reviews are in several programs today), but executed within and/or across various courses, could also become a secondary way to facilitate programmatic synergy. Finally, we would acknowledge the need for changes outside the realm of music education, where complex conceptions of musical learning must also be attempted. Therefore, we offer not a "radical" model but one we consider feasible and in line with current developments, exemplified by two individuals in two schools who serve as models for such enterprises: Ed Sarath, from the University of Michigan, and

TABLE 5.1 } **Proposed twenty-first-century courses**

First year	Second year
Ethics in Musical Action and Learning	Creating Musical Experiences I (CME I)
Musical Critical Literacy in Media and	(elementary)
Technology	Creating Musical Experiences II (CME II)
The Differentiated Needs of Musical Learners	(secondary)
	Secondary Instrument Pedagogy

Third year	Fourth year
The Dynamics of Learning within Ensembles	Sociological and Philosophical Thinking in Music
Informality and Musical Learning	Teaching and Learning
Musical Communities and Cultural	Policy and Curricular Understanding
Entrepreneurship	Student Teaching and Seminar

his wonderfully creative work with improvisation as a disposition across the curriculum; and Juan Chattah, who is leading an experiential approach to theory learning at the University of Miami. These are cojoined models that show promise and could strongly impact the formation of music teachers.

Below we offer a description of these courses as ways to further engage in a conversation about the nature and specific structure of curricular reform:

- Ethics in Musical Action and Learning
  This course would discuss the place of music within education; address (via case studies) the challenges and ethical responsibilities connected to teaching; and structure a foundational understanding of the field's innovative research and thinking (the notion of research, research questions, and inquiry-based practice should be introduced here and followed up in every single course). Observation hours would be required for this course.

- Musical Critical Literacy in Media and Technology
  This course would place technology and media beyond a tool for learning and teaching, situating them as an environment where an education in and through music can be facilitated and transformed. Starting from a complex understanding of the role of media in music and education, students would explore innovative software, virtual learning practices, engagement with critical media, music and videogames, and podcasting, among possible learning exploration foci. The early placement of the course is an attempt to instill a disposition toward innovation and an understanding of technology as a source of sustainable development in teaching.
  The foundational knowledge gained in this course would support the work of several other courses, principally CME I and II, Dynamics of learning with Ensembles, and Informality and Musical Learning.

- The Differentiated Needs of Musical Learners
  This course would address the spectrum of teaching and learning challenges presented in integrated and mainstream classrooms. Understanding efforts to teach toward learning variability—from giftedness to learning or physical impairment—would be aim of the class. The class would ideally be a composite, based on an introduction to research in the area, practical and pedagogical strategy development, and field observation and experience.
  Observation hours or a faculty-led practicum component would be part of this course. Research interviews of experienced practitioners would constitute the concluding project.

- Secondary Instrument Pedagogy
  The aim of this course would be to introduce students to pedagogical aims and procedures in the development of basic pedagogical proficiency of traditional Western instruments. Many permutations could be available in structuring the contact hours for varied instruments, extending the traditional divisions between brass, woodwinds, percussion, and strings. A collaborative approach based on small ensembles with multiple or varied instruments would facilitate peer teaching, multiple faculty involvement, and outside-the-classroom time allocation for learning. Learning integrated in the community would be essential here.
  The foundational knowledge of several instruments gained in this course would be used again in several other courses, principally, CME I and II, Large Ensemble and Informality and Musical Learning.

- Creating Musical Experiences I (CME I) (elementary)
  This course would be focused on learning and teaching at the elementary levels, developing understanding of educational practices that connect to complex formations of literacy; the introduction of rich text notions; psychology and learning theory in early years. The course would address key concepts in assessment and feedback formation, lesson planning, and curricular organization. The course would critically explore traditional music methodologies and how they function practically with learning spaces. Foundations for interactions with children's singing, composing, playing, and creating would be laid out. This course would have a practicum component and an ethnographic research protocol, where "material gathering" and "video samples of teaching practice" would lead to the collection and organization of a curricular material outline.

- Creating Musical Experiences II (CME II) (secondary)
  This course would be focused on learning and teaching at the elementary levels, developing understanding of educational practices that connect learning and creativity. The course would address key concepts in assessment and feedback formation, lesson planning, and curricular organization. Foundations for an interaction with how to lead musical and learning activities within multiple small group formats would be introduced, as would usage of electronic instruments, garage band/chamber configurations, and multi-media composition. This course would have a practicum component where students would implement and collect information on the impact of their work, using data to lead self-reflection.

- The Dynamics of Learning within Ensembles
  Based on the focus (choral or instrumental), this course would
  present key elements of the interaction with ensembles of different
  sizes, integrating conducting techniques to repertoire development, ensemble pedagogy, and arrangement and improvisation
  techniques. The course would also focus on *alternative practices*
  within ensemble pedagogy, such as student-led learning, creative
  integration of chamber work, project-based performance. This
  course would have a practicum component involving a phenomeno-
  logical investigation of the personal opportunities and challenges of
  playing in the large ensemble.

- Informality and Musical Learning
  This course would investigate informality within nonformal
  and formal contexts, exploring curricular models, musical practices, research development, and pedagogical developments. The
  groupings in this course would integrate multiple musical genres,
  exploring a synergistic interaction between playing, composing,
  improvising, and listening. Multiple musical genres would guide
  the learning activities and musical projects to be developed in this
  class. Foundational awareness of music in the home, community,
  and nonprofit environs would also be gained.

- Musical Communities and Cultural Entrepreneurship
  This course would explore global variability within musical practices. The exploration of musical understanding across cultural
  parameters, both immediate and less familiar, would be front and
  center, as would an understanding of how cultural entrepreneurship is today a global pathway for the economic and cultural lives
  of artist and teachers. In order to avoid exoticism and tokenism,
  a complex understanding of "culture" would be at the center,
  from where exploration of youth, geographic, ethnic, racial, faith,
  or gender-based (as well as other) cultures would be advanced.
  Foundational anthropological and ethnomusicological concepts
  and practices would be introduced and used for curricular and assessment development. A field experience of the collection of data
  regarding musical practices in the community would be accomplished through this course.

- Sociological and Philosophical Thinking in Music Teaching and
  Learning
  This course would be the first of two upper-level, research-based
  courses that music education students would take, focusing on the
  exploration of key historical and contemporary concepts in music

education. This in-depth investigation of social theory and philosophical ideals within and outside music education would provide
students with the myriad discourses available in the field today,
which would have to be discussed in public and web-based critical papers, collaborative podcasts, mock round-table discussions,
among others. The course would culminate in an article resembling
those in the *Music Educators Journal*, offering a vision for music
education in the twenty-first century.

- Policy and Curricular Understanding
  The second of two upper-level, research-based courses, Policy and
  Curricular Understanding would provide an in-depth investigation
  of curricular theory and practice within and outside music education.
  The course would make use of collaborative, small-group research
  projects, a survey of national and international programs. The course
  would culminate in a capstone project, in which students would develop a *policy brief*, convincingly arguing (with materials, research,
  and implementation strategies) for curriculum and policy change in a
  music education program within a midsize school district.

- Student Teaching and Seminar
  This course would consist of mediated engagements that attend to
  state requirements while at the same time helping students to frame
  these new experiences and providing a context for grounded reflective practice by encouraging students to continue to interrogate the
  contexts in which they find themselves placed, by reflecting on previous experiences, readings, and discussions. A significant research
  project (we have used narrative and action research models) should
  be part of this process, helping graduating teachers to do inquiry
  on their own and crowning the initiative that began in the first
  course of the sequence.

Conclusion

Some may argue that curricular restructuring is itself reactionary, given that in
many ways the challenge is what happens within courses, not what courses are
called or how they are organized. We would certainly agree that the innovation
that matters most is the pedagogical creativity that is fostered in our interactions with students. However, it would be naïve, or disingenuous, to argue that
the resetting of policy parameters that might lead to a new equilibrium between
the "education" part of a music education degree and the musical and the general core requirements is not significant. Of course, resetting our classroom
pedagogies has a significant impact on students' lives and their conceptions

about music education. Resetting curricular patterns leads to significant labor (workload) and staffing adjustment, has an impact on resource and time allocation, shifts the ideological placing of musical learning and educational value within the still staple conservatoire-based structures of schools of music, and establishes the music education degree in a position of academic rigor.[7]

The curricular map outlined above is a mere exercise, but one that could serve important purposes: (1) to establish the complex reality necessary to help guide the formation of conscious and critical educators; (2) to provide a pathway for a more integrated format for the process of becoming a teacher; (3) to establish the music educator as a *cultural citizen* committed to educative entrepreneurship; consequently moving the educator further away from the musician/teaching identity/duality or the failed performer syndrome. The intent is to consider *vertical conceptions* of the curriculum, by which we mean fully developed understandings that thematically guide curricular connections between skill and action in the world. In other words, a curriculum, designed by teachers, that presents musical practices that have social, cultural, or economic value and impact as the leading element in interconnecting skill development, theoretical underpinnings, and practical applications. A vertical construction of the curriculum would present critical reflection of musical practices "in the world" and would introduce different ways for musical and pedagogical tasks, actions, and conceptualizations to bring students to fully understand and experience said practices.

The task today (as the introduction of the Common Core demonstrates) is that we need to see teachers as critical cultural workers who, as Paulo Freire would have articulated, lead students to become aware of and understand their conditions and the conditions around them, and consequently work toward impacting them. But not only that, teachers also need to able to develop their own sense of conscientization, working toward their own agency. We continue to believe that higher education is the essential transformative space where the preparation for consciousness can and should take place. Some may see the curricular map above as *politicizing* music education, but alongside Henry Giroux (2014) we would argue that the intent is rather to amplify the notion that higher education must commit to a political education, that is, to establish clearly for the young adult and future professional that music is power-laden, and that an education in and through music is necessarily linked to economic, cultural, racial, political, gendered, and social parameters, all of which will impact this music educator's perceptions, actions, and relations with institutions and with others.

Notes

1. http://www.whitehouse.gov/issues/economy/innovation.

2. *E pluribus unum* is written on the Seal of the United States and was one of the nation's first mottoes.

3. We are limiting our understanding of a modern educational history to the period since the Second World War for the sake of brevity and argumentative clarify.

4. The Common Core Standards have been adopted by almost every state in the union and will be in effect throughout the United States as of 2015, with assessments in place in 2014–2015.

5. While the Next Generation National Arts Standards movement may seem to be the purview of preK–12 educative situations, it is worth noting a few of the more salient "consensus" points and goals of the Coalition for Core Arts Standards and the ways they would impact the first two years of higher education curricula, and not just in the area of teacher preparation: I. National Arts Standards should extend preK–14. Extending to 14 (college sophomore) will enable standards writers to work with higher education colleagues to delineate college general education arts expectations that articulate with preK–12 expectations and might also apply to students in technical, community, or junior colleges. http://nccas.wikispaces.com/Proposed+Standards+Details+Consensus+Document.

6. Certainly, changes here suggested are currently in motion in several institutions across the country. The University of Arizona recently restructured its undergraduate program, establishing "flexible musicianship, inquisitive minds, innovative practices, and community leaders" as the core principals guiding the program. it is now offering a twelve-credit course called "Art of Teaching" that attempts to address several of the concerns presented in this chapter. The University of Miami is experimenting with an integrative approach to musicianship. New York University has in Alex Ruthmann a great advocate for technologically mediated learning. The University of Nebraska has a relatively new music education program that focuses on composition.

7. We understand that a music educator does not always present the same kind of "return of investment" that an award-winning performance major might. The long-term worth (economic, social, and cultural) of a music teacher as a cultural citizen is immense, given that he or she is capable of articulating the cohesive and symbiotic relation between societal growth and well-being, educational and economic achievement, as well as between ethical and communal development that can be mediated by creative, mindful, and educationally sound interactions in music and the arts. The long game of cultural transformation might be unthinkable for the more and more economically minded. This would require a reduction in other elements of the music curriculum to be sure, as well as a conscious reshaping of general core and arts and science courses required of music education majors.

References

Alexander, F. K. (Ed.). (1998). The President's Commission Higher Education for Democracy, 1947. Retrieved from http://courses.education.illinois.edu/eol474/sp98/truman.html.

Allsup, R. (Fall 2009). Choosing Repertoire. In H. Abeles & L. Custodero (eds.) *Music Pedagogy: Frameworks for Practice.* New York, NY: Oxford University Press.

Amin, A., & Roberts, J. (Eds.). (2008). *Community, economic creativity and organization.* Oxford: Oxford University Press.

Apple, M. W. (2004). Creating difference: Neo-liberalism, neo-conservatism and the politics of educational reform. *Educational Policy, 18*(1), 12–44.

Asmus, E. (2000). Commentary: Foundation competencies for music teachers. *Journal of Music Teacher Education, 9*(2), 5–6.

Ball, S. J. (2003). The teacher's soul and the terrors of performativity. *Journal of education policy, 18*(2), 215–228.

Ball, S. (2008). *The education debate*. Bristol, UK: Policy Press.

Banaji, S., & Burn, A. (2007). Creativity through a rhetorical lens: Implications for schooling, literacy and media education. *Literacy, 41*(2), 62–70.

Bresler, L. (2009). 'The academic faculty as an entrepreneur: Artistry, craftsmanship and animation.' *Visual Art Research, 35*(1), 12–24.

Brophy, T. (2002). Teacher reflections on undergraduate music education. *Journal of Music Teacher Education, 12*(1), 19–25.

Burnard, P., & White, J. (2008). Creativity and performativity: Counterpoints in British and Australian education. *British Educational Research Journal, 34*(5), 667–682.

Christensen, L. (2006). Our visions of possibility for literacy: Keeping a social justice vision in the land of scripted literacy. *Language Arts, 83*(5), 384–394.

Craft, A. (2012). Childhood in a digital age: creative challenges for educational futures. *London Review of Education, 10*(2), 173–190.

Craft, A., & Jeffrey, B. (2008). Creativity and performativity in teaching and learning: Tensions, dilemmas, constraints, accommodations and synthesis. *British Educational Research Journal, 34*(5), 577–584.

Cremin, T., Burnard, P., & Craft, A. (2006). Pedagogy and possibility thinking in the early years. *Thinking skills and creativity, 1*(2), 108–119.

Debord, G. (1988). *Comments on the society of the spectacle*. Retrieved from http://libcom.org/library/comments-society-spectacle.

Deleuze, G., & Guattari, F. (1987). *A thousand plateaus: Capitalism and schizophrenia*. Minneapolis and London: University of Minnesota Press.

Florida, R. (2003). *The rise of the creative class*. New York: Basic Books.

Fish, S. (1980). *Is there text in this class?* Cambridge, MA: Harvard University Press.

Finney, J. (2009). Music education as identity project in a world of electronic desire. In J. Finney and P. Burnard (Eds). *Music Education with Digital Technology* (pp. 9–20). London: Continuum.

Giroux, H. (2014). *Neoliberalism's War on Higher Education*. Chicago: Haymarket Books.

Glenn, M. (1929). Creative education in music. *Music Supervisors' Journal, 15*(5), 15–21.

Gutstein, E. (2006). *Reading and writing the world of mathematics: Toward a pedagogy of social justice*. New York: Taylor & Francis.

Henderson, J., & Forbat, L. (2002). Relationship-based social policy: Personal and policy constructions of care. *Critical Social Policy, 22*(4), 669–687.

Hickey, M. (2001). Creativity in the music classroom. *Music Educators Journal, 88*(1), 17–18.

Hickey, M., & Webster, P. (2001). Creative thinking in music. *Music Educators Journal, 88*(1), 19–23.

Hursh, D. (2007, September). "No Child Left Behind" and the rise of neoliberal education policies. *American Educational Research Journal, 44*(3), 493–518.

Hutcheson, P. A. (2007). The Truman Commission's vision of the future. *Thought & Action* (Fall), 107.

Jenkins, K. (1999). *Why history? Ethics and postmodernity.* New York: Routledge.

Johanningmeier, E. V. (2010). "A Nation at Risk" and "Sputnik": Compared and reconsidered. *American Educational History Journal, 37*(2), 347–365.

Jones, P. (2008). Policy studies as a component of music teacher education: Building the profession's capacity for strategic action. In C. C. Leung, R. L. C. Yip, & T. Imada (Eds.), *Music education policy and implementation: International perspectives* (pp. 54–63). Aomori: University of Hirosaki Press.

Lamont, A. & Maton, K. (2010). Unpopular music: Beliefs and behaviours toward music education. In R. Wright (Ed.), *Sociology and Music Education* (pp. 63–80). London: Ashgate.

Lamont, A., Hargreaves, D.J., Marshall, N.A., and Tarrant, M. (2003). Young people's music in and out of school. *British Journal of Music Education, 20*(3), 229–41.

Lehman, P. (2000). How can the skills and knowledge called for in the National Standards best be taught? In C. K. Madsen (Ed.), *Vision 2020: The Housewright Symposium on the future of music education* (pp. 89–101). Reston, VA: Music Educators National Conference/National Association for Music Education.

Leonard, C. (1988). Methods courses in music teacher education. In J. T. Gates (Ed.), *Music education in the United States: Contemporary issues* (pp. 193–201). Tuscaloosa: University of Alabama Press.

Lin, Y. S. (2011). Fostering creativity through education: A conceptual framework of creative pedagogy. *Creative education, 2*(3), 149–155.

McWilliam, E. (2009). 'Teaching for creativity: From sage to guide to meddler.' *Asia Pacific Journal of Education, 29*(3), 281–293.

National Association of Schools of Music (NASM). *NASM Handbook 2013–2014.* http:// nasm.arts-accredit.org/site/docs/Handbook/NASM_HANDBOOK_2013-14.pdf.

National Commission on Excellence in Education (NCEE). (1983). *A nation at risk: The imperative for educational reform.* Report to the nation and the secretary of education, United States Department of Education. Retrieved from http://datacenter.spps.org/ uploads/SOTW_A_Nation_at_Risk_1983.pdf.

National Governors Association (NGA) Center for Best Practices, Council of Chief State School Officers. (2010). *Common Core State Standards, English Language Arts & Literacy in History/Social Studies, Science, and Technical Subjects.* National Governors Association Center for Best Practices, Council of Chief State School Officers, Washington, DC. Retrieved from http://www.corestandards.org/.

Organisation for Economic Cooperation and Development (OECD). (2005). *Innovation policy and performance: A cross-country comparison.* Paris: OECD.

President's Committee on the Arts and the Humanities (PCAH). (2011). *Reinvesting in arts education: Winning America's future through creative schools.* Washington, DC. Retrieved from http://www.pcah.gov/sites/default/files/photos/PCAH_ Reinvesting_4web.pdf.

Rietzschel, E. F., Nijstad, B. A., & Stroebe, W. (2007). Relative accessibility of domain knowledge and creativity: The effects of knowledge activation on the quantity and quality of ideas. *Journal of Experimental Social Psychology, 43*, 933–946.

Sawyer, R. K. (2012). *Explaining creativity: The science of human innovation.* New York: Oxford University Press.

Sloboda, J. A. (2001). Emotion, functionality, and the everyday experience of music: Where does music education fit? *Music Education Research, 3*(2), 243–255.

Stauffer, S. (2009). Placing curriculum in music. In T. Regelski & T. Gates (Eds.). *Music education for changing times* (pp. 175–186). Dordrecht, Netherlands: Springer.

Schmidt, W., Houang, R., Cogan, L., (2002). A coherent curriculum: The case of mathematics. *American Educator, 26,* 1–17.

Tierney, R. J., Bond, E., & Bresler, J. (2006). Examining literate lives as students engage with multiple literacies. *Theory into Practice, 45*(4), 359–367.

Webster, P. R. (1990). Creativity as creative thinking. *Music Educators Journal, 76*(9), 22–28.

Webster, Peter, & Rutkowski, Joanne. (2011). *Status of doctoral programs in music education.* Paper presented at the Society for Music Teacher Education Conference, Greensboro, NC.

Weintraub, A. N., & Yung, B. (2009). *Music and cultural rights.* Chicago and Urbana: University of Illinois Press.

Wenger, E. (1998). *Communities of practice.* Cambridge, UK: Cambridge University Press.

Wood, J. N. (2008). Visual memory for agents and their actions. *Cognition, 108,* 522–532.

Yorke, M. (2006). *Employability in higher education: What it is—what it is not.* York, UK: Higher Education Academy.

PART II

Innovative Practices in Music Teacher Education

6 }

Juxtapositional Pedagogy as an Organizing Principle in University Music Education Programs
Frank Heuser

A university curriculum is often viewed as merely an approved set of classes that a student must complete in order to satisfy the requirements necessary to earn a degree in a given academic discipline. The courses included in a curriculum usually comply with standards adopted by experts in that branch of learning and specify the knowledge that must be mastered in order for those graduating from the program to acquire the competence necessary to function as professionals in the given field of study. Because undergraduate instruction provides students with the foundational knowledge and skills central to an academic tradition, the classes required for a bachelor's degree tend to be carefully defined. For music teacher preparation programs in particular, which must adhere to standards set forth by both professional and governmental accrediting agencies, traditional curricular approaches tend to be highly prescriptive and rigorously defended. Attempts to envision innovative or alternative instructional practices are often challenged in university settings, where "drastic changes in thinking are typically regarded with caution, if not disdain" (Blascovich & Bailenson, 2011, p. 83) and efforts to modify existing programs of study can become a source of conflict among faculty members. This chapter explores how a juxtapositional pedagogy might allow for restructuring of university music education programs so that traditional and innovative methodologies could be creatively combined for the express purpose of revitalizing music teacher preparation. Such an approach would allow a university music teacher preparation program to become more than simply an approved sequence of courses and instead function as a catalyst for curricular reflection and innovation.

Purpose and Tradition in Music Teacher Education

Traditionally, the primary purpose of undergraduate music education programs in American universities was to prepare individuals for teaching positions in public schools. The curriculum in these programs has remained relatively unchanged for decades, is fairly uniform in colleges throughout the country, and focuses on grooming future educators to replicate the large ensemble model of instruction dominating American school music programs. Supported by a culture that views ensemble creation as the ultimate purpose of school music education, this approach to professional preparation excludes individuals with interests in world music, popular idioms, or teaching in community settings. Understanding that musical culture has experienced significant change and continues to evolve since current teacher preparation practice was implemented, re-visionists hope to replace tradition with a variety of vernacular offerings while preservationists are determined to protect and maintain current practice. A major challenge for university music education programs is to develop curricular procedures that prepare future teachers for the large ensemble tradition still prevalent in American schools while simultaneously challenging future teachers to become curricular innovators as they progress through their careers.

How might university music departments, which offer conservatory-style professional preparation designed to train musicians for positions in symphony orchestras and opera companies, challenge education majors to become curricular innovators in the future? How might music teachers prepare for a future that promises to be radically different from the learning environments in which their own musical skills were nurtured? The challenge for university music education programs is to prepare future teachers to work in educational settings as they are presently configured while concurrently developing dispositions that will allow them to explore creative curricular options in the future. This chapter describes an approach to university music teacher preparation that employs a juxtapositional stance toward curriculum development. This unique approach pairs contrasting musical learning experiences that would usually be taught in separate methods classes and places them together in a single instructional setting to create spaces where the nature of musical thinking and learning can be explored. The concept for this juxtapositional approach to curriculum design evolved out of practice as a result of attempts to provide students with a context for music education theory in an environment of actual music making. This distinctive approach to music teacher preparation provides opportunities to experience different styles of music learning, to reflect on the multiple processes involved in music learning, and to develop initial understandings of music psychology and music education philosophy. The chapter proceeds by describing an emerging undergraduate music education curriculum based on juxtapositional pedagogy, employs student reflections to provide an in-depth description of how this approach functions and how it evolved in one course, and offers an initial theoretical basis for the pedagogy. This is one example of how juxtapositional pedagogy might enable a forward-looking undergraduate curriculum to both preserve the traditional approach to music education and simultaneously provide students with the dispositions needed to envision an innovative future. Furthermore, juxtapositional pedagogy should accomplish this without adding additional stress to the already overburdened course load expected of music education majors.

A Juxtapositional Curriculum

Pre-service music teachers tend to enter professional preparation programs with deeply held conceptions of what music education is and how learning should proceed in schools. Methods courses, which comprise a major component of the music education curriculum, are designed to provide future teachers with the specific skills needed to deliver well-defined content in an efficient manner (Allsup & Benedict 2008, p. 159). Most traditional music teacher preparation programs focus on developing skills in a particular methodology, such as Kodály or Gordon, providing basic knowledge in vocal and/or instrumental pedagogy, or on acquiring rehearsal strategies to prepare large ensembles for public performance. This standardized music teacher education curriculum enables novices to begin their professional lives with a basic command of the information and music-making skills currently taught in primary and secondary schools. This preparation, however, tends to be prescriptive rather than generative and does little to nurture innovation or reflection about the potential multiple purposes of music in a person's life. Recognizing the need to accommodate tradition and to simultaneously nurture dispositions that might encourage change, the music education program at UCLA is implementing an innovative curriculum that juxtaposes informal and formal music learning experiences as well as conventional music education methods courses with newly created counterparts from world music. Rather than trying to impose a radical reconceptualization of music education practice, this juxtapositional pedagogy encourages the comparison of different instructional approaches and should allow future teachers to acquire their own understanding of effective teaching practice.

Although excellent bands, orchestras, and choirs remain in the forefront of preK–12 music programs, there are an increasing number of public schools looking for educators who are also versed in teaching mariachi or various world music styles and who have skills in music technology. Additionally, privately funded organizations, such as Education Through Music (http://www.etmonline.org/) and El Sistema music programs (http://elsistemausa.org/), seek music teachers with qualifications in both traditional and nontraditional modes of music instruction. Recognizing the need to accommodate tradition and to simultaneously nurture dispositions that might encourage change, the music education program at UCLA is implementing this innovative juxtapositional curriculum. The UCLA approach continues to provide the skills needed to teach in schools with traditional large ensembles while also offering professional preparation to students who may desire to work in community-based music programs.

The foundational premise of this curriculum is that juxtaposing two different musical styles, each having its own unique learning tradition, creates a space which opens opportunities to engage in reflection and meaningful discussions about the nature of music and music learning. The pairings currently in place or being developed include:

- Informal and formal aural learning through the guitar and clarinet;
- String orchestra and beginning mariachi ensemble;
- Snare and world drumming;
- Choral methods and gospel choir;
- Jazz pedagogy and laptop ensemble.

Because aural learning is a central component of this curriculum, several of the pairings juxtapose a written tradition with a musical style that is generally not notated. These juxtapositions place music making at the core of the music education program and serve as the basis for contextualized discussions about the foundational principles of music education. By discussing their experiences in music making and learning that take place in the context of these pairings, future teachers acquire a wider range of understandings and instructional tools than might be possible in a traditional music teacher preparation program. This approach supports one of the greater goals of music study in a university setting, which is that of engaging students in the processes of discovery and creative thinking in a discipline so that they become adept at exploring ways to increase the relevance of their discipline to society. These course pairings extend the field of music teacher preparation beyond the acquisition of rudimentary performance skills on instruments and beyond the development of a narrow range of specific rehearsal methods needed to replicate traditional school ensembles. Instead, the juxtapositions help future teachers develop flexible pedagogical understandings that can be applied in a wide range of settings rather than specific methodologies that are applicable only in traditional ensemble settings.

There are three major components to this curriculum: (1) a core set of courses for all students interested in music learning and teaching; (2) the additional classes necessary to qualify students to eventually pursue a teaching credential; and (3) a fieldwork component for those interested in community music making. This multifaceted approach expands undergraduate music education beyond the standard realm of preK–12 teacher training and offers professional preparation in teaching for individuals intending to work in private and/or community settings. Representing a radical break from current practice, which teaches directly and only to the state certification set of competencies, the curriculum provides preparation for preK–12 teaching positions as they are currently defined (band, orchestra, and choir), the skills and concepts necessary to redesign programs in the future, and the understandings necessary to work in community venues.

Core Music Education Curriculum

In addition to requiring work in music theory, history, and performance, students complete the core music education curriculum (see below), which includes: (A) two courses that examine the foundations of music education; (B) four comparative classes that juxtapose traditional methods courses with a contrasting approach; and (C) a course in creative musicianship. Credential students also take: (D) classes required for a teaching certificate, and students interested in community-based teaching take: (E) classes that provide them with field experiences in music teaching. The curriculum outlined below is followed by a description of each key component.

A. Foundations courses
  1. Learning approaches in music education
  2. Major childhood approaches to music learning
B. Comparative approaches: four juxtapositions grounded in music making
  1. String ensemble (written notation) and mariachi (aural tradition)
  2. Formal choir (written notation) and Gospel choir (aural tradition)
  3. Snare drum (written notation) and selected world drumming (aural) traditions
  4. Jazz pedagogy (written notation with improvisation) and iPad Band (creativity, composition)
C. Musicianship, creativity, and improvisation: a year-long course that develops musicianship through improvisation;
D. Credentialing requirements for students interested in certification:
  1. Woodwinds
  2. Brass
  3. Vocal pedagogy
  4. Conducting
  5. Curriculum design, evaluation, and assessment
E. Music in schools and community for students not pursuing certification;

    F. Capstone courses: overview of program design and assessment in school and community settings

        1. Program design and assessment

        2. Field applications: work in community settings

FOUNDATIONS COURSES

Theoretical foundations of music education are developed in two courses that emphasize conceptual understanding of music learning within the context of music making. These courses have extensive academic requirements in addition to music-making responsibilities. Functioning as the introductory course in music education at UCLA, "Learning approaches in music education" challenges students to acquire music-making skills on secondary instruments aurally without notation and to contrast a formal approach to music instruction with informal learning processes. These two learning modes include systematic aural transmission, which is employed extensively in jazz and numerous non-Western musical traditions, and informal learning, which as described by Lucy Green (2002) is the way most popular musicians acquire their performing skills. Because most future music teachers acquire their music-making skills in notation-based instructional settings, the difficulties they experience while learning music aurally serves as an excellent forum for reflecting on the nature of music learning and exploring how music learning is related to the major learning theories (e.g., behaviorist, cognitive theories, and constructivist theories).

In "Major childhood approaches to music learning," Kodály and Orff methodologies are juxtaposed with examples of approaches to music learning that are used with young children in different parts of the world, to develop a global understanding of music learning. The course provides an understanding of brain development in early childhood, examines different ways of understanding musical development, and explores the nature of musicality by using resources from the fields of music education, ethnomusicology, and folklore. It is in this class that future music teachers explore how children acquire their musical preferences and motivations to study music, develop literacy, and learn to respond emotionally to music.

COMPARATIVE APPROACHES

Two juxtapositions are currently included in the comparative-approaches component of the curriculum. Each course pairs a form of music making that is transmitted through notation with a tradition that is acquired aurally. The inclusion of mariachi, Gospel choir, and world drumming allows the music education program at UCLA to take advantage of the incredible resources available through one of the world's great departments of ethnomusicology. The goal of these juxtapositions, however, is not to simply add additional prescriptive methods courses from different musical traditions to the curriculum, but instead to use these pairings as catalysts for reflecting about music making and pedagogy.

String Ensemble and Mariachi

In the string ensemble–mariachi course students compare and contrast several of the beginning string method books that are used in schools as they develop basic playing skills. By working with different texts, they begin to acquire the pedagogical understandings necessary to analyze a variety of approaches to teaching beginning string technique and to understand the crucial role the choice of a method book, the skills of the teacher and the effective selection of ensemble literature can play in student learning.[1] The mariachi portion of the course is taught aurally and requires that students learn to play and sing a repertoire with which most are only peripherally familiar. This learning challenge is a direct contrast to the orchestral portion of the class and provides the opportunity to discuss how pedagogical traditions evolve, how aural skills are acquired through each approach, and how the social conventions that are unique to each tradition result in very different performing practices.

Jazz Pedagogy and iPad Band

The jazz pedagogy and iPad Band course pairing is emerging and evolving almost as quickly as applications for tablet computers are created. High-quality pedagogical materials are readily available for teaching both the ensemble and improvisational aspects of jazz (see Dunscomb & Hill, 2002; Sorenson & Pearson, 1998; Steinel, 2000). In many respects, the methods for teaching this improvisational art form have become quite prescribed. In contrast, formal instructional materials for iPad Band are not yet published. Some of the excellent texts designed for music technology offer insights that can be adapted to iPads (for example see Watson, 2011). However, many of the musical applications available for tablets are highly intuitive and require almost no formal instruction, especially when the tablets are used by digital natives.

The very presence of iPads in a class seems to encourage a constructivist approach to learning, and students are extremely willing to use them to create and arrange music for ensemble performance. The contrast between student-constructed technology-based learning experiences and the well-documented methods available for jazz instruction provides opportunities to discuss how a pedagogical approach becomes formalized as performance practice in an area moves from infancy toward maturity. Other comparative pairings are currently in development. Although not the only juxtapositions possible, these specific pairings will allow the curriculum to use the resources available in this particular academic setting.

Musicianship, Creativity, and Improvisation

"Musicianship, creativity, and improvisation" is the foundational course that provides skills necessary to engage learners in both school and community settings in a wide variety of musical activities, including improvisation, composition, and group singing. The course is modeled on the approach pioneered by Ed Sarath (2009) in his text *Music theory through improvisation: A new approach to musicianship training* and the work of Lee Higgins and Patricia Shehan Campbell (2010) in their book *Free to be musical: Group improvisation in music*. In this class, students develop basic keyboard skills by studying rudimentary figured bass and basic jazz comping in twelve keys while learning to improvise on their own instrument. The skills necessary to teach improvisation and composition are acquired in the course.

Credential Requirements and Music in Schools and Community

Students interested in public school teaching must complete several methods and pedagogy courses required to earn state certification, including conducting, secondary instruments, and a course in preK–12 curriculum design and music assessment. Although these are traditional teacher preparation classes, the concepts developed and insights acquired in other courses provide the foundation necessary to critically examine long-held conceptions of music education. Individuals intending to teach in community centers complete a capstone course that requires them to develop a professional portfolio, design programs for different potential teaching experiences, and plan an instructional program that they deliver in an actual community setting.

Because this music education program is not restricted to students training as elementary and secondary public school instructors, individuals from the entire spectrum of music studies may participate, including those majoring in musicology and ethnomusicology. This approach to undergraduate university music education represents a major departure from the current practice of teaching only the specific competencies required for state teacher certification. When in place, beginning in the fall of 2014, the program will provide professional preparation in music education for individuals intending to work in private or community settings, as well as within the time-honored traditions of public school music programs.

This curriculum recognizes that elementary and secondary schools, like their counterparts in higher education, are hesitant to embrace change and will continue to hire ensemble directors and build specialized facilities in which to rehearse those performing organizations. However, this curriculum moves beyond training individuals to teach only large ensembles and provides all potential music teachers with the skills and concepts necessary to redesign curriculum as needed in the future. Additionally, this approach places music making at the center of all music teacher preparation courses. The concepts and theories about music education that are usually relegated to a separate foundations class are instead woven into these courses.

The different modes of music making experienced in the program's juxtaposed pairings serve as the catalyst for contextualized discussions about the nature of musical knowledge and of music learning. This interweaving of "doing" with "concept acquisition" parallels the ideals expressed by the comprehensive musicianship model of music education (Thomas, 1970), which sought to incorporate instruction in music history, theory, composition, and improvisation into the school music performance curriculum. A juxtapositional approach should provide future teachers with a working example demonstrating that it is possible to actually meet such an ideal.

Evolution of Juxtapositional Pedagogy

As Lee Shulman has suggested, any change in "pedagogy typically begins in frustration. Educators rarely invent new modes of teaching simply out of a sense of mastery or longing. More often, they are fed up with the kind of teaching they have been doing in the past." (Shulman, 1992, p. 1). The juxtapositional pedagogy described in this chapter began as a result of frustrations resulting from attempts to introduce Gordon's Music Learning Theory to students who understood only traditional notation-based music instruction. Student reflections on this experience indicated initial hostility toward aural learning:

> *I'm a little wary of it. I think that it's hard for anyone to think that the way that they were taught something wasn't the best way to learn. In the back of everyone's mind we're all thinking, "well I wasn't taught using this theory and I turned out okay." It's hard to admit that the way you learned isn't the best.* (Student 1)

To encourage deeper thinking about the value of aural music learning, I added discussions about music psychology and music learning, included peer-teaching exercises, and set daily journaling assignments as regular components of the class. The peer-teaching component was the mechanism that seemed to change student thinking, as the following reflection from the final journal assignment of the course suggests:

> *I was not expecting to find out just how effective solfeggio really was in the learning process. The benefits are limitless, from students developing an ear for pitch relations to internalizing a pulse. One realization I just came upon, however, is that by having students sing a phrase before playing it,*

you have effectively disguised an extra repetition of your material without anyone realizing it. You more or less fool them into practicing something twice. (Student 2)

Recognizing that carefully guided experiences in aural learning could actually shape student views, thereby enabling them to understand the value of aural learning, encouraged me to try a radical experiment. I developed a course combining formal and informal aural music learning experiences, with the intention that this juxtaposition would become the basis for in-depth discussions about the nature of musical knowledge, musical understanding, and music learning. The course that has evolved from these experiments now includes the following major activities:

- learning the clarinet via aural transmission;
- peer teaching, using Gordon's learning sequences;
- learning the guitar via informal processes;
- creating assessment rubrics and doing peer evaluations;
- working in groups to prepare without notation a song for performance;
- reflective journaling.

The purpose of the class is not to provide students with a template for teaching in an alternative manner upon entering the profession, but rather to help them acquire understandings and dispositions that might allow for creative approaches to the challenges they will encounter when working in the ever-changing world of education. A major objective is to help future teachers overcome apprehensions they might have toward unfamiliar approaches to music learning. Once their awareness has expanded, they will be better equipped to work with larger variety of students, many of whom may have already experienced different approaches to music learning.

In "Learning approaches in music education," formal music learning is experienced as students learn and teach one another on the clarinet using the Gordon approach. This highly structured method provides music education majors with the framework necessary to learn the instrument and to plan and present effective lessons to their peers. This also provides the opportunity for students to understand the mental processes involved when playing by ear. The following reflection demonstrates that learning to perform familiar songs by ear on a new instrument can be challenging and a catalyst for examining the learning process:

I am learning clarinet, with my ear guiding what notes will be played in accordance to simple melodies that I am already familiar with. Instead of "learn to play the passages from this page of music... " the assignment was to pick a couple songs that only require the notes that I've already learned. This involves generating the music internally before translating it into the act of playing, which to me requires more effort than simply reading sheet music to generate a song. (Student 3)

The combination of learning an instrument and also having to present lessons for one's peers on that instrument encourages students to take the entire process quite seriously. As one stated:

I found it to be very interesting trying to teach an instrument that we were trying to learn at the same time. For me, at least, it forced me to put in extra practice time in an attempt to not make a fool of myself while trying to teach. (Student 2)

As this course evolved, it became increasingly clear that the different activities were having a positive effect on student learning.

An understanding of informal music learning is developed by learning the guitar using the listen–copy–play approach employed by popular musicians. Lucy Green (2002) found that informal learning is distinguished by: (1) students choosing the music they learn; (2) listening to and imitating recordings; (3) working in friendship groups; (4) learning without structured guidance; and (5) mixing listening, performing, improvising, and composing throughout the learning process. So that the students can immediately begin working on the instrument, they are not allowed a choice of songs but instead given a CD with five carefully sequenced pieces, each of which is presented in three versions: (1) the entire song; (2) just guitar; (3) vocals and accompaniment without the guitar (like Music Minus One). Songs on the CD include:

- He's got the whole world in his hands
- Free fallin
- Peggy Sue
- Let it be
- Temptation

This sequence allows students to commence their guitar learning with a song using only two chords and prevents them from selecting materials that might have overwhelming technical challenges. Time is allotted in each class for students to work individually and in groups. This aural approach to music learning is not something with which most of my students are familiar and initially it causes considerable discomfort. The words of one student echo feelings of most of the class members:

Alright, honestly, at first, I really hated it. I hated not knowing exactly what I was doing. In general, I just like to be told what I have to do. (Student 3)

However, as they proceed in the class many discover that informal processes can actually be a powerful way to learn. Another student reflection confirms this evolution in thinking:

> *My initial reaction to learning guitar using the informal approach was very negative because I had no idea how to learn the guitar without formal instructions of a teacher. I've been so used to having all the information that is needed to learn anything.* I actually had to take the initiative to learn [emphasis in original]. *After a lot of work I've realized that it's easier for me to retain all the information. I think the informal approach to learning guitar, so far, has been successful and I've been enjoying learning it this way.* (Student 4)

As students progressed through the required songs, they realized that, although it was unlike the way most of them initially learned music, informal learning is a valid mode of developing skills and understandings. Additionally, most students quickly discovered that the Internet is an excellent way of supplementing their "self-instruction."

> *I have really enjoyed learning the guitar informally. Interestingly, when I listen to the songs on the CD for the first time, it is not very difficult for me to hear what chord belongs where. This is due to my training in theory. I am LOVING this experience. "On Your Own" learning is very different from my musical training, but I am quickly realizing that I am learning things faster, and am forced to practice more often. It is easier for me to memorize chords when I look them up on the Internet than having someone give me a long explanation.* (Student 5)

One of the more surprising discoveries for the students was that informal learning can be completely engaging. It seems that once an individual becomes "hooked" by the task to be learned, all of their mental energies are focused on that task and the motivation to continue and succeed becomes quite high. One student described her sense of flow while learning the guitar in the following manner:

> *The positive side to this learning method is that I feel more fully engaged mentally and physically when I am trying to figure out notes and chords on my own. There is a greater feeling of accomplishment when a new piece is learned, which motivates me to keep learning.* (Student 6)

Developing formal assessments might seem out of place in a course that explores informal learning. However, instead of providing instructions and templates for rubric creation, the students use the Internet to explore the topic of assessment. This process allows them to explore assessment and rubric creation in a constructivist manner. In this course, students create rubrics for evaluating learning on both the clarinet and guitar, use their rubrics to evaluate each other's performance, and then reflect on effectiveness of their own and other students' rubrics. Their rubrics are never formally graded. Instead, self-reflection and input from their peers result in refinements in the evaluation tools they are creating and using.

> *In grading [Mina], I realized that my rubric needed revisions. In its original form, it didn't quite suit the purposes of this lesson. [Mina], a beginner at the guitar, has made obvious progress in the past few weeks. I felt as if the standards of my original rubric were too strict. I realized that the original form would better suit a slightly more experienced guitar player. This being said, I still like the breakdown of skill level and description that I created in my rubric.* (Student 5)

As the students assess each other, they discover the weakness in the rubrics they created and refine their work in subsequent re-visions. Perhaps even more important, these future teachers realize that the way they interact with learners can have an impact on the way the information they are trying to convey is interpreted.

> *One of the best reflections we had to do was after we did the partner tests for guitar. I was able to sit down and truly think about what my partner that day did well and what she could improve on in her guitar playing. More than that though, I was able to reflect on how I relayed information to her and if she understood what I was saying.* (Student 7)

By having students create formal assessments in this class, while juxtaposing these with informal reflections and discussions about the application of these assessments, music education majors begin to develop an understanding of and an appreciation for evaluation in our field.

The final assignment in this course asks the students to work in groups and prepare a song of their own choosing for performance. The preparation must be done aurally without the use of notation and participants may not perform on their primary instruments. Class time is allotted to this project and it is interesting to watch the students interact and create music in ways that would otherwise not be a part of their formal music education. For the most part, the students choose standards from the Great American Song Book and seem to enjoy the experience. One student reported:

> *All in all, this experience has been very positive. It was fun to recreate a standard to a level that I think will be well received by the class. This ability to hear music and immediately be able to know how to recreate it is a skill that is invaluable to teaching and developing in students and teachers alike.* (Student 8)

Because the students prepare a piece while working in secondary performance areas, the final product may not match each individual's usual level of musical accomplishment. However, by engaging in what Thomas Turino describes as "participatory music making," they learn that it is possible to experience satisfaction in an ensemble that "creates a camaraderie and an empathy for people with different levels of skill (2008, p. 49)." It appears that in the context of a course juxtaposing formal and informal music learning experiences, students can become comfortable with both aural and social music making.

Juxtapositional Pedagogy

The curriculum described in this chapter evolved from attempts to provoke critical thinking about music education. The application of a juxtapositional stance to other courses in the UCLA music teacher education program represents an instance of a theoretical approach toward instruction emerging from practice and being applied to other courses in the curriculum. Juxtapositional pedagogy is a curricular stance to teacher preparation that deliberately pairs contrasting learning experiences to create spaces that challenge the critical thinking skills and enhance the evaluative cognitive capacities of future music educators. In *How we think*, John Dewey (1981, [1933]) develops the concept of critical thinking as a form of "reflective thought," which requires individuals to maintain a critical yet open mind while examining issues from multiple points of view. This way of thought demands continuous and thorough deliberation of the evidence supporting any beliefs.

The intention of this curriculum is to develop future educators' abilities to make meaningful programmatic and instructional decisions. The juxtapositional experiences are designed neither as polarized points of view requiring the future teacher to make a pedagogical choice of which approach is best nor with the intention of developing a combined, middle-of-the-road approach to the pairings that might result in a blended but prescriptive methodology that could be unreflexively applied in the classroom. Instead, these carefully constructed juxtapositional experiences are meant to form catalysts for intellectual conversations between class members so that their discussions and social interactions are central to forming new understandings about the nature of teaching and learning.

A precedent for developing musical understandings through juxtapositional pairings of styles can be found in Mantle Hood's advocacy of bi-musicality (Hood, 1960). This ethnomusicologist described how imperial court musicians in Japan developed fluency in both their native Gagaku and Western classical traditions. A bi-musical approach to performance-skill acquisition contrasts with the more limited objectives of most professional conservatory training, in which the goals center on developing virtuoso performance skills in a specific musical style. Hood insisted that with extended persistent study, fluency in multiple performing traditions is achievable. More recently, Huib Schippers (2010) has campaigned for a more holistic and global approach to musical development that would include study in multiple styles and traditions. Although the acquisition of bi-musical skills can be intrinsically valuable, it is insights into the music learning process rather than performance expertise that is the objective of the juxtapositional curriculum presented in this chapter. It is understood that students will leave these classes with just a basic foundational understanding of the pedagogies studied and will need to develop and refine the methodologies associated with any given musical tradition as they continue in their teaching careers. What is hoped for is that the curricular pairings will nurture reflective processes that will result in a disposition towards skepticism, questioning, and problem-solving, so that they might develop the curricular structures to meet the needs of their own students throughout their future teaching careers

Education is entering an era in which the hierarchal separation of master/apprentice is being replaced by flexible and fluid mentor/mentee relationships. In these associations, teachers offer learners a variety of potentially meaningful experiences and then themselves become immersed in an emerging community of practice that allows all participants to play multiple roles based on their background and experience. This approach allows the teacher to work collaboratively with students and use their expertise to scaffold activities in a manner that focuses the learner's attention on the important aspects of the experiences and activities within the learning community. Juxtapositional pedagogy permits the learner to develop a conscious awareness of how the instructor interprets methodological tasks but does not impose a specific belief system on the students. Instead, it encourages the active consideration and persistent reconsideration of belief systems in our field.

Excellent teaching requires both reflective and real-time decision making. Whether working with students in class, reflecting on their past instructional actions, or developing future curricula, teachers must have the skills necessary to make pedagogical decisions while taking into consideration multiple points of view. Rather than obstinately adhering to a predetermined methodology, teachers need the intellectual ability and emotional stability to examine successes and failures through ongoing reflection, so that they are able to choose from multiple paths of action, thus providing students with the best possible instructional experiences.

This chapter suggests that a juxtapositional approach to curriculum development offers a means for simultaneously preparing music educators to teach in traditional large ensemble settings and to develop the dispositions and understandings necessary to create alternative learning environments in the future. The chapter presents one possible approach for using juxtaposition to diversify the undergraduate course offerings within a music teacher preparation program. This approach to music teacher education might be applied at different points and in different ways during professional training. Mathematics educator Thomas Ricks juxtaposes videos showing contrasting approaches to instructional practice as a means of demonstrating the uncertainties that will be experienced in the classroom (Ricks, 2009). Because music is an art form that is constantly evolving, teachers must learn to become comfortable with ambiguity, even though they will be entering an academic culture that desires deterministic outcomes. Ideally, a juxtapositional pedagogy will allow prospective teachers to move beyond the stereotype of "teaching as they were taught" and will enable them to generate creative curricular solutions to meet the needs of their own future students.

Notes

1. By examining a variety of method books in the class, future teachers discover that the way information is presented in a text reflects specific pedagogical philosophies and understandings. For example, String Explorer (Dabczynski et al., 2002) has students add fingers on an open string where as Orchestra Expressions (DeBerry Brungard, 2004) has beginners place the third finger on an open string and then learn descending pitches. This reflects different approaches to developing left hand technique. Learning to critically examine texts for issues of this nature is essential to making effective pedagogical choices.

References

Allsup, R. E., & Benedict, C. (2008). The problems of band: An inquiry into the future of instrumental music education. *Philosophy of Music Education Review, 16*(2), 156–173.

Blascovich, J., & Bailenson, J. (2011). *Infinite reality: Avatars, eternal life, new worlds, and the dawn of the virtual revolution*. New York: William Morrow.

Dabczynski, A., Meyer, R., & Phillips, B. (2002). *String explorer*. Miami, FL: Warner Bros.

DeBerry Brungard, K. (2004). *Orchestra expressions, book one*. Miami, FL: Warner Bros.

Dewey, J. (1981). How we think. In J. A. Boydston (Ed.), *John Dewey: The later works, 1925–1953* (Vol. 8, pp. 105–352). Carbondale: Southern Illinois University Press. (Original work published 1933.)

Dunscomb, J. R., & and Hill, W. L. (2002). *Jazz pedagogy: The jazz educator's handbook and resource guide*. Miami, FL: Warner Bros.

Green, L. (2002). *How popular musicians learn: A way ahead for music education*. Burlington, VT, and Aldershot, UK: Ashgate.

Higgins, L. & Campbell, P. S. (2010). *Free to be musical: Group improvisation in music*. Lanham, MD: Rowman & Littlefield Education.

Hood, M. (1960) The challenge of bi-musicality. *Ethnomusicology, 4*(2), 55–59.

Ricks, T. (2009). Juxtapositional pedagogy: Designing contrasts to enable agency in methods courses. In Swars, S. L., Stinson, D. W., & Lemons-Smith, S. (Eds.), *Proceedings of the 31st Annual Meeting of the North American Chapter of the International Group for the Psychology of Mathematics Education* (pp. 1244–1252). Atlanta, GA: Georgia State University.

Sarath, E. (2009). *Music theory through improvisation: A new approach to musicianship training.* New York: Routledge.

Schippers, H. (2010). *Facing the music: Shaping music education from a global perspective.* New York: Oxford University Press.

Shulman, L. S. (1992). Toward pedagogy of cases. In J. H. Shulman (Ed.), *Case methods in teacher education* (pp. 1–30). New York: Teachers College Press.

Sorenson, D., & Pearson, B. (1998). *Standard of excellence jazz ensemble method: For group or individual instruction.* San Diego, CA: Kjos.

Steinel, M. (2000). *Essential elements for jazz ensemble: A comprehensive method for jazz style and improvisation.* Milwaukee, WI: Hal Leonard.

Thomas, R. B. (1970). *MMCP synthesis: A structure for music education.* Bardonia, NY: Media Materials.

Turino, T. (2008). *Music as social life.* New York: Oxford University Press.

Watson, S. (2011). *Using technology to unlock musical creativity.* New York: Oxford University Press.

7 }

Where It All Comes Together

STUDENT-DRIVEN PROJECT-BASED LEARNING IN
MUSIC TEACHER EDUCATION

Michele Kaschub

It is easy to talk and think about music education divorced from the contexts and purposes of teaching and learning in practice. Curricular offerings standard in most teacher preparation programs serve to transmit a consensually defined and fixed striation of music content and skills[1] even as new musics and musical practices continue to evolve outside the boundaries of school and formalized music studies. This juxtaposition has led some to theorize that the very privileging of these narrowly defined offerings within tertiary institutions has contributed to, and continues to be a significant factor in, music education's dated and disconnected present reality (Kratus, 2007; Williams, 2011).

Methods courses reveal a microcosm of similar trajectory. Typical coursework offers indoctrination in a roster of daily activities (i.e., pattern and scale exercises, rhythm games, etc.) partnered with strategies for efficient content delivery. Yet the majority of these standard instructional practices are sustained and transmitted in absence of critical analysis (Allsup & Benedict, 2008; Bennett, 1986; Regelski, 2005). Over time the application of routine and linear procedures has quietly codified the expectations of music teachers and music teaching while shackling teachers' creativity and the evolutions of practice that such creativity might have wrought.

Despite the best intentions of all involved, emphasis on specific teacher and student behaviors is now geared toward ensuring the survival of novice teachers and documenting the development of easily measurable skills. Little evidence exists to suggest that these practices will ensure novice teachers' professional longevity or the lifelong engagement of their students with music (Lebler, 2007). As Darling-Hammond has noted "effective teaching is not routine, students are not passive, and questions of practice are not simple, predictable, or standardized" (1994, p. 4). Given these circumstances, there is reason to question the extent to which current practices meet the needs of pre-service music teachers and, in turn, the ethicality of the teacher education enterprise.

New Roles within Deepened Learning Engagements

Project-based learning is by no means a new idea in education (Dewey, 1956; Kilpatrick, 1926), but its potential as a tool for ethical teacher preparation is far from exhausted. Commonly conceived as a set of activities designed by teachers through which students discover key concepts and ideas, project-based learning takes on new dimensions when students assume the driver's seat—that is, when projects are largely planned, controlled and executed by pre-service teachers.

PLACING PRE-SERVICE TEACHERS IN THE DRIVER'S SEAT

In *Drive*, Pink (2009) describes autonomy, mastery, and purpose as three key motivational factors that contribute to learning. Within student-driven, project-based learning structures, pre-service teachers actively engage all three components. They exercise varying degrees of autonomy as they decide who, what, and how they will teach. Multiple opportunities are offered to develop mastery of pedagogical strategies through actively researching music and related topics, planning activities and lessons, organizing materials, interacting with students, reflecting and revising, and enacting lessons learned by returning to the classroom to teach again. Most importantly, pre-service teachers develop a deep sense of purpose as they guide and support the learning of younger musicians.

The idea of the "driver's seat" is important in this conception. Pre-license drivers learn the rules of the road, how to recognize potentials dangers, and they practice behaviors, decision-making skills, and reactions appropriate to an array of situations. All this takes place while an experienced driver sits alongside to offer feedback and guidance until the learner develops sufficient familiarity to feel safe and secure in the driver's seat. The teaching equivalent of "road hours" is classroom experience. As Britzman has noted, "practice makes practice" (2003). Providing opportunities for pre-service teachers to confront the realities of teaching specific learners in specific contexts is a foundational component of the student-driven learning process.

THE CURATORIAL ROLE OF THE MUSIC TEACHER-EDUCATOR

To foster the development of the dispositions, knowledge, skills, and understandings that benefit teachers throughout their careers, music teacher-educators might adopt a role more akin to that of a curator. While curators are typically thought of as people who present collections of significant artifacts and materials, the role of the curator is experiencing a turn toward designing direct experiences and interactions for museum visitors. In this revised role, curators prepare collections and present artifacts in ways that allow and invite learners to experience and explore topics in new ways. As described by Siemens, the ideal "curator balances the freedom of individual learners with the thoughtful interpretation of the subject being explored" (2007, ¶9). Emphasis is placed on interactions that are self-directed and organized by the learner in accordance with his or her needs and interests as artifacts, concepts, and materials representative of the discipline are explored.

The value of the curatorial role lies in the facilitation of opportunities for others to make personal sense of information and experiences. When music teacher-educators apply this conception of curation to project-based learning engagements, pre-service teachers are presented with an opportunity to assume ownership of their own learning. The teacher-educator's job then becomes one of challenging pre-service teachers to think through the real implications of their musical and pedagogical choices and actions to help them consider alternative ways of being and acting (O'Sullivan, 2003) for the benefit of their students' learning.

COMPONENTS OF SUCCESSFUL STUDENT-DRIVEN PROJECT-BASED LEARNING ENGAGEMENTS

There are many variables to consider when utilizing student-driven, project-based learning as a tool for developing actively engaged and mindful teachers. The following collection of key components can be used as a checklist to ensure that projects maximize learning potentials.

Projects must allow for teacher autonomy. Accustomed to networked information and human relations (Boyack, 2004; Dede, 2005; Friedlander, 2003; Jenkins et al., 2006), twenty-first-century learners prefer engagements that allow them a fair degree of independence as they explore options, make choices, and act in ways that suit their perceived needs, interests, goals, and motivations. In acknowledging and welcoming the natural diversity of pre-service teachers, music teacher-educators can encourage the pursuit of different paths while collectively engaging pre-service teachers in an exploration of the varied outcomes that result. Such work may contribute to the development of curiosity, innovation and ownership that has been identified as indicative of creative teachers (Grainger, Barnes, & Scoffham, 2006; Jeffrey, 2003, 2005; Woods, 2002).

Projects must invite self-identification in the role of the developing teacher. The formation of teacher identity is the focus of considerable research in teacher education (Beauchamp & Thomas, 2009). The ability to define oneself as a teacher comes with some trepidation (Roulston, Legette, & Trotman Womack, 2005), as novices believe that the current pedagogical knowledge and skill they employ in practice is reflective of who they are as teachers. Pre-service teachers must be guided to understand that the ability to effectively enact pedagogical knowledge and skills develops in and through practice. As such, projects must allow pre-service teachers to exercise existing skills while simultaneously introducing new skills and teaching challenges.

Projects must activate a powerful personal narrative. Pre-service teachers benefit from developing a philosophy of music education that reflects their personal experiences with music and that applies to their professional lives. This philosophy is a key component of their teacher identity, shaping their preparation and experience (Hargreaves et al., 2007) and steering their professional actions, behaviors and decisions (Ballantyne, 2005; Reimer, 1989). As pre-service teachers assume increased responsibility for student learning, they are challenged to justify an ever-widening array of musical choices and pedagogical actions. Yet it is easy for these choices and decisions to pass unnoticed. Therefore, a critical task for music teacher-educators lies in bringing philosophical positions into consciousness and question so that pre-service teachers can explicitly and meaningfully reflect on their practice.

Projects must provide opportunities to engage in fulfilling work. Pre-service teachers need to sense that they are on a meaningful journey and not just committing to memory decontextualized behaviors and routines. The potential to expand and nurture musical and educational capacities for oneself and others is a powerful force in becoming an artist-teacher. Teachers who know that their work has made an impact on others find gratification and personal fulfillment in their work (Bernard, 2003). Their level of engagement deepens as their passion for music making and sharing is realized.

Projects must be challenging and should carry the possibility of both success and failure. When pre-service teachers have the opportunity to lead a lesson multiple times or to adapt a lesson for children of different ages, skills, and abilities, they can meaningfully explore what works and what does not within important aspects of the teaching and learning process. Pre-service educators tend to judge their own teaching quite harshly as they prioritize their personal impact more highly than self- or task-related concerns (Campbell & Thompson, 2007). More often than not, the problems that pre-service teachers encounter and label as "failures" are the very same challenges that more experienced teachers take in stride. Failure, a word often avoided in education, provides an opportunity for substantial re-visioning and significant growth. Should pre-service teachers experience a "teaching disaster," they can make rapid and significant developmental progress provided that music teacher-educators and field-based mentors offer feedback and guidance during the period of critical reflection and as pre-service teachers plan future learning engagements. In these instances empathy and assurances of the long trajectory of professional growth can help novice teachers maintain motivation and volition.

Projects must provide opportunities for transformative learning. Defined as "a process of examining, questioning, validating and revising our perspectives" (Cranton, 2006, p. 23), transformative learning changes how people think, and therefore has the potential to change how people act (Boyd, 1991; Daloz, 1986; Freire, 1970; Mezirow, 1991). To ensure transformation, learners must be active contributors in the process of creating and constructing what they are to learn. They must become aware of the limitations of their current experiences, knowledge, and perspectives and they must examine any assumptions they bring to the learning process.

As pre-service teachers engage in this work, they may need to "unlearn" approaches stemming from their own preK–12 experiences. Evaluative discourse can be used to explore the viewpoints and experiences of others as additional evidence is sought. Widened perspectives change how teachers think and alter their definitions of what is possible (Cranton, 2002). The magnitude of the resulting thought and behavioral shifts can be likened to what videogame designer and researcher McGonigal (2011) calls "an epic win"—an event of such magnitude that it was believed impossible. Pre-service teachers who experience the educational equivalent of an "epic win" in fieldwork return with the desire to lead, with advice to share and strategies and stories that become part of the communal teaching narrative.

Projects must unfold in intellectually open environments. College classrooms are fraught with power imbalances. Music teacher-educators must ensure that all facets of project design and experiences occur in an environment that encourages intellectual openness and relational candor. Most importantly, the music teacher-educator must carefully balance support and challenge to facilitate growth. Pre-service teachers must trust the music teacher-educator and feel that they are secure in taking musical and pedagogical risks. At the same time, they must learn to trust their own judgment so that they can fully embrace the role of teacher in the absence of the music teacher-educator (Dolloff, 2007).

Projects must occur within a community where people are willing to work together. In the process of undertaking student-driven projects, powerful social and professional connections can be established. Pre-service teachers collaborate with their peers, field-based practitioners, music teacher-educators, and preK–12 students as they learn how to teach (Burton & Reynolds, 2009). They benefit from exposure to differing pedagogical choices and perspectives (Loughran, 2006).

While music teacher-educators and field-based practitioners are often considered important resources and guides for pre-service teachers, it is often peers who suggest nuanced adjustments to a lesson or provide meaningful feedback from an observation. Further, the best teachers in any classroom are preK–12 students as they journey through learning activities with the pre-service teachers. The feedback students provide may range from overt to subtle, but in all cases, it is immediate for the pre-service teachers who are mindful of the rich data that are directly before them.

Projects must be closely aligned with the needs of specific learners and specific contexts. Successful teaching, at least in part, is predicated on knowledge of the learner. Powell (2011) has noted that while peer teaching allows pre-service teachers to refine their plans and approaches to lesson delivery, they remain uncertain as to how to gauge children's learning level and struggle with finding the right vocabulary to connect with students.

To overcome this and many other "knowledge of the student" challenges, Darling-Hammond (2006) has suggested that pre-service teachers must experience sustained contact with specific students in specific contexts to develop situated teaching tools and strategies. While pre-service teachers learn valuable lessons as they "tour" a lesson plan between several different classes and/or schools, multiple opportunities to observe and assist in a single classroom will allow pre-service teachers to become part of the community before they assume the leadership role in totality. Music teacher-educators and field-based hosts can collaborate to make such opportunities widely available.

Projects must include opportunities for teachers to hear, and reflect and act upon community-based feedback. While pre-service teachers can develop basic-level teaching skills without the guidance of an expert, Kirschner, Sweller, and Clark (2006) suggest that guided instruction is critical to advanced and nuanced learning. Experts, such as music teacher-educators and field-based practitioners, can highlight effective pedagogical thinking and action while staving off misconceptions that may unduly limit or hinder the future actions of pre-service teachers. The inclusion of focused self-evaluation has been found to be more important in the development of good teaching than heavy emphasis on instructor grading or feedback alone (Killian & Dye, 2009). Once feedback has been offered, reflection that emphasizes self-evaluation and professional responsibility is critical.

Representative Models of Student-Driven Project-Based Learning

This section highlights four projects, one from each year of the four-year teacher preparation program at the University of Southern Maine. Students typically complete two to three projects each semester. Music teacher-educators play a critical role as curators of all experiences, but continually cede control, independence, and responsibility for student learning to pre-service teachers as their teaching capacities advance.

In the seven semesters prior to the capstone professional internship, pre-service teachers complete projects in four general configurations. Throughout the first year the music teacher-educator frames and models learning activities that pre-service teachers adapt for specific students and implement in specific contexts under the watchful eye of a field-based practitioner. Projects that occur in the second year of the program are collaboratively designed and implemented by teams of pre-service teachers. Each teacher is responsible for individually leading part of the lesson within the team structure. The music teacher-educator serves as a critic and guide for these projects. In year three, pre-service teachers design independent study projects inclusive of literature reviews, fieldwork, and scholarly presentations. The music teacher-educator serves as a sounding board and resource for this work and facilitates field placements. In the final year and prior to the professional internship semester, pre-service teachers collaboratively design and implement projects within the framework of a multiweek workshop for home-schooled students. The music teacher-educator fills the role of "teacher whisperer," providing quiet guidance and support while individual pre-service teachers adopt the role of lead teacher.

SAMPLE PROJECT 1: BOOKSCORING FOR EARLY ELEMENTARY MUSICIANS

Bookscoring is a term to describe the process of adding music to children's literature. As children are led through an exploration of the characters, events, and settings that comprise a particular story, they engage in a process of guided composition. The children are invited to identify the expressive potentials of the story, determine complimentary or contrasting sounds and gestures, and then to create the music that they perform as the story is read. Through this activity children discover how music can enhance the impact of the feelingful components of literature.

The bookscoring project occurs in the first semester of study and focuses on three teacher preparation goals: activating pre-service teachers understandings of key philosophical ideas in music education as they relate to curriculum decisions; developing pre-service teachers' conceptions of effective teaching practices through an examination of prior knowledge and the analytical observation of peer teaching; and providing an opportunity for pre-service teachers to use their emerging philosophical ideas and further develop their conceptions of "good practice" as they assume the role of artist-teacher.

Pre-service teachers draw on their work in a concurrent course exploring philosophy in music education, as they decide what educational and experiential aspects of the bookscoring project they will emphasize with their students. The choices they make evidence their prior experiences as well as the new ideas they are encountering. Often their work also reveals some of the conflict that has arisen between their own educational histories and the varied perspectives they encounter through interaction with their peers.

Emphasis placed on building new skills and competencies often eclipses the knowledge of teaching that pre-service teachers have amassed informally throughout their own preK–12 education (Dolloff, 1999). This prior knowledge, when mined, reveals highly insightful and fruitful topics for further exploration and development. This knowledge can be viewed as a point of departure in the analysis of what makes for good and effective teachers.

In the early stages of the bookscoring project, pre-service teachers identify educators who have made a particular impact on their learning. They then analyze how certain actions, beliefs, and characteristics have contributed to their impressions. To further personalize concepts of good practice, students prepare brief peer-teaching episodes in which they share a topic or skill area in which they hold (non-musical) expertise. Peers analyze each presentation for "evidence of effective teaching" and the class compiles a list of engaging and effective practices. This list then serves as an action guide as pre-service teachers plan lessons and interact with school children.

In some ways, this first project occurs in the "deep end of the pool." While pre-service teachers have access to the music teacher-educator and host teacher, they ultimately assume leadership in designing and implementing their version of bookscoring. Project preparation may unfold in many different ways, but it is critically important that the music teacher-educator allow pre-service teachers time and space to discover how to shape their lessons most effectively.

Pre-service teachers begin by collaboratively discussing what they will need to know to successfully lead young learners in scoring books. They then develop criteria for book selection. At this point individual work begins. Each pre-service teacher selects his or her own book and has it reviewed by the host teacher. At the same time, pre-service teachers are observing and assisting in the two to three music classes where they will lead their version of the bookscoring project. Observation and interaction with the host teacher and children is essential as it allows pre-service teachers to gain a general sense of the students' prior knowledge and allows them to familiarize themselves with the unique characteristics of individual students and the learning environment that they will share.

Based on these interactions, the pre-service teachers develop the activities and questions that they will use in guiding students through the bookscoring process. They analyze the story and develop guiding questions to prompt students' thinking. They prepare needed materials and developing strategies for guiding students as they determine where music can be added to their story. They create plans for helping students explore the sounds of available instruments, consider how they will fairly manage the distribution of instruments that children have selected to match their compositional intentions, and weigh how they might best encourage and coach the creation of brief compositions that are often just a few seconds in length. Perhaps most practically, they rehearse the dual task of narrating the story while keeping eyes and attention on the students so that they can help them make their entrances during performance.

The fieldwork component of the project typically unfolds over a three-week period. Pre-service teachers travel into the field in pairs and assist each other by recording video (where permitted), writing field notes, and assisting as needed. At the conclusion of all the field teaching work, the novice teachers gather as a community to discuss their experiences and the feedback they received from their field partners and host teachers. The conversation begins with the prompt, "What did the students help you learn about teaching?" but evolves a life of its own as the teachers share their experiences. Below are a few responses that demonstrate the range of what they note:

> *"After we performed the book for the first time, the third graders spontaneously burst into revision. Their suggestions came with artistic rationales, 'We should add a high xylophone to make it feel like flying' and questions such as, 'Could we add a big drum played slowly and then faster and faster to make everyone feel scared?' I think they might have performed and revised all day if time had permitted."*

> *"They think of very musical things if I just stop talking. They went way beyond sound effects and got into character motif and the creation of soundscapes. The less I talked, the more they asked questions and made musical decisions. It is important to give them room to wonder, test ideas and arrive at their own understandings of how music feels."*

> *"Twenty-four kids and twenty-four percussion instruments. Let's just say it was a powerful example of forte. I won't forget to establish a quiet signal next time!"*

> *"After I led the bookscoring with my first grade class, the host teacher asked if I could repeat it with the third graders arriving at the door. Though I hadn't really thought of the adaptations that might have been useful, I said 'sure.' Here's what I learned: First graders and third graders are just alike and totally different. I had to listen differently to understand their questions and meet them with guiding questions that helped them figure out the challenge we had created together. [The third graders'] music was more complex. Sophisticated, even. Their ability to imagine was unlimited, but they weren't really able to perform what they imagined. It is so important to listen to them describe their compositional ideas. Their performances are not a good measure of their musical thinking."*

SAMPLE PROJECT 2: LISTEN UP

The "Listen Up" project seeks to engage children in active listening as they explore instrument families, musical genres, historical periods, or specific musical concepts through lessons featuring live performance. Children in grades three to six are the target learners for this project, but presentations have been adapted for younger children as well as middle and high school students. Given the role of performance in this project, host teachers frequently ask that presentations be made to large groups rather than to individual classes.

This project takes place during the second year of study and challenges pre-service teachers to capitalize on their musical expertise as performers within the role of teacher. Pre-service teachers engage in collaborative planning and presentation and teach individually as members of a cooperative team. Through these activities, they must fill the role of performing musician and teacher simultaneously. It is important to note that the project frequently calls upon the roles of composer and arranger as well.

Pellegrino (2009) reports that explorations of music teacher identity formation commonly note tensions between performer and teacher identity. This notion is reinforced in many teacher preparation programs as the development of the performer-musician identity is emphasized while less attention is given to the development of the teacher-self (Scheib, 2007). Unfortunately, this dichotomy is an oversimplification of a much more complex role. Occupational identity stems from three constructs: musician identity, self-perceived teacher identity, and teacher identity as inferred from others (Isbell, 2008). Developing teachers need to explore all three facets as their music teacher identities form. This project invites pre-service teachers to participate in multiple musical roles, develop personal experiential frames and expertise, and enact those roles in teaching environments.

While pre-service teachers are given considerable freedom in the design of the presentations, the project guidelines are given as follows:

- Form a teaching team or music ensemble of three to five members.
- Create a listening lesson that features your teaching team in live performance.
- Select a lesson focus. Consult with your host teachers and situate your lesson within their curricula.
- Prepare active listening lessons that can be adapted to suit learners of different ages, interests, and listening skills. (Note: Lessons will be presented three or four times.)
- Arrange and complete onsite observations prior to each presentation.
- Determine within the group teaching responsibilities. (Note: The ensemble must perform together, each member must perform individually, and each member must lead part of the listening activity.)

With the general framework of the project defined, students immediately form groups and determine an essential question to explore. They draw on listening skills and strategies developed in previous and concurrent coursework as well as their own listening and performance experiences to inform their lessons. When their plans are complete, they are shared in a teaching circle, where each team talks through its plan and gathers ideas and feedback from other teams and the music teacher-educator. Once any needed revisions and adjustments are made, fieldwork commences and feedback starts to arrive.

The following comments represent impressions of the same teaching episode from the perspectives of the host teacher and a pre-service teacher.

Host teacher:

"I just had a most enjoyable morning working with the four students sent to [our elementary school]. They presented their program to two third-grade classes and a fifth-grade class. The lessons were excellent and very valuable to the students, as well as age appropriate and entertaining! I particularly enjoyed the question and answer portion of the class. Your students think well 'on their feet,' asked good questions, listened, used good eye contact, and adapted quickly to the different age levels... and their playing was great too!"

Pre-service teacher:

"It was so awesome to play for an entire gym full of third graders. They listened so intently and asked great questions. When I walked through the gym to demonstrate some of the sounds that the flute can make, they really came alive. I loved their enthusiasm. Before this experience, I didn't think that I would ever want to teach this age group. Now, I see that I can use my performance to inspire their love of music without losing or giving up mine."

Host teacher:

"Today my sixth graders heard opera, jazz, and music theater selections from three sopranos. They were amazed by the singers' performances, but more importantly, they were able to describe key similarities and differences between the three genres. Two of the three teachers were a little nervous at first, but settled in quickly as they asked lots of questions and got the students engaged by challenging them to solve 'a mystery.' The students were so intrigued that their questions spurred a whole side lesson which the teachers tackled in a playful and humorous manner that was spot-on for middle school."

Pre-service teacher reflection:

"The connections that kids make are endless and sometimes lead to unexpected places. We set out to take our listening lesson in one direction, but after five minutes it was clear that we were headed down a different road. With a quick exchange of raised eyebrows and glances,

we decided to follow the kids for a bit and then [one of us] asked a few questions that put the train back on the track. The side trip was a little challenging in the first run of our lesson, but as we talked through what had happened, we decided that in the next class we would ask a few questions differently in hopes of preventing the miscommunication that had led us astray."

SAMPLE PROJECT 3: INDEPENDENT STUDY, INTERNSHIP, AND PRESENTATION

The junior-year pre-professional internship varies from other student-driven project-based learning activities in that it is part of a three-credit core requirement tied to the study of ethics. The project involves four parts: the selection of a topic that is of particular interest to the pre-service teacher; a formal literature review; a minimum of twelve hours of fieldwork that includes partnered teaching and independent teaching corresponding to the individual study topic; and a twenty-five-minute conference-styled presentation drawing together literature review and fieldwork. This presentation is given in a miniconference held for the full membership of the music education program. Throughout the project, pre-service teachers are tasked with examining the ethical dimensions of teaching and learning in their particular setting as part of their work.

This guided independent study and internship experience marks the most significant transition point in the development of teacher autonomy. In this project the music teacher-educator facilitates internship placement and serves as a resource as pre-service teachers pursue information and experiences to inform both their conceptual understandings and lived experiences of a particular topic area within music education. A significant level of project ownership and professionalism is required to fulfill project requirements.

The project begins with pre-service teachers identifying an area of study that they would like to pursue in greater depth. Choices have included pre-schools, preK–12 public schools, community music schools, and senior assisted-living facilities. Pre-service teachers have sought to increase their knowledge and skills in areas as diverse as working with students with special needs to exploring jazz band rehearsal strategies and curricular options for middle school guitar classes. The definitions of "music education" and "teaching and learning site" are broadly construed.

Pre-service teachers learn how to assemble a literature review in a concurrent course examining research in music education. The literature review is approached as an evolving process so that related topics can be drawn when questions arise from fieldwork.

Simultaneously, pre-service teachers complete a minimum of twelve hours of observation and assistive teaching in a setting appropriate to their topic area. Most pre-service teachers spend the first few hours in observation of their field-based mentor or host teacher before they begin assisting with sectionals or other smaller activities. Hosts and mentors are appreciative of extra eyes, ears, and hands and tend to put pre-service teachers into action as soon as possible. Pre-service teachers often continue working in school-based settings long after their required hours are completed.

The final aspect of the pre-professional internship semester is a conference-styled presentation for the university-based music education community. Interns schedule a miniconference with three to four presenters per time block. All music education majors are required to attend sessions and complete presentation evaluation forms that are given to the presenters at the end of the conference. While the interns have lead discussions within classes prior to this miniconference, this presentation is formal and echoes what teachers might expect to see at division conferences. Presenters are evaluated on appearance, confidence, effectiveness of slide presentation (if used), audience engagement, and a host of other parameters deemed valuable by the presenters prior to the conference.

Once presentations have concluded, the interns gather to discuss their experience from designing and pursuing their independent study, through fieldwork, to the presentations that they have just completed. These thoughts represent some of their experiences:

> *"As most of you know, I came to the violin through a studio where violin and fiddle playing are taught side by side. When I grew tired of one style, my teacher would just shift our focus for a bit. Without that variety and room to explore, I think I would have quit the violin. My fiddle-playing experiences have made me wonder how I could engage students with chamber music. It's hard to put an entire orchestra in your living room, but a fiddle, banjo, and bass fit nicely. I was able to complete my internship hours between a community school and private high school offering an evening course in chamber music. I coached a group of four students all semester and through their recital. What struck me most was how much they loved the freedom to pursue their own musical interests. The second thing that struck me was how little is written about using chamber music in middle school and high school music programs. It was extremely difficult to find research studies and practitioner articles were few and far between. I think this is an area that I will continue to pursue and I hope to share what I learn with other teachers."*

> *"Through my internship I was able to start and run a middle school show choir with the group of kids who didn't make it into the first group. I read everything I could find. I talked with a dozen different music teachers who*

had groups who had done well at recent state festivals. I worked hard to pump up my students' self-esteem as the sting of rejection and the idea of being 'the second group' wore on them a bit. I used music from the school's library and borrowed a couple of pieces for us to work on. The kids were doing so well that the music teacher decided to enter the group in their district festival and, after a bit of paperwork, I've been listed as the primary teacher. When school resumes in January, I will hold a sti-pend position as the second show choir coach and we will be at the festival. [Addendum: This teacher and his group earned second place at their district festival three months after this meeting and he returned to the school to coach the group again in the fall.]"

"I have to say that I was really nervous at the start of my presentation. I have attended a handful of conferences and watched lots of presenters, but I never really thought about the improvisatory nature of talking about my work until I was tripping over my tongue! It took me five minutes to settle down, but then I think it went well. I had my audience of about twenty music ed. majors playing the rhythm improvisation game that I invented for my second graders. They asked great questions and made some good suggestions about other ways that the game could be used with beginning instrumentalists. More importantly, as I watched everyone else present, I learned so many interesting things. I wish I could have done everyone's fieldwork."

SAMPLE PROJECT 4: THE YOUNG COMPOSER'S WORKSHOP

The Young Composer's Workshop is designed to provide eight weeks of composition study for young composers. As the project unfolds, pre-service teachers are enrolled in a course examining teaching music composition preK–12, they participate in a collegiate level composer's en-semble in the roles of composer and performer, and they assume the role of lead teacher within the Young Composer's Workshop. The experience differs from previous fieldwork in that "the field" comes to the university in the form of home-schooled students, accompanied by parents who sit around the perimeter of the teaching space as lessons and composition work takes place.

Curation of the project involves three tasks for the music teacher-educator. Once the pre-service teachers have created workshop brochures and regis-tration forms, the music teacher-educator distributes the materials via homeschooling networks. While waiting for registration forms to arrive, the pre-service teachers develop an overarching curriculum to span the eight-week period. The music teacher-educator serves as a facilitator as the pre-service teachers collaboratively create their plan. Finally, as each pre-service teacher fills the lead role in guiding the young composers and their peers through a variety of composition activities, the music teacher-educator is free to observe and offer in-the-moment feedback and guidance. In the role of "teacher whisperer", the music teacher-educator can affirm from the sidelines, but can also whisper words of guidance and wisdom to help lead teachers lead more effectively.

Perhaps the most striking feature of the Young Composer's Workshop is the opportunity to have all pre-service teachers teach in the same classroom as their peers, partaking of the learning activities in collaboration with the young composers. This allows the nonlead pre-service teachers to directly engage, observe, and collaborate with young composers to gain a better understanding of their thoughts, feelings, intuitions, and understandings in the musical domain of composition. It also allows pre-service teachers to learn about teaching while in the role of participant-observer.

These common experiences allow pre-service teachers to engage in individual and collaborative analysis of curriculum design, teaching, and learning. Conversations take place at the conclusion of each class meeting and focus on what has been accomplished to date, how the learning that has been achieved fits into the overall unit arch, and what adjustments have to be made to the upcoming lesson to advance student learning and individual teacher's skills. The pre-service teachers examine what they have noticed about individual students, what approaches and practices different pre-service teachers have used effectively, and how students have responded to differing task designs. Rather than focusing solely on what has occurred in the past, the accomplishments of the past are used to springboard future action.

In this setting, many learners emerge:

From a pre-service teacher:

"It is scary to start a lesson and not know where it will go. At the same time, it is really powerful to trust that students will have ideas, to follow and help them develop their ideas, and hear real music emerge along the way. Teaching composition has taught me that if you think you know all the answers, you aren't really teaching—you are playing dictator. Teaching is an act of vulnerability and mystery. If you open yourself to discovering with students, you also discover yourself."

From a twelve year-old YCF participant:

"[The teacher] was so helpful as I tried to write my ukulele song. I sort of knew which chords I wanted to use, but she helped me figure out how to test my ideas and try some new things. She also really helped me get my lyrics going. Once the words were done, we worked with the idea of unity and variety to change things up. It's really cool how just changing the strumming patterns makes the song even better."

From a parent:

"It was such a pleasure to watch [a pre-service teacher] work with the kids. His passion for music making was clearly evident in the way he cheered their ideas. I didn't know that the music my son creates had so many complex things behind it. When he plays an idea over and over making the tiniest changes, it drives me a little crazy (laughing). Now I know that he is in pursuit of a particular feeling and a way of shaping that feeling with the piano. The intensity and complexity of this process is astounding."

Situating Student-Driven Project-Based Learning in Music Teacher Education

Student-driven project-based learning engagements are not add-ons or occasional activities to be attached to a course or two in music teacher education programs. Rather, they are a critical component of a much broader conception of music teacher education that emphasizes the importance of fieldwork in every semester. Working within this conception, music teacher-educators use pre-service teachers' observations, needs and interests to draw important questions.

In this way, pre-service teachers learn to explore ideas, research theories, and test teaching methods and strategies that are new to them. The ability to adapt to rapidly changing information and contexts with curiosity and flexibility lies at the heart of ethical practice, that is, practice that is not limited by routine, which leaves room for students' active engagement and teacher's personal and professional creativity within the complex, unpredictable and varied exchanges that frame teaching and learning interactions.

FINDING STABILITY FOR FUTURE MUSIC TEACHING AND LEARNING

Without question, the most significant challenge facing music teacher education is that of the moving target. Evolutions in music, musical practices, and the tools that people use to create, perform, and interact with music have been in a process of change since music's inception. It is difficult for music teachers to develop a curriculum and concomitant tools for delivering that curriculum that keep pace with the rapid changes now unfolding. Change, however, is not the only constant in the educational equation.

Regardless of the genre, origin, or style of the music, the processes and practices that bring that music into being or the tools that humans use to create, perform, preserve, or share musical products, human interaction with music can be defined as limited to five direct engagements: composing, improvising, listening, playing, and singing (Kaschub & Smith, 2009). These engagements are stable in that they are evidenced throughout the history of music. As such, a curriculum built with these five interactions at its core can explore culturally defined, emerging, historical, technological, traditional, sociological, and any number of other descriptors or influences, interactions, or perspectives in, on, about, and through music. In these five direct engagements lies the foundation for a timeless and responsive approach to music education.

TRIANGULATION OF COURSEWORK

Preparing pre-service teachers to be able to adapt, change, and evolve at pace with all the evolutions in music or that influence music requires the curation of a program that triangulates direct experiences of the five engagements with methods courses and fieldwork. Pre-service teachers must have the opportunity to sing and play instruments in a variety of ensemble, chamber music, and solo settings. They must compose original music and improvise both freely and in multiple styles. Considerable time should be spent in the act of creative and critical listening, as this interaction provides the most accessible path to exploring existing familiar and unfamiliar musics. These personal experiences with music are foundational and should occur prior to, or at least concurrently with, coursework in methods and fieldwork.

Methods courses must help pre-service teachers establish strategies for exploring musical content and teaching strategies in relation to specific types of musical engagement. Pre-service teachers can employ analytical approaches as they explore *how* and *why* people learn *about, in, of,* and *through* music. These approaches can be tailored to interactions with all kinds of music, musical practices, and pedagogies. Questions such as, "What are ten questions that a musicologist (sociologist, theorist, performer, listener, critic, conductor, etc.) would ask when encountering a new music? And how would he or she then proceed?" help pre-service teachers prepare for change and encourage a breadth of perspective that can inform present and future action.

In this conception, methods courses are permanently unstable. Content cannot be fixed as it is contextually dependent. This allows the methods that arise from inquiry and analysis to be responsive to the flux and instability that characterize contemporary music and music education practice. While training prepares pre-service teachers to merely survive in the short term, education rooted in critical analysis prepares pre-service teachers to ask questions and engage in messy pedagogies—those that are able to address complex, everyday conditions of the field of music education.

PROGRAMMATIC EMPHASIS ON FIELDWORK

Many researchers have noted the need for integration between methods courses and field-based work (Gardiner & Shipley Robinson, 2009; Grossman & McDonald, 2008; Moore & Sampson, 2008; Zeichner, 2010). Tight coordination between integrated courses and careful mentorship can produce educators who successfully enact complex teaching practices (Zeichner & Conklin, 2005). Within the field of music teacher education, Scheib (2007) has suggested that such courses emphasis dialogue focused on problem posing, debate, cooperative learning, and reflection to help pre-service teachers develop a range of pedagogical skills and understandings.

These types of integrative structures are effective when fieldwork includes multiple observations and sustained interaction with specific children in specific school environments, as well as opportunities to repeat lessons with children of the same age in different settings. Chaffin and Manfredo (2010) have reported the positive impact of individual feedback during these engagements. Focused and immediate feedback can help pre-service teachers come to understand their own developing practice as well as the diversity of learners, schools, and teachers. Pre-service teachers actively involved in the full range of teaching actions, behaviors, and practices through fieldwork experience an "enculturation into practice" (Brown, 2006, p. 4) that contributes to the formation of teacher identity and professional confidence.

Challenges in Student-Driven Project-Based Learning

The implementation of student-driven project-based learning within music teacher education programs is not without its challenges. Hierarchical structures, logistical hurdles, assessment strategies and conflicting philosophies all contribute to the complexities of this approach, particularly in relation to the field components of project work. All of these challenges should be carefully considered and addressed before substantial programmatic changes are implemented.

The first challenge that participants face within this curricular structure is that of changing roles and hierarchical relationships. The roles of "teacher" and "student" are constantly changing. The person who was the "learner" five minutes ago may now be filling the role of "lead teacher." All participants must understand that these roles are fluid. The dichotomy of teacher and student is of limited usefulness in a community of teacher-learners.

Following closely behind the question of role is the question of how teaching and learning are best assessed in collaborative student-driven projects. Should pre-service teachers be assigned specific roles and tasks? To do so diminishes the autonomy they need to develop their own learning process and strategies. Should music teacher-educators be the primary assessors? Should students assess peer contributions and even their own work? These questions are not new in field of assessment, but how these questions are answered bears both philosophical and curricular weight in the development of teachers who will carry their own experiences as touchstones for their present and future practice.

On a more practical front, the logistical challenges of placing pre-service teachers in host schools are considerable. It takes a significant amount of time to visit schools, establish rapport with host principals and teachers, and to establish workable partnerships. It is important to develop host sites at the intersection of research and practice. Hosts must be able to give pre-service teachers opportunities to try activities that stretch beyond existing practices and routines. This type of openness to innovation requires field-based practitioners to rethink their own practice, consider ideas from different perspectives and perhaps even shift their professional values. Such actions are not only professionally challenging, but emotionally charged. Host teachers may feel threatened as they see "my way of doing it" set aside in favor of other practices.

Even when compatible matches have been made, relational challenges may still exist. Pre-service teachers often feel that they have to alter or abandon their plans to fit the conceptions held by host teachers. As guests in the host teacher's classroom or rehearsal hall, pre-service teachers may find it difficult to articulate why they wish to try an activity or method that differs substantially from what they have observed the host do. This difficulty does not stem from a lack of understanding or an inability to offer a rationale, but rather is a sign of the respect that pre-service teachers hold for those who have allowed them teaching space in their programs and with their students. Adding to this challenge are host teachers' tendencies to offer feedback reflective of their own comfort zone. Even the best preK–12 practitioners may not know how to best support learning in the early stages of teacher education.

Each of the above challenges can be overcome. Open collaboration can soften role boundaries and strengthen professional partnerships through active professional discourse. Logistical issues eventually ease as host teachers begin to realize that their students and their programs benefit from the presence of additional ears, eyes, and hands, as pre-service teachers assume supportive teaching roles within preK–12 settings. And most importantly, ongoing relationships between music teacher-educators, host teachers, and pre-service teachers lead to the development of a rich community of learners ultimately pursuing similar goals in the best interest of preK–12 students. As with nearly any carefully tended endeavor in education, new approaches and practices grow and evolve over time when the expertise and input of all participants is valued.

Conclusions

Despite the variety of challenges that may arise, student-driven project-based learning launches pre-service teachers on an intense developmental trajectory through which many personal and programmatic goals are achieved. Pre-service teachers directly encounter philosophical ideas and dilemmas. They develop direct experiential knowledge of learners and child development. Curriculum design, development, implementation, and evaluation are explored, as are academic, intellectual, social, and self-management skills, as they assume responsibility for the learning of others. Moreover, a critical awareness of educational stakeholders' values grows as they interact with students, music and non-music colleagues, principals, parents, and others (Reimer, 2003). These encounters allow ethical dimensions of teaching and learning to be viewed broadly, but also in specific contexts as related to actions that teachers routinely perform in their work.

Through all of these encounters, pre-service teachers develop dispositions of confidence, respect, curiosity, self-awareness, intrinsic motivation, humor, enthusiasm, passion, perseverance, and an appreciation of others and other points of view. A professional collegiality that crosses the boundaries of collegiate study and future practice is established and facilitates the transition from college classroom to teaching positions. Most importantly, pre-service teachers who have assumed considerable responsibility for their own learning become teachers who understand the difference between the "tasks of teaching" and teaching that invites and inspires students to be curious and engaged explorers and learners.

Perhaps the best testament to the effectiveness of this approach is found in the comments offered by practitioners who have hosted pre-service teachers during their final internships:

> "Totally in-tune with the kids. She was engaging and set challenges at just the right level to capture the imagination and interest of nearly every child. No one would guess that she was a student teacher."

> "Unlimited creativity, energy, and commitment to every learner's development—including his own ongoing growth as a learner of music and teaching."

> "He was so responsive to the students. He met them question for question and was really able to help them discover so much about music and themselves."

> "My students hung on her every word, but ultimately, under her guidance they made their own music."

Notes

1. See *NASM Handbook*, 2012–13, pp. 98–101, for suggested guidelines for music teacher education programs.

References

Allsup, R. E., & Benedict, C. (2008). The problems of band: An inquiry into the future of instrumental music education. *Philosophy of Music Education Review, 16*(2), 156–173.

Ballantyne, J. (2005). *Identities of music teachers: Implications for teacher education.* In the 33rd Australian Teacher Education Association Conference 2005: Teacher Education: Local and Global, July 6–9, 2005, Surfers Paradise, Gold Coast, Australia.

Beauchamp, C., & Thomas, L. (2009). Understanding teacher identity: An overview of issues in the literature and implications for teacher education. *Cambridge Journal of Education, 29*(20), 175–189.

Bennett, P. (1986). When method becomes authority. *Music Educators Journal, 72*(9), 38–40.

Bernard, R. (2003). Striking a chord: Elementary general music teachers' expressions of their identities as musician-teachers. Paper presented at the Annual Meeting of the American Educational Research Association, Chicago.

Brown, J. S. (2006). Learning in the digital age (21st century). Paper [keynote] presented at the Ohio Digital Commons for Education (ODCE) 2006 Conference. Retrieved June 27, 2011, from http://www.oln.org/conferences/ODCE2006/papers/jsb-2006ODCE. pdf.

Boyack, K. W. (2004). Mapping knowledge domains: Characterizing PNAS. *Proceedings of the National Academy of Sciences, 101*(Suppl. 1), 5192–5199. Retrieved from http:// www.pnas.org/cgi/reprint/101/suppl_1/5192.

Boyd, R. D. (1991). *Personal transformation in small groups: A Jungian perspective.* London: Routledge.

Britzman, D. (2003). *Practice makes practice: A critical study of learning to teach.* New York: State University of New York Press.

Burton, S., & Reynolds, A. (2009). Transforming music teacher education through service learning. *Journal of Music Teacher Education, 18*(2), 18–33. doi: 10.1177/1057083708327872.

Campbell, M. R., & Thompson, L. K. (2007). Perceived concerns of pre-service music education teachers: A cross-sectional study. *Journal of Research in Music Education, 55*(2), 162–176. doi: 10.1177/002242940705500206.

Chaffin, C., & Manfredo, J. (2010). Perceptions of pre-service teachers regarding feedback and guided reflection in an instrumental early field experience. *Journal of Music Teacher Education, 19*(2), 57–72. doi: 10.1177/1057083709354161.

Cranton, P. (2002). Teaching for transformation. *New Directions of Adult and Continuing Education, 93*, 63–71.

Cranton, P. (2006). *Understanding and promoting transformative learning* (2nd ed.). San Francisco: Jossey-Bass.

Daloz, L. (1986). *Effective teaching and mentoring: Realizing the transformational power of adult learning experiences.* San Francisco: Jossey-Bass.

Darling-Hammond, L. (1994). *Professional development schools: Schools for developing a profession*. New York: Teachers College Press.

Darling-Hammond, L. (2006). Constructing 21st-century teacher education. *Journal of Teacher Education, 57*(3), 300–314. doi:10.1177/0022487105285962.

Dede, C. (2005, January 1). Planning for neomillennial learning styles. *Educause Quarterly, 28*(1). Retrieved from http://www.educause.edu/pub/eq/eqm05/eqm0511.asp.

Dewey, J. (1956). *The child and the curriculum*. Chicago: University of Chicago Press.

Dolloff, L. (1999). Imagining ourselves as teachers: The development of teacher identity in music teacher education. *Music Education Research, 1*(2), 191–207.

Dolloff, L. (2007). All the things we are: Balancing our multiple identities in music teaching. *Action, Criticism, & Theory for Music Education, 6*(2), 1–21.

Freire, P. (1970). *Pedagogy of the oppressed*. New York: Seabury.

Friedlander, A. (2003). Knowledge lost in information: Report of the NSF workshop on research directions for digital libraries. Retrieved from http://www.digitalpreservation.gov/news/2004/knowledge_lost_report200405.pdf.

Gardiner, W., & Shipley Robinson, K. (2009) Paired field placements: A means for collaboration. *The New Educator, 5*, 81–94.

Grainger, T., Barnes, J., & Scoffham, S. (2006). Creative teaching for tomorrow: Developing a creative state of mind CCCU. A report for Creative Partnerships, Canterbury, UK.

Grossman, P., & McDonald, M. (2008). Back to the future: Directions for research in teaching and teacher education. *American Educational Research Journal, 45*(1), 184–205.

Hargreaves, D. J., Purves, R. M., Welch, G. F., & Marshall, N. A. (2007). Developing identities and attitudes in musicians and classroom music teachers. *British Journal of Educational Psychology, 77*(3), 665–682. doi: 10.1348/000709906X154676.

Isbell, D. S. (2008). Musicians and teachers the socialization and occupational identity of pre-service music teachers. *Journal of Research in Music Education, 56*(2), 162–178. doi: 10.1177/0022429408322853.

Jeffrey, B. (2003). Countering student instrumentalism: A creative response. *British Educational Research Journal, 29*(4), 489–504.

Jeffrey, B. (2005). *Creative learning and students' perspectives research project: Final report*. Approved by the European Commission, April 2005. London: Tufnell.

Jenkins, H., Clinton, K., Purushotma, R., Robison, A. J., & Weigel, M. (2006). *Confronting the challenges of participatory culture: Media education for the 21st century* (Part two). Retrieved from http://digitallearning.macfound.org/atf/cf/%7B7E45C7E0-A3E0-4B89-AC9C-E807E1B0AE4E%7D/JENKINS_WHITE_PAPER.PDF.

Kaschub, M., & Smith, J. P. (2009). *Minds on music: Composition for creative and critical thinking*. Lanham, MD: R & L Education.

Killian, J., & Dye, K. (2009). Effects of learner-centered activities in preparation of music educators: Finding the teacher within. *Journal of Music Teacher Education, 19*(1), 9–24. doi: 10.1177/1057083709343904.

Kilpatrick, W. (1926). The project method. *Teachers College Record, 19*, 319–335.

Kirschner, P., Sweller, J., & Clark, R. (2006). Why minimal guidance during instruction does not work: An analysis of the failure of constructivist, discover, problem-based, experiential, and inquiry-based teaching. *Educational Psychologist, 41*(2), 75–86.

Kratus, J. (2007). Music education at the tipping point. *Music Educators Journal, 94*(2), 42–48. doi: 10.1177/002743210709400209.

Lebler, D. (2007). Student-as-master? Reflections on a learning innovation in popular music pedagogy. *International Journal of Music Education, 25*(3), 205–221. doi 10.1177/0255761407083575.

Loughran, J. J. (2006). Toward a better understanding of science teaching. *Teacher Education, 17,* 109–119.

McGonigal, J. (2011). *Reality is broken: Why games make us better and how they can change the world.* New York: Penguin.

Mezirow, J. (1991). *Transformative dimension in adult learning.* San Francisco: Jossey-Bass.

Moore, L., & Sampson, M. B. (2008). Field-based teacher preparation: An organizational analysis of enabling conditions. *Education, 129,* 3–16.

National Association of Schools of Music (NASM). (2013). *NASM handbook.* Reston, VA: National Association of Schools of Music.

O'Sullivan, E. (2003). Bringing a perspective of transformative learning to globalized consumption. *International Journal of Consumer Studies, 27*: 326–330. doi: 10.1046/j.1470-6 431.2003.00327.x.

Pellegrino, K. (2009). Connections between performer and teacher identities in music teachers: Setting an agenda for research. *Journal of Music Teacher Education, 19*(1), 39–55. doi: 10.1177/1057083709343908.

Pink, D. (2009). *Drive: The surprising truth about what motivates us.* New York: Penguin.

Powell, S. R. (2011). Examining pre-service music teachers' perceptions of initial peer- and field-teaching experiences. *Journal of Music Teacher Education, 21*(1), 11–26. doi: 10.1177/1057083710386751.

Regelski, T. A. (2005) Critical theory as a foundation for critical thinking in music education. *Visions of Research in Music Education, 6.* Retrieved from http://www.rider.edu/~vrme/v6n1/visions/Regelski%20Critical%20Theory%20as%20a%20Foundation.pdf.

Reimer, B. (1989). *A philosophy of music education* (2nd ed.). Englewood Cliffs, NJ: Prentice-Hall.

Reimer, B. (2003). *A philosophy of music education: Advancing the vision* (3rd ed.). Englewood Cliffs, NJ: Prentice-Hall.

Roulston, K., Legette, R., & Trotman Womack, S. (2005). Beginning music teachers' perceptions of the transition from university to teaching in schools. *Music Education Research, 7*(1), 59–82. doi:10.1080/14613800500042141.

Scheib, J. W. (2007). Music teacher socialization and identity formation: Redesigning teacher education and professional development to enhance career satisfaction. Paper presented at the 2nd Biennial Symposium on Music Teacher Education, Greensboro, NC, September 13–15.

Siemens, G. (2007, August 24). Networks, ecologies, and curatorial teaching. Retrieved from http://www.connectivism.ca/blog/2007/08/.

Williams, D. A. (2011). The elephant in the room. *Music Educators Journal, 98*(1), 51–57. doi: 10.1177/0027432111415538.

Woods, P. (2002). Teaching and learning in the new millennium. In C. Sugrue & D. Day (Eds.), *Developing teachers and teaching practice: International research perspectives* (pp. 47–62). London and New York: Routledge Flamer.

Zeichner, K. (2010). Rethinking the connections between campus courses and field-experience in college- and university-based teacher education. *Journal of Teacher Education, 61,* 89–99. doi: 10.1177/0022487109347671.

Zeichner, K. and Conklin, H. (2005). Teacher education programs. In M. Cochran-Smith & K. Zeichner (Eds.), *Studying teacher education* (pp. 645–735). New York: Routledge.

Inquiry and Synthesis in Pre-service Music Teacher Education

A CLOSE LOOK AT CULTIVATING SELF-STUDY RESEARCH

Mark Robin Campbell

About five years ago several colleagues[1] and I within the music education department of the Crane School of Music at SUNY Potsdam embarked on a curriculum experiment that began with the idea of placing inquiry and synthesis at the center of our four primary professional development courses. We believed that these twin processes should be the guiding idea behind what the students did in all of their professional learning—beginning with the students' introductory course entitled "Principles of Music Education" on into their "Music Teaching and Learning" course, and then into their differentiated practices courses (choral and instrumental), and finally into student teaching. This experiment is ongoing, but it has been as exhilarating as it has been daunting. Vignette 8.1 illustrates the power of inquiry and synthesis when music teacher-educators provide students with tools that empower them to take charge of their own learning in ways that build personal and professional understanding, and create a sense of efficacy and passion.

The need to re-vision music teacher education has been the topic of a number of important writings in the profession. For example, Leonhard (1985) identified the need for music teacher-educators to be more in control of the curricular learning experiences that prepare teachers to teach in the musical world of today. Leonhard's concern was in reaction to what he perceived as a near total control of the teacher education program by external accrediting agencies and music disciplinary constructs derived from eighteenth- and nineteenth-century European traditions. Colwell (1985) spoke about the dominating power of the nineteenth-century European conservatory system and how it shaped curriculum experiences and competency expectations in the music education degree program within higher education. He questioned its appropriateness for American music education—as have more recent critics (see, for example, Kratus, 2007). Colwell's analysis regarding the history

149

Will Sutton: A Teaching Practicum Inquiry

Will Sutton is known for his superior performance ability and expressivity on the euphonium and his seriousness toward music study. He is also the recipient of a number awards that recognize his leadership and academic achievement. Will is a music education scholar. He conducted this practicum study during his third and fourth years in the program. As he notes below, Will had had a rather frustrating—and in his own word, "unsuccessful"— general music teaching experience working with 3rd graders in a local school. He had contemplated changing majors, but after a conversation with me focused on his positive dispositions toward learning and his keen sense of personal reflexivity, he decided to undertake a self-study focused on his own development. Below is Will's summary of his study.

"The Dynamic Theory of Goodness"

The purpose of this project was to become a better teacher. My motivation to become a better teacher came from a terrible general music practicum experience. It was my first time teaching children and I experienced almost no success during the semester. The framework used to structure this project was an inquiry-based self-study with focus put on my development as a "student of teaching." My primary question was: "How can I become a better teacher?" The data sources used during this project consisted of journals, logs, lesson plans, unit plans, observed student reactions, and my own emotions.

My project was done in many steps. I began by reading several theories of teacher development (Berliner, 1994; Fessler, 1992; Frede, 2003; Fuller, 1969; Furlong & Maynard, 1995; Huberman, 1993). I then chose four of the theories I believed were a best fit to my own path of development, as well as parts of theories I thought were best to strive toward. I then used the ideas in the theories as a framework for doing a content analysis of my blogs, lesson plans, and reflections. This allowed me to see where I stood in my own path of development, helping me to see what meaningful experiences I needed in order to become a better teacher.

After completing the analysis, I created my own theory of development called the "The dynamic theory of goodness." This theory has three main parts: (1) beliefs, (2) experiences, and (3) reflections. The theory is dynamic because it is ongoing and constantly changing within. It begins with identifying all your beliefs. You then test your beliefs. That is, seek out a particular experience that you have not had yet or seek an experience that addresses some of your current blank spots. Once the experience is over, you reflect on it and revise, dispose, and develop new beliefs. This then starts all over with the identification of your beliefs. The big idea within this theory is that *experience + reflection = growth.*

Several outcomes from this project I believe are important. This project helped me to discover more about myself as a developing teacher. It also helped me to learn about many theories of teacher development and how they can be useful in my own journey toward becoming a better teacher. This project also showed me the importance of inquiry. Through inquiry-based research I was able to develop my own theory, which I can now use in my future learning. Its usefulness in my development has been immensely important and has shaped the student of learning and teaching I have become.

Since completing this project I have a few tips for future undergraduates majoring in music education as well as professors working with pre-service music teachers. We all need to promote undergraduate research. The current image of research shows and privileges doctoral students and college professors conducting research. That image needs to be thrown out. There is a huge disconnect between primary- and secondary-level educators and the research being conducted by those in higher education. The importance of inquiry-based research and its usefulness in music education must be shared and adopted by all as a meaningful and important part of being a better music educator.

---

of music teacher education has remained unchanged since the 1985 publication; although he has continued to look for research and policy initiatives that seem promising for reconceptualizing the music teacher preparation program (see Colwell, 2006). Most recently he has proposed an approach focused on a "scholarship of teaching and learning," built on Shulman's (1987) concept of pedagogical content knowledge with a focus on the use of: (1) motivation (inspiration, persistence, doing good work); (2) critical thinking leading to wisdom; (3) transfer of subject-matter content and learning strategies—direct and constructed; and (4) assessment, in its broadest definition of feedback and reporting to multiple audiences including students (Colwell, 2011, p. 138).

Disconnect between theory and practice, along with the continuingly widening gap between research and practice, has been the source for a number of initiatives focused on music teacher education and programmatic reconceptualization (Boardman, 1985). Boardman (1985, 1992) proposed that music teacher-educators develop a clear understanding of contemporary constructs of learning and base their instruction on teaching and learning principles derived from them. Concerns about research-practitioner disconnects or gaps have generated suggestions to reconceptualize teachers' roles along the lines of action researchers or "teacher as researchers" (Conway, 2000).

More recent concerns have situated the need to reconceptualize the music teacher education program around ideas of learning that place the sentient, cognitive, and intentional individual at the center of the learning. This is in reaction (or in relation) to behaviorists' visions of teaching and learning and curriculum and assessment dominant among mid-twentieth-century theorists and educationists (on orientations to teacher education, see Cochran-Smith, 2006). Constructivist learning theory has served as the larger umbrella idea for these visions of music teacher education that center on the cognitive, social, and affective construction of learning (see, for example, Barrett, 2005; Boardman, 1992; Campbell 2007).

Most recently, Campbell, Thompson, and Barrett (2010, 2012) have put forward the notion of *personal orientation* as a theoretical framework for conceptualizing music teacher education. They draw upon a wide array of traditions but are rooted in postmodern assumptions that the self cannot be separated from the inquiry/learning process. In their articulation of the personal orientation theory, learning to teach music is viewed as a matter of personal action that is informed by a developing awareness of self, learners, subject matter, and communities within the profession. Cultivating an understanding of the complexity and interrelatedness of school contexts and teaching environments is also dominant in the personal orientation framework. From this stance, learning to teach music becomes a matter of role negotiation and identification, within a cultivated notion of good practice, with adumbration of issues related to power and politics. The learning to teach process is best summarized as "connecting self knowledge with social knowledge" (Campbell & Thompson, 2014). By extension, the music teacher education curriculum is conceptualized as inquiry and action. Vignette 8.2 captures the results of the personal orientation theory in action. It also illustrates how inquiring and learning are epistemologically rooted in self, collaboration, knowledge construction, autobiographical history, and context.

VIGNETTE 8.2

Matthew Wurtzel: A Curriculum Study

Matt Wurtzel possesses a gregarious personality, quizzical nature, and a contagious enthusiasm for all things musical and socially just. He is at home in many genres of performing, ranging from classical to ska, and uses a variety of techniques, including looping. He writes songs and regularly arranges and performs them on both acoustic and digital instruments. He can DJ and turntable a dance party upon demand and, if necessary, improvise on the spot accompanied by a self-constructed video. His observations of music education in the schools, along with his own personal experiences of formalized music teaching served as impetus for "A curriculum study." Matt was a third-year student when he undertook this project.

"Revise, Reform, and Replace: Re-inventing Music Theory Teaching and Learning for Secondary Students"

Over the last seven or eight years I have taken many different music theory courses, including "Intro to music theory" and "AP music theory" in high school and then "Music theory 1–4" in college. I have also observed many different high school music theory classes in different districts, with different teachers, and at different levels of depth. I always excelled in music theory and enjoyed how I could use music theory to enhance and enrich my own musical studies. I once, however, observed a high school AP music theory class in a very wealthy district, where the teacher had the students all sit at different computers and do part-writing exercises on the computer for forty minutes straight. The students didn't speak, didn't interact with each other, they just stared at the computer screen. The teacher walked around the room making sure students were always working and not just sitting in their chairs staring blankly at the work to be done. I came to learn later that this was the routine. At first glance, however, I thought this was good; students were using technology in the classroom to practice what would be on the test in May. Upon further investigation, I realized that the students weren't engaged much in the class. Doing these exercises wasn't helping them understand the music they were actually listening to and making outside of class, and they received little to no feedback from the teacher or from their peers. Nothing that they were doing was put into an authentic or social context and the drills they were doing lacked relevance in their musical lives.

I remember walking into Dr. Campbell's office one day, telling him what I observed, and saying: "There must be another way!" I then looked back at music theory classes I had taken or observed and realized that there were certain practices that existed in the teaching of music theory to secondary students that were of concern. These included the almost exclusive use of direct instruction, use of decontextualized and standardized content of minimal relevance to students, over-reliance on skill and drill exercises, and instruction that was driven by high-stakes testing. After identifying these issues I sought to create a model of a curriculum that was more student-centered, offered authentic and socially oriented musical experiences, and developed skills that were relevant to what students wanted to do in music. This curriculum would follow a constructivist-based framework and would use project-based learning. My problem and question were the same: "How can I design a substantive and well-grounded, yet relevant music theory curriculum for secondary students?"

I began my study by gathering information. I interviewed university music faculty, high school teachers, and secondary-school-age students about what they thought music theory was, how it should be taught, what should be taught, who it should be taught to, and what purpose music theory should serve musicians. I also looked through existing high school theory courses, advanced placement exams in music theory, and read literature on constructivism, behaviorism, project-based learning, and assessment (some sources new to me came from the following readings: Biamonte, 2001; Bransford, Brown, & Cocking, 2000; Campbell, 2002; Green, 2002, 2008; Janesick, 2006; Nettl, 1995; Schafer, 1967; Upitis, 1992). I took all this information and began to analyze it so that I could understand what I was learning. I then synthesized and critiqued the information and organized it into a concept map using an online digital mapping tool. With the concept map I was able to show what I wanted to use, what I might use, and what

I would definitely not use in my curriculum. I then began to create new curricular materials for teaching.

I created a set of projects that had students assume different musical roles, including listeners, performers, and creators of music. Each project allowed students to travel down multiple pathways so they could pursue what they were interested in while still broadening their horizons by interacting with students who had different interests from themselves. The projects were constructed using big ideas (drawn from Merriam, 1964), authentic and socially oriented musical experiences, and authentic means to assess student learning and growth. Below are short descriptions of four of them.

Create Your Own Radio Station
Music as communication and expression of themes of a culture
- What does it take to be a radio DJ?
- Students assume the roles of listeners and describers of music and create playlists to categorize music.

Book Your Own Gig
Music as aesthetic enjoyment and entertainment
- What does it take to play at the House of Blues?
- Students form ensembles to cover a song they choose and perform at a venue of their choice.

Create Music for Sound Sources
Music as symbolic representation and communication
- What does it take to be a professional creator of music?
- Students form an ensemble for which they compose music and perform at a venue of their choice.

Be a Commissioned Composer
Music as symbolic representation and communication
- What does it take to be a professional commissioned composer?
- Students collaborate with a performer to create music that the performer premieres at a venue of choice.

This project was very meaningful to me. Why? Because it helped me (1) develop a better understanding of constructivism and project-based learning; (2) analyze my own music theory experiences to see exactly what was helpful and what was not; and (3) create curricular materials that I can use when I begin teaching in public schools.

I believe that inquiry-based learning is important because it allows students in a music teacher education program to: (1) research topics of interest; (2) develop professional skills and dispositions that are necessary for life-long engagement in the profession; (3) create and use tools and find useful resources; (4) collaborate with others; (5) be creative and experimental with curricular design and use of materials; and (6) take ownership over their own undergraduate learning.

It was from this larger music teacher curriculum project of trying to conceptualize music teacher education's purposes/objectives, intents/outcomes, and instructional/learning processes, that several members within the music education department and I took a look at what we thought was important for future music teachers to experience and what we thought would be the most powerful approaches to use in achieving our goals. We wanted intellectual depth and we wanted learning experiences that would connect theory and practice. We wanted student-learning experiences that could be personalized and collaborative, and we wanted the experiences to cultivate life-long dispositions toward the continuous study of music teaching and learning.

We began with the idea that music teachers should develop an identity founded on adaptive expertise (Schwartz, Bransford, & Sears, 2005) and should hold three primary intellectual dispositions: curiosity, pursuit of excellence, and reflective action. To provide both clarity and direction, we envisioned that our graduates would be guided by a sense of personal agency. We viewed agency as informed action and characterized it as a music teacher enacting positive dispositions toward inquiry and putting into action teaching practices that advanced a particular vision of music education. Intertwined with this view of agency we held a specific notion of reflection, one that possessed the following key attributes: deliberating on classroom practice dilemmas; questioning of assumptions and values; attending to institutional and cultural contexts, initiating curricular transformation; and taking personal responsibility for professional development (Zeichner & Liston, 1996).

At the center of this conception of music teaching, as noted above, was the idea that inquiry and synthesis should serve as a primary theme in students' experiences within the program. We also felt that all of the inquiry and synthesis experiences within the curriculum needed to be: (1) flexible and challenging for both students and teachers, (2) substantive in terms of student knowledge growth, and (3) personalized in terms of student interest and skill development. We felt that the diverse range of inquiry methodologies and strategies offered by Campbell, Thompson, and Barrett's (2010, 2012) personal orientation framework met these goals and criteria, plus their methodologies offered maximum utility within and across the entire program regardless of course specificity (i.e., focus, track, or specialty).

Vignette 8.3 illustrates how a pre-service music teacher in our program sought to make sense of her course work, and music and teaching experiences using inquiry and synthesis. By analyzing and synthesizing her work, readings, and experiences across three different courses within the program she was able to understand more clearly how her degree functioned and helped her grow as a professional.

In short, our conceptualization of the program is not too dissimilar to Schwab's idea of "curriculum as practical inquiry" (1969, 1970) and his notion

Kathryn Hess: An Independent Study

Kathryn Hess has enough energy, curiosity, persistence, and initiative to serve an entire school of music—and then more! A more heartfelt and helpful young woman would be difficult to find. Katie conducted this year-long self-study during her third and fourth years. She had many ideas and interests that she wanted to study, but had difficultly landing on a meaningful project that would act as a synthesizing agent in her professional studies in the program. She was positively eager to do some kind of study prior to her student teaching experience. Upon receiving a special grant from an on-campus research program, Katie decided to look at her own development across several different courses. Below is Katie's summary of her study.

"Looking at Music Teacher Development: A Self-Study of Three Undergraduate Teaching Experiences"

The purpose of this project was to discover what it means to be a developing teacher. My goal was to work out a description of the ways I had viewed teaching and learning, including questions I had, challenges I encountered, pedagogy I had applied, and new perspectives I was developing. The frameworks I used came from chapter 4, "Orientations to teacher preparation," in Campbell, Thompson, and Barrett's *Constructing a personal orientation to music teaching* (2010) and Hersh's (n.d) *Suzuki teaching principles*. I used the ideas in these courses as lenses through which to look at my experiences and make sense of what was useful and important to me.

The data sources I used came from responses I generated from course assignments in three different teaching practica: (1) general music teaching practicum, (2) a special education practicum, and (3) a string teaching practicum. I also did an in-depth conceptual analysis of the music education curriculum at the school of music I attend and an analysis of models of teaching gained from attending at Suzuki Institute during a summer between semesters. In addition, I met with professors for both informal and formal conversations, and relied upon my own personal reflections on completed course work and teaching experiences.

My analysis goal was to identify concepts and skills that emerged in my music teacher preparation program. I wanted to know what I had learned and how I might use what I learned moving forward in my career. Although each teaching and learning context was different, convergence arose from reflecting on my course work, experiences, and readings. Here is what my analysis revealed. I developed knowledge, skills, and dispositions that evolved out of: problem solving, decision making, and adjusting to changing circumstances, reflection, time management, differentiating instruction, and developing and utilizing criteria. I found that each course provided both similar and different pedagogical problems that helped me analyze (and understand) teaching (and music learning) from different perspectives. I also learned that each course provided opportunities to explore one or more of the five orientations to teacher preparation discussed in Campbell, Thompson, and Barrett (2010), as well as the Suzuki teaching principles presented by Hersh (n.d.). For my own teaching, I see advantages of pulling from all five orientations, as well as the Suzuki teaching principles, in assisting students as they engage with music. No one idea serves all individuals.

Analyzing and synthesizing my course work has better prepared me for student teaching. This project helped me to understand how to facilitate strategies for instruction and use reflection to propel my development. It has also strengthened my disposition to "always be" curious about education and to be a thoughtful educator. And last, it allowed me to personally assess the generativity, vibrancy, and residue of the course work I had undergone in my music teacher education program in a meaningful and professional level.

---

of "curriculum commonplaces" (1983) as an anchor for teacher investigation and action. Thus, inquiry into and about self, learners, music, and contexts became sites not only for class activities and discussions, but also for both individual and collaborative student investigations. Figure 8.1 shows in schematic form our conceptual framework.

Making Inquiry and Synthesis Practical in the Program

Because inquiry and synthesis function as a central theme within the program and across different courses students take, we felt the need to characterize it as systematic study built on: (1) seeking knowledge and refining skills through questions; (2) examining and analyzing something close up and far away; and (3) synthesizing investigative inquiry into a theory, set of principles, or a conceptual framework for personal practice. Given this characterization, we were able to make it practical. That is, faculty could tailor student inquiry to the specific goals and objectives within their courses. As space does not allow for describing how individual faculty members integrate inquiry into their course work, a list of the kinds of inquiry projects that occur within the overall program is shown in Table 8.1. In this table, note two courses: (1) teaching and learning, and (2) practicum. "Teaching and learning" refers to a sophomore-level course that is focused on the research and study of music teaching and learning. This course replaced standalone elementary and standalone secondary general music methods courses about ten years ago. The practicum is a junior-level music teaching course that all students take for a semester, working with music education faculty members in a local pre-K–6 parochial school prior to student teaching.

Individually these inquiry projects comprise the armature for each pre-service music teachers' personal and scholarly study of music teaching and learning. Through direct design efforts, we believe the sum of the individual

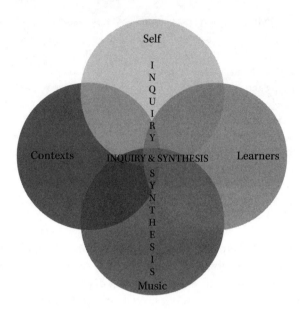

FIGURE 8.1 **Conceptual framework**

projects (listed in Table 8.1) adds up to a greater synthetic whole. How so? Because students have investigated self, learners, music, and context within different programmatic (and cultural or institutional) settings and have been asked to analyze and synthesize various ideas within these four commonplaces continuously over the entire program. Collectively these inquiry projects allow pre-service music teachers to reflect on their upbringings, as well as to acknowledge the cultural and historical spaces that have contributed to shaping their professional identities. Both personal and professional growth and development are embodied in the projects, with learning to teach music viewed as a continuously reshaped and reshaping phenomenon (see Britzman, 2003).

For both accrediting and institutional accountability purposes, the electronic portfolio project listed in Table 8.1 serves as a process document of student learning and development, as well as a product document for employment usage (see Campbell & Brummett, 2007). In the larger scheme of program goals, the portfolio functions as a form of self-study. In the even larger scheme of lifelong professional learning, the self-reflection and assessment activities involved in the portfolio project strengthen the kind of mindset required for both educational change and reform as well as for personal and professional renewal (Samaras & Freese, 2006). As a professional habit of mind, however, cultivating self-study begins in the pre-service program (see Lassonde & Strub, 2009).

The idea of self-study is both appealing and compelling for the music teacher education profession because it stands in contrast to preparation

TABLE 8.1 } **Kinds of inquiry projects**

Inquiry project	Course	Purpose—activities
Musical circles	Throughout	Identifying and reflecting on the power of music experiences in people's lives
Education and musical personal history	Introduction	Reflecting on the impact of personal learning experiences and personal musical experiences
Autobiographical time-lining	Introduction	Constructing a biographical timeline that identifies important musical and educational events
Successful/unsuccessful teacher reflection	Introduction, practicum	Identifying and reflecting on successful qualities required for teaching
Images and metaphors	Introduction, practicum, student teaching	Creating initial personal teaching metaphor; constructing a representation of self as teacher
Interviewing	Introduction, teaching-learning (methods)	Learning from students, practicing teachers, music education faculty, older pre-service students about educational and musical aspects of the profession
Shadow study	Introduction, practicum, student teaching	Investigating a particular (K–8) student's lived experience in school (at elementary and middle school levels)
Grammars of schooling	Teaching-learning (methods)	Uncovering the structural and reproductive nature of schooling
Blogging-journaling	Throughout	Reflecting on teaching: open, formatted, prompted
Lab ensemble	Practices	Experimenting with new pedagogies and reflecting on their efficacy and experimenting with personal teaching
Participant-observation	Practicum, practices	Describing and understanding a particular topic or situation through the meanings ascribed to it by the individuals who live and experience it
Content analysis of teaching	Practicum, practices, student teaching	Identifying patterns in text, visual, or audio records of a music teaching experience and synthesizing findings into descriptions of practice
Personal musicianship	Teaching-learning (methods)	Informally (1) learning a new (fretted or digital) instrument, (2) investigating unfamiliar genres of popular, world, or vernacular music, and (3) creating compositions using creative digital technologies; documenting the learning processes of all three
Independent study	Throughout	Designing, carrying out, and presenting an investigation project on any musical or educational aspect of personal interest
Curriculum study	Throughout	Identifying, analyzing, and critiquing existing curricular ideas or instructional practices, and proposing alternatives based upon theoretical frameworks
Curriculum design	Teaching-learning (methods)	Synthesizing educational theory, educational principles, musical experiences into comprehensive preK–12 curriculum activities, units, or documents

(Continued)

TABLE 8.1 } **(Continued)**

Inquiry project	Course	Purpose—activities
Literature inquiry	Teaching-learning (methods), practices	Investigating a topic of musical or educational interest across three different professional communities and evaluating ideas for constructing guidelines for practice
Trend spotting	Teaching-learning (methods)	Cultivating dispositions of inquiry and renewal of interest
Teacher development synthesis	Practicum, student Teaching	Synthesizing program experiences in relation to normative theories of teacher development
Self-study	Throughout	Designing, carrying out, and presenting a personal investigation project that shows personal and professional growth
Developmental portfolio	Throughout	Creating a portfolio that reflects personal development and growth in becoming a student of music teaching

programs built on "top-down best practices," decontextualized research, routine, method implementation, impulse, or tradition. When viewed and designed as a systematic and critical examination of a teacher's actions in a specific context, self-study becomes a "consciously driven mode of professional activity" (Samaras & Freese, 2006, p.11). The idea of self-study is equally compelling because of its focus on the *scholarship of teaching and learning*, and its capacity to cultivate critical thinking and complex reasoning within the domains of education and music (on critical thinking as key component of music teacher education, see Colwell, 2011). It is especially compelling because of its capacity to engender personal agency within a professional context. Given the appeal and potential power of self-study as an efficacious methodology in the development of learning to teach music, a closer look at its philosophical foundations, characteristics, and benefits is useful.

A Closer Look at Self-Study

WHAT IS SELF-STUDY (IN MUSIC TEACHER EDUCATION)?

Self-study belongs to a cluster of educational research paradigms and approaches to the scholarship of teaching that includes teacher inquiry (or teacher as researcher), reflective practice, and action research. From teacher inquiry comes the idea of questioning one's practice (Cochran-Smith & Lytle, 2004; Zeichner & Liston, 1996). From reflective practice comes the idea of examining and problematizing teaching practice (Dewey, 1933; Schön, 1983, 1987). From action research comes the idea of systematically changing practice based on problem posing and problem solutioning (Carr & Kemmis, 1986; McNiff, 1988; Mills, 2003).

Although related and derivative of these three traditions, self-study is distinctive. Hamilton and Pinnegar (1998) provide the following characterization: "Self-study is the study of one's self, one's actions, one's ideas, as well as the 'not self'" (p. 236). Samaras and Freese (2006) add that self-study is "designed to lead to the reconceptualization of the role of the teacher" (p. 29) as a source of knowledge in collaborative dialogue, as distinct from the receiver of knowledge. Distinctive dispositions characteristic of this reconceptualized role, according to Samaras and Freese, are: (1) *openness* (willingness to learn from self-doubt and vulnerability, and willingness to learn from others), (2) *collaboration* (working within contextualized communities of practitioners), and (3) *reframing ideas* (collaborative dialoging focused on framing or reframing problems and situations from multiple perspectives that leads to change or improvement in practice). Although these descriptions provide information on what the self-study of teaching is, Bullough and Pinnegar (2004) argue that as a research practice it is in continuous redefinition due to its conceptual inclusiveness and the communal conversations that surround it.

In essence, teachers (whether pre-service or in-service) engaged in self-study seek to investigate problems and/or explore successful practices in order to generate knowledge about their practices so that they can articulate and share with others what they have found (LaBoskey, 2004; Loughran, 2005). Furthermore, teachers address and honor the contextual nature of their studies (whether it be in a classroom, a program, a school, etc.) because it affords them the opportunity to assess the efficacy of their personal and practical theories (see Connelly & Clandinin, 1985). Self-study teachers also recognize that the self cannot be separated from the research process or from the teaching process (Cochran-Smith & Lytle, 2004), and they primarily employ post-positivist qualitative research approaches to analyzing and reporting their findings. Within the context of the pre-service practicum, Beck, Fresse, and Kosnik (2004) describe the research/learning process as inquiry-oriented, personal, reflective, collaborative and constructivist. Its core purposes are: (1) personal growth and development, (2) professional growth and development, and (3) educational improvement.

CURRICULUM EXAMPLES OF PRE-SERVICE MUSIC TEACHER SELF-STUDIES

The three vignettes in the first part of this chapter, used to illustrate inquiry and synthesis, are examples of self-studies. Each has been crafted around the basic ideas used to characterize self-study. In our program we have aspired to create both conditions and opportunities for self-study; however, our work has been tempered by a number of factors. These include: (1) students' maturation and intellectual development—including their abilities and dispositional willingness to critique their own experiential knowledge of the "grammars of schooling" (see Tyack & Cuban, 1995); (2) student positioning within the university evaluative system and the dominantly conservative cultural and technical-rational political context of the public school student teaching experience; (3) student knowledge and experience with formal aspects of qualitative research; and (4) the creation of time within preconceived notions of content coverage within a highly packed curriculum of required courses dictated by a number of outside agencies and constituencies.

Nonetheless, we have integrated into the program many aspects of teacher inquiry and reflective practice, and where possible, aspects of formal action research—especially where students have capacity and access to educational contexts and situations where they can problematize and systematically change curricular thinking and pedagogy. Where we have been most successful is using the different inquiry projects identified in Table 8.1 as components of more integrative self-studies.

When conceptualized broadly, however, self-study within the music teacher education program can happen both informally and formally when music teacher-educators offer opportunities for pre-service music teachers to interrogate (i.e., access and critique) their beliefs and study (i.e., narrate) their developing teacher identities. Self-study can also be promoted when music teacher-educators specifically guide reflection—often by focusing on problematic situations versus ideal situations, then identifying limitations and qualities necessary for overcoming these limitations, and finally proposing actions for positive change (see Egan, 2007). In both cases (critique of beliefs and guided reflection), narratives about self and situations can occur in response to readings, discussion, practica, or student teaching experiences.

To engage in the necessary dispositions of openness, collaboration, and reframing of ideas required of substantive self-studies, we have had to step back and specifically focus on cultivating *wonderment* and *curiosity*. We have learned that these two dispositions are prerequisite to openness and reframing. (We have hypothesized—in our own self-study of pre-service music students in teaching and learning situations—that the paucity of wonderment and curiosity observed may be due to the students' precollegiate "apprenticeships of observations" [Lortie, 2002] of teaching as a transmissive practice [Thompson & Campbell, 2003], as well as their experiences in precollegiate curricular content derived from competitive and/or test-driven instruction.) Collaboration (working within contextualized communities of pre-service "soon-to-be practitioners") has also required some significant work in helping students learn how to be an intellectual community. Two examples serve to illustrate the cultivation of these dispositions within the larger goal of self-study as a core activity in professional development. The first comes from a sophomore-level methods class, which we have reconfigured as "the research and study of music teaching and learning." The second one comes from a choral practices course taken during the junior-level year.

Curriculum Design Project. In the Music Teaching and Learning class, we ask students to form friendship groups and spend six to seven weeks on creating comprehensive preK–12 music curriculum for entire school systems in which they would like to teach. (This is the "Curriculum design project" found in Table 8.1). They begin this project by exploring the descriptive and demographic makeup of several existing but contrasting school districts around the United States; plus they share characteristics of school districts they have attended prior to college. Afterwards, students create a school and community context replete with demographics to serve as a basis for their design work. Then specific curricular content work commences. To do this, students take an ethnomusicological perspective. Using one of Merriam's (1964) functions of music, buttressed with Gregory's (1997) descriptions of social roles in music, students generate a curricular focus for an entire preK–12 school and then create disciplinary questions that are developmentally appropriate for primary, elementary, middle school, and high school students. The questions are then used as a basis for creating extended (ten to twelve weeks) music-learning activities using project-based learning and "assessment as exhibition" models.

For example, using Merriam's function of "music as aesthetic response," students might fashion a set of learning activities around the question: "How do different conceptions of beauty influence the creation, performance, and reception of music?" Their basic intellectual task is to individually and collaboratively *wonder* (and reflect): They have to wonder about the question, wonder about how to create comprehensive musical experiences that could emerge from the question, wonder about how to organize instruction in a logical manner, wonder about how to create a balance among different musical activities, and finally wonder about how to create relevant and meaningful experiences for preK–12 learners.

Their second basic task is to be *inquisitive* and seek out information that will help them design (and later teach) their curriculum. Here students have to work within an inquiry framework that asks them to use *criteria* for assessing the quality of learning goals, materials, activities, presentations, performances, assessment vehicles, and teaching processes and procedures. For describing criteria we draw upon Eisner's (2002) definition of the function of criteria as that of judging the qualities of something in terms of its capacity for deepening experience rather than making comparisons. For the project, we ask students to use Campbell, Thompson, and Barrett's (2010) three criteria for assessing musical/educational experiences: generativity, vibrancy, and residue (pp. 126–127). While in the design phase, students have opportunity to interview preK–12 students and innovative practicing music teachers for "good learning ideas" and "good musical things to do" that are at root educative. The information from their interviews must be worked into their designs. Later they present their instructional ideas to the younger students and practicing music teachers for feedback. Plus, college students are required to surf the Internet, "play with," assess, and integrate free online creative digital technologies into their curriculum. Upon completion, students give an exhibition of their work to invited guests (including as many deans, directors, and upper-level collegiate administrators as are available to attend).

This project embodies Schwab's (1959/1978) notion of the teacher as *curious* and *inquiring*, as well as the teacher as *maker* and *inquirer* of curriculum. It also embodies Schwab's idea that teachers are professionals who are concerned about their own practices and the complexities and subtleties of their effects, and not trained technicians charged with delivering prepackaged materials and skill work to groups of learners. Furthermore, the project embodies the ideas of investigating and questioning practice, examining and problematizing practice, and systematically posing and solving problems. Although the project's focus is on curriculum design, it is a self-study project appropriate for pre-service music teachers given their developmental trajectories in professional learning.

Participant-Observation Project. "Choral practices" is the first of two courses focused on educating pre-service music teachers on how to run a successful choral program in elementary and middle schools. Goals include development of instructional and assessment skills and development of children's music program standards. Students do many learning activities that are not specifically inquiry oriented, but inquiry projects in the course are designed to personalize student learning and to connect learning to the work of practicing choral teachers and choral literature. The main goal is to develop research skills of problem posing, investigation, interviewing, collecting data, and analyzing and synthesizing information. The inquiry projects are whole-class and team-based projects. Projects are presented in class and at other campus venues. The participant-observation project is the main inquiry project students do for the course, which is conducted over the course of an entire semester.

Using Schwab's four curriculum commonplaces as a framework, students investigate team-generated questions based on their own interests and/or the ideas presented in the course readings. Once a week the class visits a local middle school and participates in a 6th–8th grade mixed chorus by carrying out and engaging in variety of "teacherly" activities (e.g., assessing students' singing, leading sectionals, exploring choral literature). Students keep journals as a record of their participation. While at the middle school, teams also carry out their commonplaces investigations—getting data from interviewing, field logging, observing classroom interactions, and analyzing materials and ideas offered by the host choral music education teacher. These data, along with the data from their participation journals, are analyzed and synthesized into lessons learned, and then compared to the course readings and other scholarly literature devoted to choral music education. Commonplaces topics of recent student inquiry, for example, include: (1) questions related to vocal health, use of amplification (Teacher); (2) questions about warm-ups, use of body, posture, choral arrangements (Subject Matter); (3) questions on students' perception of chorus, performances, rehearsals, and extra-curricular music activities (Learner); and (4) questions about combined gender groupings (i.e., male and female mixed choruses) or separated gender groupings (i.e., male only or female only choruses), classroom environment, and school-cultural environment (Milieu). Upon completion of their participation-observation projects, students give presentations on what their teams learned and how they will use it in their own choral music education practices.

This project also exhibits the characterizing features of self-study. At the same time it introduces pre-service music teachers to the larger research and practice literature on choral music education. It also helps them begin to analyze, assess, and integrate their own understandings in relation to larger professional (scholarly and practical) contexts.

What are the Central Characteristics and Benefits of Self-Study?

Given its flexibility for use in many different music teacher-learning contexts, self-study as a research (and teaching and learning) methodology might be seen as a rather "fluid concept." It is. However, in trying to describe self-study more formally as a research methodology, scholars of teaching have identified five basic characteristics that seem to capture the nature of the activity and its benefits for professional thinking and action. Self-study is (1) situated inquiry, (2) process-oriented, (3) knowledge-generating, (4) multiple, and (5) paradoxical.

Situated inquiry. Self-study begins with a (music) teacher's personal inquiry and is driven by interest and self-generated questions, and it emanates from within the context in which the individual is situated. Because knowledge is generated by personal inquiry, rather than "outside" researchers, it has immediate utility and it authenticates the teacher's or inquirer's role as researcher (Cochran-Smith & Lytle, 1993, 2004). Because self-study is context-bound it is also grounded in the "living issues" of the individuals in the study. Furthermore, vesting and intrinsic motivations are embedded in self-study, as are the essential elements required for intellectual development and meaning making: interest and questioning (see Dewey, 1938). The capacity for change in thinking is both immediate and compelling because it is connected to practice and the situation and context at hand. Thus, teaching and learning are integrated, with inquiring and learning epistemologically rooted in the self and context.

Process-oriented. Self-study is a journey comprising continuous ongoing activity, whether formally or informally undertaken. It begins with, or is initiated and prompted by, uncertainty, curiosity, or wonderment, and its goal is to understand, to develop new perspectives, and to investigate and reframe practice over time, and not necessarily to assert a final knowing (Pinnegar, 1998). Because process is embedded in self-study, it is also generative. The self-study process produces—it creates findings and results that propel music teachers to seek out new knowledge and/or to develop and refine skills. It is dynamic and spiral-like and not automatically linear. Because self-study is generative it is also action-focused: inquiry and implementation move in tandem with improvement and change. Thus, knowledge and action are interdependent and emergent out of the inquiring process.

Knowledge-generating. Self-study is *self-knowledge.* "No thought, no idea, can possibly be conveyed as an idea from one person to another.... Only by wrestling with the conditions of the problem at first hand, seeking and finding [his/her] own way out, does [a person] think" (Dewey, 1916, p. 188). Music teachers construct their own knowledge and come to know more deeply their own professional potentials, motivations, and emotions. Educative experiences are the catalysts and sources for generating self-knowledge (Dewey, 1938).

Self-study is *professional knowledge* when it has been grounded in reflection. As Schön (1983) has argued, "the knowledge inherent in practice is understood by artful doing" (Usher, Bryant, & Johnston, 1997, p. 143). In other words, knowledge generated by the practitioner when engaged in reflection-on-action and reflection-in-action *is* professional knowledge. Professionals, according to Schön (1983), cannot simply "take" expert knowledge developed by others and apply it as if they were mere technicians. Instead, professional knowledge involves examining experiences, connecting with feelings, and attending to personal theories (for an example of a practicing music teacher's self-study focused on reframing practice around democratic learning ideals in a high school guitar class, see Easton, 2012).

Self-study is, finally, *institutional knowledge.* Cochran-Smith and Lytle (1993) note that professional teacher inquiry generates knowledge about teaching, learning, and schooling that is both local and public. Local knowledge generated from inquiry is useful to teachers and their immediate communities. Public knowledge generates knowledge for the larger community of educators beyond the immediate locale (p. 43). In addition, self-study research that engages in critical examination of curricular and instructional practices contributes to both teacher education and reform efforts (Zeichner, 1999). Self-study also contributes to departmental communication, reframing program goals, and curriculum activities (for an example of a department-wide collaborative self-study in a preK–12 music education setting, see Natale-Abramo & Campbell, 2012).

Multiple. Self-study is multiple. A detailed study of the descriptions and illustrations used in this chapter would reveal multiple perspectives and theoretical frameworks used to inform self-study research, as would it reveal a range of different emphases and focal points. A quick glance at Table 8.1 shows how multifaceted self-study can become when methodologies of inquiry for pre-service music teachers are viewed synoptically. As can be imagined, self-study can serve the needs of individuals as well as groups of teachers, administrators, teacher-educators, policy makers, and pre-service music teachers.

Paradoxical. According to Samaras and Freese (2006), self-study is paradoxical because it is: (1) individual and collective, (2) personal and interpersonal, and (3) private and public. What the term *self-study* does not reveal in its focus on the individual is that it is a collective task. As noted previously, self-study knowledge is situated, individually and socially constructed, and culturally produced. Although many aspects of the process are individually initiated, directed, and monitored, critical friends play roles in clarifying and improving the process. Understanding issues (like the example used in the choral practices participant-observation project) may require examining work *with* others and the work *of* others and aligning individual beliefs accordingly. In addition, colleagues or peers can play an important role in checking for credibility (as well as other qualitative assessments of trustworthiness).

Although self-study produces personal theorizing and knowledge it is done in the context of social mediation and interpersonal interaction. Many aspects of Vygotsky's (1978) social interaction theory have particular relevance here during self-study research. Cognition, assisted opportunities for learning by or from others, and the reciprocal relationships found in the learning process all speak to the relationship between (or the paradox of) the personal and the interpersonal.

The ideas contained in reflection are often a private matter, as are the personal questions we generate or the dilemmas we encounter in music teaching. When written down for potential inquiry, analysis, and synthesis and shared with others, they become public. However, self-study music teachers need an audience in order to improve their questioning and investigation strategies, to share findings, to shape reports, to influence others, and to strengthen their work. Plus, in more formal self-studies, self-study teachers (and researchers) may require an activist stance about their work due to the ethical, moral, and political nature of educational reform.

Some Concluding Thoughts and Lessons Learned from Our Experiment

Programmatically, the infusion of inquiry and synthesis throughout the program has been effective in achieving its aims. It has also been effective in creating a community of learners focused on music teaching and learning as a kind of scholarship and professional activity rooted in intellectual dispositions, complex reasoning, critical thinking, and reflective practice. Placing inquiry and synthesis as a central theme, along with self-study research and its methodologies, within a music teacher education program poses several challenges to long-standing technicalized images of music teacher education and behaviorist-derived (-driven) curriculum and instruction. A number of philosophical issues have been mentioned previously (e.g., epistemological stance). In addition, self-study implicitly questions the long-term validity and social utility of the technical-rational approach to learning found in training and corporatized models seen in music education and in some music teacher education programs. It also challenges teacher education reform efforts that seek to evacuate and/or dismantle substantive and rigorous professional preparation as a requisite for certification and practice. Plus, it problematizes the compliant curriculum standards of the content-coverage and skills-acquisition approach offered by accreditation agencies such as NASM (2012). On the other hand, NCATE's specification to use tools of inquiry as a necessary mechanism for constructing content knowledge and scholarship of practice (NCATE, 2008; CAEP/NCATE, 2013) is congruent with the manner in which we have integrated inquiry and synthesis into the different projects found in the curriculum.

Our experiment with inquiry-based learning, however, has taught us a few lessons. Table 8.2 lists in chart form some positive aspects that students (and faculty) have mentioned in our program, as well as some concerns that diminish or make inquiry-based learning challenging. Table 8.2 also contains tips from pre-service music teachers designed to help music teacher-educators who want to use inquiry-based learning in their courses.

In closing, two ideas are of import when thinking about inquiry and synthesis in relation to the aims of music teacher education and how music teacher-educators assess the quality of their own programs. Quality of student work and quality of effect on students seem preeminent.

If inquiry and synthesis engender and reveal substantive scholarship, personal ownership, demonstrated knowledge and skills within professional music teaching contexts, and creative innovation, then it has made a difference in a music teacher's professional development. If inquiry has repositioned the curriculum in a way that allows future music teachers to see themselves as *sources of knowledge* and that empowers them to be the "agents of education" through curriculum and instructional deliberations and actions (Schwab, 1959/1978), then it has had impact. Quality, however, is the linking adjective between work and impact, and should serve as both a standard and an attribute. Continued and increased discussion of how inquiry-based learning contributes qualitatively to the knowledge base of music teaching and learning is necessary, as is discussion on how inquiry contributes to the

TABLE 8.2 } **Lessons learned**

Positive aspects	Negative aspects
• Increases professional investment	• Creates anxiety in having to be self-directed
• Develops and strengthens professional identity	• Increases work beyond "typical content delivery" courses
• Actively engages students in the process of seeking knowledge, creating knowledge, and constructing new understandings	• Creates anxiety in having to negotiate group dynamics (positive and negative)
• Creates opportunities for problem posing and solutioning	
• Strengthens analytic and synthesizing skills	
• Is motivating	
• Cultivates critical thinking and creativity	
• Creates a vision of self and future students as "curious and collaborative inquirers"	

Lessons learned

- Topics need to be relevant to students, and generated by students. Provide prompts when necessary.
- Research projects take time; plan for it.
- Most effective projects result in meaningfulness to the students (and hopefully others).
- Plan an event or medium for sharing work.
- Provide students with resources and materials necessary for success in tackling the confusing and challenging philosophical concepts embedded in an inquiry project.
- Develop and stick to a schedule and timeline to help students best organize and complete tasks. Prepare for a learning curve regarding unfamiliar ideas found in resources or skills needed to develop proficiency with a specific technology. These skills are best learned in context of the study, but might take more time.
- Create checkpoints to help students manage time and inform all involved what will be expected at certain points.

professional lives of both current and future music educators. The evidence provided by the student samples in this chapter is a step in the right direction because it provides positive assurance that situating inquiry and synthesis at the center of professional development can have a qualitatively significant effect on pre-service music teachers' learning. Inquiry and synthesis in the education of music teachers warrant serious attention.

Notes

1. Debra Campbell, Caron Collins, Nancy Conley, Sarah Hersh, Kathleen Hubbard, Jennifer Kessler, and Rebecca Reames were instrumental in the work involved in reconfiguring different courses within the curriculum.

References

Barrett, J. R. (2005). Planning for understanding: A reconceptualized view of the music curriculum. *Music Educators Journal, 91*(4), 21–25.

Beck, C., Fresse, A. R., & Kosnik, C. (2004). The pre-service practicum: Learning through self-study in a professional setting. In J. J. Loughran, M. L. Hamilton, V. K. LaBoskey,

& T. Russell (Eds.), *International handbook of self-study of teaching and teacher education practices* (Vol. 2, pp. 1259–1293). Dordrecht, Netherlands: Kluwer Academic.

Berliner, D. C. (1994). Expertise: The world of exemplary performances. In J. N. Mangieri & C. C. Block (Eds.), *Creating powerful thinking in teachers and students* (pp. 161–186). Fort Worth, TX: Holt, Rinehart, and Winston.

Biamonte, N. (Ed.). (2001). *Pop-culture pedagogy in the music classroom.* Lanham, MD: Scarecrow.

Boardman, E. (1985). Teacher education: A wedding of theory and practice. *Bulletin of the Council for Research in Music Education, 81,* 65–73.

Boardman, E. (1992). New environments for teacher education. *Music Educators Journal, 79*(2), 41–43.

Bransford, J. D., Brown, A. L., & Cocking, R.C. (2000). *How people learn: Brain, mind, experience, and school.* Washington, DC: National Academies Press.

Britzman, D. P. (2003). *Practice makes practice: A critical study of learning to teach* (2nd ed.). Albany, NY: SUNY Press.

Bullough, R. V., Jr., & Pinnegar, S. E. (2004). Thinking about the thinking about self-study: An analysis of eight chapters. In J. J. Loughran, M. L. Hamilton, V. K. LaBoskey, & T. Russell (Eds.), *International handbook of self-study of teaching and teacher education practices* (Vol. 1, pp. 313–342). Dordrecht, Netherlands: Kluwer Academic.

Campbell, M. R. (Ed). (2002). *On musicality and milestones: Selected writings of Marilyn Pflederer Zimmerman with contributions form the profession.* Urbana: University of Illinois Press.

Campbell, M. R. (2007). Introduction: Special focus on music teacher preparation, *Music Educators Journal, 93*(3), 26–29.

Campbell, M. R., & Brummett, V. M. (2007). Mentoring pre-service teachers for development and growth of professional knowledge. *Music Educators Journal, 93*(3), 50–55.

Campbell, M. R., & Thompson, L. K. (2014). A critical analysis of qualitative research on learning to teach music in pre–service music teacher education (pp. 448–478). In C. Conway (Ed.), *The Oxford handbook of qualitative research in American music education.* New York: Oxford University Press.

Campbell, M. R., Thompson, L. K., & Barrett, J. R. (2010). *Constructing a personal orientation to music teaching.* New York: Routledge.

Campbell, M. R., Thompson, L. K., & Barrett, J. R. (2012). Supporting and sustaining a personal orientation to music teaching: Implications for music teacher education. *Journal of Music Teacher Education, 22*(1), 75–90.

Carr, W., & Kemmis, S. (1986). *Becoming critical: Education, knowledge and action research.* London: Falmer.

Cochran-Smith, M. (2006). *Policy, practice, and politics in teacher education.* Thousand Oaks, CA: Corwin.

Cochran-Smith, M., & Lytle, S. L. (1993). *Inside/outside: Teacher research and knowledge.* New York: Teachers College Press.

Cochran-Smith, M., & Lytle, S. L. (2004). Practitioner inquiry, knowledge, and university culture. In J. J. Loughran, M. L. Hamilton, V. K. LaBoskey, & T. Russell (Eds.), *International handbook of self-study of teaching and teacher education practices* (Vol. 1, pp. 601–649). Dordrecht, Netherlands: Kluwer Academic.

Colwell, R. (1985). Program evaluation in music teacher education. *Bulletin of the Council for Research in Music Education, 81,* 18–62.

Colwell, R. (2006). Music teacher education in this century: Part I. *Arts Education Policy Review,* 108(1), 15–27.

Colwell, R. (2011). Reflections on music teacher education. *Action, Criticism, & Theory for Music Education,* 10(2), 127–160. Retrieved from http://act.maydaygroup.org/articles/ Colwell10_2.pdf.

Connelly, F. M., & Clandinin, D. J. (1985). Personal practical knowledge and the modes of knowing: Relevance for teaching and learning. In E. Eisner (Ed.), *Learning and teaching ways of knowing: The eighty-fourth yearbook of the National Society for the Study of Education* (pp. 174–198). Chicago: University of Chicago Press.

Conway, C. M. (2000). The preparation of teacher-researchers in pre-service music education. *Journal of Music Teacher Education,* 9(2) 22–30. doi: 10.1177/105708370000900205.

Council for the Accreditation of Educator Preparation/National Council for the Accreditation of Teacher Education (CAEP/NCATE). (2013). CAEP accreditation standards and evidence: Aspirations for educator preparation. Retrieved from http:// caepnet.files.wordpress.com/2013/02/commrpt.pdf.

Dewey, J. (1916). *Democracy and education.* New York: Macmillan.

Dewey, J. (1933). *How we think: A restatement of the relation of reflective thinking to the educative process* (Revised ed.). Boston, MA: D. C. Heath.

Dewey, J. (1938). *Experience and education.* New York: Macmillan.

Easton, K. (2012). *Co-constructing curriculum in the high school guitar class: An Investigation and reflection on democratic learning in music education.* Unpublished master's thesis, State University of New York at Potsdam.

Egan, M. (2007). Reflective thinking: The essence of professional development. *Excelsior: Leadership and Learning,* 2(1), 1–14.

Eisner, E. (2002). *The arts and the creation of mind.* New Haven, CT: Yale University Press.

Fessler, R. (1992). Teacher career cycle. In R. Fessler & J. C. Christensen (Eds.), *Teacher career cycle: Understanding and guiding the professional development of teachers* (pp. 21–44). Needham Heights, MA: Allyn & Bacon.

Frede, E. (2003, Spring). How teachers grow: Four stages. *High/Scope ReSources,* 21–22.

Fuller, F. F. (1969). Concerns of teachers: A developmental conceptualization. *American Educational Research Journal,* 6, 207–226.

Furlong, J., & Maynard, T. (1995). *Mentoring student teachers: The growth of professional knowledge.* London: Routledge.

Green, L. (2002). *How popular musicians learn: A way ahead for music education.* Burlington, VT, and Aldershot, UK: Ashgate.

Green, L. (2008). *Music, informal learning and the school: A new classroom pedagogy.* Burlington, VT, and Aldershot, UK: Ashgate.

Gregory, A. H. (1997). The roles of music in society: The ethnomusicological perspective. In D. J. Hargreaves & A. C. North (Eds.), *The social psychology of music* (pp. 123–140). New York: Oxford University Press.

Hamilton, M. L., & Pinnegar, S. (1998). Conclusion: The value and the promise of self-study. In M. L. Hamilton (Ed.), *Reconceptualizing teaching practice: Self-study in teacher education* (pp. 235–246). Bristol, PA: Falmer.

Hersh, S. (n.d.) *Suzuki teaching principlces.* Unpublished manuscript.

Huberman, M. (1993). *The lives of teachers* (J. Neufeld, Trans.). New York: Teachers College Press.

Janesick, V. K. (2006). *Authentic assessment.* New York: Peter Lang.

Kratus, J. (2007). Music education at the tipping point. *Music Educators Journal,* 94(2), 42–48.

LaBoskey, V. K. (2004). The methodology of self-study and its theoretical underpinnings. In J. J. Loughran, M. L. Hamilton, V. K. LaBoskey, & T. Russell (Eds.), *International handbook of self-study of teaching and teacher education practices* (Vol. 1, pp. 817–869). Dordrecht, Netherlands: Kluwer Academic.

Lassonde, C. A., & Strub, D. (2009). Promoting self-study as a habit of mind for pre-service teachers. In C. A. Lassonde, S. Galman, & C. Kosnik (Eds.), *Self-study research methodologies for teacher educators* (pp. 207–224). Rotterdam, Netherlands: Sense.

Leonhard, C. (1985). Toward reform in music teacher education. *Bulletin of the Council for Research in Music Education,* 81, 10–17.

Lortie, D. C. (2002). *Schoolteacher: A sociological study* (2nd ed.). Chicago: University of Chicago Press.

Loughran, J. J. (2005). Researching teaching about teaching: Self-study of teacher education practices. *Studying Teacher Education,* 1(1), 5–16.

McNiff, J. (1988). *Action research: Principles and practices.* London: Routledge.

Merriam, A. P. (1964). *The anthropology of music.* Evanston, IL: Northwestern University Press.

Mills, G. E. (2003). *Action research: A guide for the teacher researcher* (2nd ed.). Upper Saddle River, NJ: Merrill.

Natale-Abramo, M., & Campbell, M. R. (2012). Music teachers investigate their work: Collaborative inquiry as curriculum making and professional development. In L. K. Thompson & M. R. Campbell (Eds.), *Situating inquiry: Expanded venues for music education research* (pp. 35–58). Charlotte, NC: Information Age.

National Association of Schools of Music (NASM). (2012). *National Association of Schools of Music handbook, 2011–12.* Reston, VA: National Association of Schools of Music. Retrieved from http://nasm.arts-accredit.org/site/docs/Handbook_Archives/NASM_HANDBOOK_2011-12.pdf.

National Council for Accreditation of Teacher Education (NCATE). (2008). *Professional standards for the accreditation of teacher preparation institutions.* Washington, DC: National Council for Accreditation of Teacher Education. Retrieved from http://www.ncate.org/Portals/0/documents/Standards/NCATE%20standards%202008.pdf.

Nettl, B. (1995). *Heartland excursions: Ethnomusicological reflections on schools of music.* Urbana: University of Illinois Press.

Pinnegar, S. (1998). Introduction: Methodological perspectivves. In M. L. Hamilton (Ed.), *Reconceptualizing teaching practice: Self-study in teacher education* (pp. 31–33). Bristol, PA: Falmer.

Samaras, A. P., & Freese, A. R. (2006). *Self-study of teaching practices.* New York: Peter Lang.

Schafer, R. M. (1967). *Ear cleaning.* Scarborough, ON: Berandol.

Schön, D. A. (1983). *The reflective practitioner: How professionals think in action.* New York: Basic Books.

Schön, D. A. (1987). *Educating the reflective practitioner: Toward a new design for teaching and learning in the professions.* San Francisco: Josey-Bass.

Schwab, J. J. (1959/1978). The "impossible" role of the teacher in progressive education. In I. Westbury & N. Wilkof (Eds.), *Science, curriculum and liberal education: Selected essays* (pp. 167–183). Chicago: University of Chicago Press.

Schwab, J. J. (1969). The practical: A language for curriculum. *School Review, 78*(1), 1–23.

Schwab, J. J. (1970). *The practical: A language for curriculum.* Washington, DC: National Education Association.

Schwab, J. J. (1983). The practical 4: Something for curriculum professors to do. *Curriculum Inquiry, 13*(3), 239–265.

Schwartz, D. L., Bransford, J. D., & Sears, D. (2005). Efficiency and innovation in transfer. In J. Mestre (Ed.), *Transfer of learning from a modern multidisciplinary perspective* (pp. 1–51). Greenwich, CT: Information Age.

Shulman, L. S. (1987). Knowledge and teaching: Foundations of the new reform. *Harvard Educational Review, 57,* 1–22.

Thompson, L. K., & Campbell, M. R. (2003). Gods, guides and gardeners: Pre-service music educators' personal teaching metaphors. *Bulletin of the Council for Research in Music Education, 158,* 43–54.

Tyack, D., & Cuban, L. (1995). *Tinkering toward Utopia: A century of public school reform.* Cambridge, MA: Harvard University Press.

Upitis, R. (1992). *Can I play you my song? The compositions and invented notations of children.* Portsmouth, NH: Heinemann.

Usher, R., Bryant, I., & Johnston, R. (1997). *Adult education and the postmodern challenge.* London: Routledge.

Vygotsky, L. S. (1978). *Mind in society: The development of higher psychological processes* (M. Cole, V. John-Steiner, S. Scribner, & E. Souberman, Eds.). Cambridge, MA: Harvard University Press.

Zeichner, K. M. (1999). The new scholarship in teacher education, *Educational Researcher, 28*(9), 4–15.

Zeichner, K. M., & Liston, D. P. (1996). *Reflective teaching: An introduction.* Mahwah, NJ: Erlbaum.

9 }

Invoking an Innovative Spirit in
Music Teacher Education
Carlos R. Abril

Imagination is not only the uniquely human capacity to envision
that which is not, and, therefore, the foundation of all invention
and innovation. In its arguably most transformative and
revelatory capacity, it is the power that enables us to empathize
with humans whose experiences we have never shared.

—J. K. Rowling, Harvard Commencement Address

Questions regarding the things teachers need to understand and skills they
must possess are fundamental to creating the teacher education programs that
best prepare teachers for work in the schools. In her article on teacher preparation, Linda Darling-Hammond (2006) outlines the many things teachers
need to know and be prepared to do in the classroom. They must understand
the ways students learn, think, feel, and are motivated, as well as the pedagogy and content of the discipline. They must also be prepared to be effective communicators and reflective thinkers capable of using a wide variety of
materials and technologies. Finally, she asserts that teachers need to posses
a disposition to solve problems and respond to unexpected situations. While
she speaks of these matters in relation to the classroom practices, teachers
also need to be aware of broader problems and unexpected situations beyond the classroom. That is, they must be aware of the ways their teaching
can remain relevant, meaningful, and responsive to changing societal needs
and specific communities. This is of critical importance for music teachers in
the twenty-first century, a time when the very nature of traditional models of
music education has been questioned and challenged (Kratus, 2007). It will
require that a new generation of music educators be prepared to be innovative thinkers and practitioners.

I will start with an observation about pre-service music educators. At the
beginning of each semester, in a required music education course at my university, I asked my first- and second-year undergraduate students to envision "music education in action" and draw a picture depicting that vision.[1]

175

Year after year, the pictures possess some telling commonalities: Virtually all include a teacher standing at the front of the class space, conducting or playing a keyboard or guitar, surrounded by students singing and playing instruments. The rooms often include posters of classical composers, instruments, rhythms, and/or musical terms. In general, when students discuss their illustrations, they describe them as ideal states, where children are on task, instruments and other equipment are plentiful, and the classroom is spacious enough to realize any lessons they dream up. They also explain that the illustrations represent music education as they remember it in their own schools, albeit with minor improvements here and there.

What is and is not included in these images and discussions reveal the values, expectations, and borders surrounding music education. The images are reflective of their personal experiences and memories with school music and also reflect the contexts and traditions that are perpetuated and reinforced in many teacher education programs. They recreate the normative pedagogies and systems that have come to define music education in schools, including the type of music learned (classical, art), instruments (elementary instruments, symphonic instruments), methods (directive, teacher-centered), and educational settings (formal, large group). This makes sense, given that music education programs typically attract students who were products of the traditional music education systems. Those who have interest in teaching but did learn music from within the traditional school music education systems (e.g., electric guitarist, composer) often have difficulties fitting into traditional models of music teacher education (Clements & Campbell, 2006). Though most music teacher education programs are unlikely to turn them away, the boxes we attempt to fit them into may serve to deter many from considering, enrolling, or persisting in a music education degree program. To date, I have yet to find an image or explanation from one of my students that challenged the norms or provided innovative alternatives to familiar systems of music education, at the beginning at least.

Music teacher education programs could be designed to encourage critical thought and reflection on current systems and invoke a spirit of innovation in music curriculum and instruction. The purpose of this chapter is to describe why it is imperative that music educators develop an innovative disposition and to offer some ideas for how this might be realized within a music teacher education program.

Conditions and Opportunity

MUSIC IN SCHOOLS

Despite media depictions and anecdotal reports, the support and infrastructure for music education in US schools remains fairly strong. Teachers, education administrators, and the general public are overwhelmingly supportive of music instruction in schools (Abril, 2009a). Most elementary schools (94 percent) offer required courses in music taught by music specialists (NCES, 2012). Secondary schools (91 percent) also offer instruction in music, most commonly in the form of large ensembles (e.g., band and choir) and other traditional non-performance courses (e.g., general music or appreciation, theory) (Abril & Gault, 2008; NCES, 2012). Music courses continue to be offered and taught by specialists in the vast majority of schools around the United States, which suggests continued interest in and support for music in schools. However, this support can last only as long as there are quality programs that serve students' needs and interests.

A respectable number of students around the country continue to enroll in music courses, though declining enrollments have been noted. In 2004, approximately 36 percent of the US senior class, or 1.12 million students, had completed at least one music course (Elpus, 2013). However, large ensemble participation (21 percent of students in the 2004 senior class) has experienced around a 10 percent decline from 1982 to 2004 (Elpus & Abril, 2011). A study, sponsored by the National Endowment of the Arts, reported that overall participation in music education in schools declined by 30 percent between 1982 and 2008 (Rabkin & Hedberg, 2011).

Why this decline in participation? Some blame it on a shift in educational priorities toward subjects that are used to judge academic progress of a given school, which has led to decreased time and resources for arts subjects (Abril & Bannerman, in press; Beveridge, 2010). Others have attributed the decline to state budget shortfalls, which have led to reductions or elimination of programs (Johnson, Oliff, & Williams, 2011). Many in the last decade have suggested this decline in enrollments and participation can be attributed to music education's disconnect from music outside and beyond the school years (Kratus, 2007; Myers, 2008; Williams, 2011). This is especially pertinent for elective music courses in secondary schools. In a study examining musical meaning, adolescents expressed the need for change in school music programs. They felt music instruction in their schools was too limited, and expressed desire for more innovative course offerings, including guitar, piano, songwriting, and composition (Campbell, Connell, & Beegle, 2007). Music teachers of the twenty-first century need to be prepared to respond to students' musical needs through innovative course work, engaging teaching approaches, and carefully prepared curricula.

MUSIC OUTSIDE OF SCHOOL

Interest in music and music learning is extremely high given the public's investment of time and money in these endeavors. Music product and digital music are multibillion dollar industries (IFPI, 2013; NAMM, 2011). Paid subscriptions to online music services such as Pandora have risen 44 percent from 2011 to 2012, with over twenty million people subscribed (IFPI, 2013). Guitars represent the dominant music instrument sale in any category, with unit sales of 2.38 million in 2010; keyboard instruments are also among the most popular instruments sold (NAMM, 2011). It should be surprising then that guitar and keyboard courses are offered in less than 20 percent of US schools that offer music (Abril & Gault, 2008).

Despite recent economic downturns and decreasing participation in school music programs, interest and participation in community music learning centers and ensembles appear to be thriving. According to the GALA, the umbrella organization of GLBT community choruses, the number of choruses around the world increased from 39 in 1983 to 180 in 2012 (http://www. galachoruses.org/about/history). According to the Old Town School of Folk Music in Chicago, enrollments in music classes that include anything from Latin groove ensemble to blues guitar, djembe to oud, have increased from little over 1000 in 1997 to over 6000 in 2010. Five of the last six years were reported to have broken all previous enrollment records. In fact, interest is so high that they have plans to expand their facilities to service thousands more (Kot, 2010). School of Rock, a community music education franchise focused on rock music, has grown from one school in 1998 to 100 schools in 2012, with a reported enrollment of 10,000 students. They are projected to grow by twenty to forty locations in 2013. In fact, CNN Money named School of Rock one of the "five hot franchises" of the year (Kavilanz, 2013). These are just a few examples of community music programs (for and not for profit) that are meeting the musical learning and engagement needs of the people, in ways that differ from the traditional school offerings. If school-based music education lacks the ability to capture the interest of students, many will turn elsewhere for systematic and sustained music education. If students are not turning towards school-based music education, programs will no longer be sustainable or viable components of the school curriculum.

OPPORTUNITY

The challenges facing music education described above are ameliorated by the fact that (1) members of the general public and educational community are overwhelmingly supportive of music as part of preK–12 schools; (2) the vast majority of schools continue to employ full-time music specialists; and (3) children, adolescents, and adults want to learn and engage with music. This support and the infrastructure offer an opportunity that should not be overlooked. It is only with public support, resources for music specialists, and student interest that school-based music education can remain sustainable. Therefore, given current patterns and mounting evidence, music teachers must be prepared to offer curricula that are relevant, meaningful, and of interest to children and adolescents. While music teacher education programs can do little in the way of macro shifts in educational priorities or the economy, they can prepare teachers to respond to changing needs through curriculum and instruction. They can provide the environment for teachers not only to learn from the traditions of the past but also to also think about and experiment with new ways of musically education students. The key may be educating for innovation.

Innovation as Part of Our Signature Pedagogy

Innovation is the creation of something new within a given context that is both practical and successful in its implementation (Wagner, 2012). It is thought to require creative thinking (Amabile, 1996), improvisation (Wagner, 2012), and collaboration (Sawyer, 2006). In the context of teaching (and this chapter), it is a deliberate change in methods, techniques, courses, or curricula that is responsive to some perceived problem (Erault, 1975).

In a collective case study of innovative individuals, Wagner (2012) found that these individuals were provided with ample space and time to play, experiment, question, observe, and reflect in their developmental years. After that period, they were given space to find and pursue their passion. Finally, that passion led to a specific purpose or reason to innovate. In studying the lives of these innovators, Wagner found a "consistent link and developmental arc in their progression from play to passion to purpose" (p. 30).

Though the literature on educating for innovation in teacher education is scarce, many agree that schools must have teachers who are prepared to educate for creativity and innovation. Wagner (2012) calls on education to prepare students to think critically, communicate effectively, and collaborate, so that they are prepared to innovate and create opportunities for themselves. This would require teacher education programs to prepare teachers to be innovative and teach for innovation, to meet the changed economic and social structures of the twenty-first century (Sawyer, 2006). Music teacher education programs must do the same; they must prepare teachers to think and act innovatively to meet the changed ways in which music is experienced and created today. Young teachers may be best suited to innovate because they are yet to be fully entrenched in the systems and models of music education. In writing about scientific revolutions, Thomas Kuhn (1970) stated, "[a]lmost always the men [and women] who achieve these fundamental inventions of a new paradigm have been either very young or very new to the field whose paradigm they change" (p. 90). Music teacher education programs would be remiss not to prepare music teachers to be nimble and able to respond to changes in the educational and music landscapes in which they will find themselves. This can begin with a focus on pedagogy that defines music teacher education.

Teaching for innovation should become a new facet of our signature pedagogy in music teacher education. Signature pedagogy is a term used by Lee Shulman to describe the characteristics of teaching reflective of fundamental values and structures of a particular discipline or profession (Shulman, 2005). It serves to inculcate the deep-seated values of and encourage practice in a given profession. For example, if you are preparing a music educator, your pedagogy should in some way model the practices of the mind (knowledge and understanding of music and pedagogy), hand (musical skills), and heart (affect, compassion) that are necessary for success in the field of music education. Music teachers should be prepared for both the routines of thought and action as well as the unexpected moments. If we agree that music teachers need to think and act innovatively, then our music teacher education programs should make innovation in its own program transparent and help students capture the spirit of innovation.

The next part of this chapter offers ideas (not answers) for how we might prepare music teachers to be innovative thinkers and doers. These ideas are meant to serve as representative examples of signature pedagogy in music education, where diversity is used as a resource and exploration and innovation are encouraged and supported.

VALIDATE DIVERSE MUSICAL BACKGROUNDS AND EXPERIENCES

Students are initially validated when accepted into a school or department of music based on high achievement as a performer. However, their "other" musical backgrounds and experiences are often ignored or suppressed, and thus not valued or drawn upon in traditional music programs. Clements and Campbell (2006) describe how members of a rock band, who were also undergraduates in the music program where they were majoring in classical music and music education, felt little support in both high school and college for "other" facets of their musicality. They found "themselves challenged by the need to switch... musical codes from rock to classical music (often on a daily basis)" (p. 18). One member of the band said he "often feels tension, if not outright hostility, from his violin teacher" for playing rock (p. 18). Julia Koza (2008) notes how many school of music students "quietly and sometimes surreptitiously engage in the musical pleasures not valued by our institutions, and faculty members tend to look the other way just as long as the other music does not interfere with the 'real' business of university music-making" (p. 148). This is a missed opportunity. Once these students are music teachers in schools, they may see no connection and make nary a transfer between their school of music education and other music experiences and expertise in their lives (Abril, 2009b, 2010).

This is not even to speak of the multitude of potential students our schools of music reject because of they do not play an instrument that is taught (e.g., djembe), meet performance audition criteria (often the only way to enter a tertiary music program), or sing in a style not deemed worthy of formal study in a school of music (e.g., musical theater). If we believe that music educators must innovate to ensure music programs in schools and communities are relevant and meaningful in the twenty-first century, we must validate musical expertise, interests, and backgrounds that do not conform to the traditional models of our secondary and tertiary music programs.

Knowledge of self is essential to creating an environment for creativity (Hickey, 2012) and creativity is necessary for innovation (Amabile, 1996). Highly innovative people have been found to grow up in environments where they were encouraged to find their passion and where their experiences, expertise, and backgrounds were recognized and drawn upon (Wagner, 2012). Culturally responsive pedagogy offers ideas for how teachers can draw upon students' rich cultural and musical backgrounds so that curriculum and instruction are more relevant and meaningful. This constructivist pedagogy validates and affirms each student for what he or she brings to the classroom, including but not limited to cultural backgrounds and personal identities, and teaches to and through their lived experiences, worldview, and strengths (Gay, 2010).

Validating students first requires *seeing* students and what the experiences and expertise they bring—beyond their "school of music" self. We could begin by learning about students' musical interests and experiences, and pushing them beyond those they think a university music professor wants to hear or know. Campbell, Thompson, and Barrett (2010) provide many valuable ideas for helping students to draw on their past. These include having students reflect upon and write about the impact of powerful learning experiences (in and outside of school) in their educations, and having them draw diagrams that document the wide range of musical experiences, preferences, and learnings that have shaped who they are, musically. Music teacher-educators can help to take that one step further by drawing on that information to help students learn, develop their own teaching ideas, or create distinct curricula.

Blogs are another effective approach to providing students with an informal space to reflect on their musical, cultural, and educational lives; to make transfers to education and music education; and to share with peers their unique music backgrounds and knowledge with others. Research has found that blogging creates a community of practice for student teachers, where they are able to interact, solve problems, and share resources (Fitzpatrick, 2013). Blog entries can provide members of a group with many opportunities to learn about one another and draw upon each other's backgrounds. Music teacher-educators can learn about students to help make individualized connection in classroom discussion or recommendations for innovative directions that students might pursue in field experiences, student teaching, or the first years in the classroom. These are just a few examples of the ways music teacher-educators can come to know and validate their students, encouraging them to draw upon their rich and diverse backgrounds and create communities of practice.

OPENING SPACE TO EXPLORE ALTERNATIVE APPROACHES

The very structures of many music teacher education programs provide little space or even close up the space for considering alternatives. Take the common tracks that music education students choose at some point in their degree program: instrumental, choral, or general. These immediately close the space for imagining alternatives to music education because they prescribe specific roles such as band directors, choral directors, or elementary general music teachers, and typically attract students who are products of these models. Even the term "music education" is a closed space in that it typically means music teaching in preK–12 schools, which in the United States connotes the aforementioned roles.

Validating students is part and parcel of opening spaces in instruction and curriculum for students to explore alterative approaches to music education. Opening space is like play, an essential part of the process, leading to creative and innovative thinking in a given area (Wagner, 2012). Maxine Greene (1995) writes about opening spaces so that students are able to think differently about traditions and conventions, and consider alternatives. She says, "trying to open students to the new and the multiple, we want ourselves to break through some of the crusts of convention, the distortions of fetishism, the sour tastes of narrow faith. Such openness requires us to be in continuing question of ourselves even as it requires that we do what we can to enable as many of the young as possible to crack the codes" (p. 146). In contrast to knowing exactly what students need to learn and standardizing that learning for all, opening space offers the chance for serendipitous discoveries, collaborative work, unexpected learning, and innovation, which may be critical for the future of music education.

Opening spaces in music teacher education is one way to move toward innovation. We can open small spaces through readings of innovative music teaching or programs. Reading has been found to be an expression of play that has been correlated with innovation (Wagner, 2012). *Alternative approaches in music education* is a collection of case studies documenting innovative ways music educators are reimagining teaching methods, courses, and curriculum (Clements, 2010). Cases of music courses in preK–12 settings included alternative ensembles, such as mariachi and rock; courses, such as film scoring and technology; as well as pedagogical approaches, including intergenerational collaborations and international exchanges. The alternative view recognizes the limitations of our traditions and stresses the need to innovate to meet the changing needs of students, community, and society.

We can also open up larger spaces, such as semester-long projects examining alternate forms of music education. In a music teacher education course I taught, with a focus on cultural diversity in music education, I asked students to conduct a semester-long project where they would examine, through a cultural lens, one bound organization or program with an innovative approach, space, or practice to music teaching and learning, with possible implications for music education.

One of my students was interested in studying innovative music learning settings of cultural hybridity, so she conducted a case study of a student-created and -mediated "hip hop dance/music crew," largely comprising Asian and Asian American students in a university setting. She documented how they taught and who taught whom, the ways they learned collaboratively, and the impact of participation in this organization on their identities. What was more important than the actual case described was the ways this study changed this student's thinking about music education. She wrote the following:

> As the diversity of student populations grow, it has become clear to me the responsibility I have as a teacher to provide a safe third space—a place for students to explore growing relationships with new culture and old, and to legitimize the cultural hybridity we all bring to schools . ... the overarching sense of community and inclusion, and how this enabled independent learning, has made me reconsider the traditional didactic relationship between educators and learners. This project has also helped me to recognize how limiting band teaching can be at times, especially in relation to the things that excite, engage, and challenge people after high school... for the first time, I started to consider how I can make a music program more expansive and more connected to the ways people are making music and dancing to music in their lives outside of school. This open space in a course can give students an opportunity to "play," to think about alternative purposes and functions of music education.

Another way of opening space is through the four-year curriculum. Instead of one-size-fits-all, these programs of study can be made more customizable for diverse interests, including those who are geared toward creating a community music school, working for the educational division of a cultural organization, or becoming a teaching artist. Some might worry that this will weaken or water down the music teacher licensure curriculum in some way. I would argue that this does not have to be the case if we steer those students toward the courses that are most critical for their success in the school classroom. There are certain principles about teaching music to children or leading an instrumental ensemble that transfer to a wide variety of settings, Alternatively, we might even open space in the nomenclature we use to describe our courses. What if "elementary general music" were renamed "teaching and learning in childhood"? What if music education were reframed as music learning? What if music teacher education programs were not only in the business of preparing teachers for certification but started to better prepare a broader segment of the music student population (e.g., performers) in learning about ways to motivate, teach, share, or engage people through music?

Invoke Innovation in Music Teacher Education

COLLEGE COURSE WORK

How can we expect future music teachers to lead the way experimenting and innovating in schools if they have yet to experience signature pedagogies that are innovative themselves? Teachers typically propel educational models that they have experienced themselves and have great difficulties breaking from these traditions (Abril, 2009b). Some universities have led the way by offering (sometimes requiring) atypical courses for music education majors.[2] For instance, in the United States, where composition is rarely taught (Strand, 2006), music education students at Northwestern University are required to complete a course in teaching composition in the schools. At Indiana University, choral and general music tracks music education majors are required to sing in the International Vocal Ensemble, where they have the opportunity to learn music of the world, using a distinct music pedagogy that remains faithful to the traditions from which the music being learned originate (see http://www.music.indiana.edu/departments/ensembles/ive.shtml). Music education majors at the University of Washington take a course in "ethnomusicology in the schools," which addresses "[i]ssues, teaching materials, and techniques involved in incorporating music cultures of United States and related world music repertoires in preK–12 classroom instruction" (http://www.washington.edu/students/crscat/mused.html). Popular music teaching methods, music technology, and entrepreneurship are required courses of the music education curriculum at the University of Miami. The content of the courses may be just as important as the opportunity for students to experience alternative ideas and structures for music education.

Myriad requirements from various accrediting bodies (music, education, state) have crowded the undergraduate music education curriculum such that students have little to no freedom. The rigidity of the curriculum has many consequences, one of which is fewer opportunities for students to explore course work that is of interest to them. Innovative individuals need time and space to play and find a passion, overly rigid and prescribed upbringing (like overly rigid course requirements) may not be conducive to innovative thinking or action (Wagner, 2012). Furthermore, it becomes a self-reinforcing cycle of preparing students for the predetermined music education roles that have defined music education for almost a century. Music education programs might consider stripping the curriculum to the bare bones and offering students flexibility and choice around areas of related interest.

EXPERIENCES IN THE FIELD

Field experiences and internships are designed to give music education students varied hands-on experience in music teaching and learning settings. These experiences are often limited to school music programs that reinforce existing models of music education. While these are important and should continue to be included, they should not be the only options for students. In order to invoke innovation, students should be provided with experiences that offer a broader perspective on the boundaries of music education. For example, music teachers can practice with elders in an instrumental ensemble, providing instruction in large and small groups. They can assist students in a local high school interested in starting a music recording studio and label. Another idea for an internship might be to work in the educational division of a cultural organization such as the symphony, a museum, or a music festival. Students would be immersed in varied settings that are focused on music teaching and learning but with diverse goals, philosophies, populations, and experiences, which could lead to new ideas for teaching music in schools.

STUDENT BODY

In part, innovation comes from collaborations among people of diverse backgrounds and areas of expertise (Sawyer, 2006). Current admission or audition requirements in university-based schools of music typically exclude students who do not sing or play art music. In so doing, we miss out on talented music students whose diverse musical backgrounds would enrich music education programs. These students could bring unique perspectives on music into our music courses and offer ideas for new forms and systems of music education. Schools and departments of music should consider ways that they can create admissions standards that remain high yet allow for alternative instruments or areas of musical expertise. This might require a rethinking of the studio-based music school.

Conclusion

At the conclusion of their degree program in music education, in a student teaching seminar, I return the students' drawings of music education as they envisioned it and have them discuss the ways that vision has changed over four years. For some, the vision has remained virtually the same. Some, however, have a more expansive view of the things students can and should be doing and learning in band, choral, and general music classroom. They speak of students composing on computers, students working in various part of the rooms on different tasks simultaneously (drumming circle, individual composition work on computers, and listening), students playing in popular music ensembles guided by the teacher. Some students see music education as more connected to the greater educational enterprise, linking subjects, collaborating with other teachers, and involving all members of the school community. Music teacher education can lead a change in the ways music education is thought about and practiced and make it more relevant to the lives of the people it serves.

Acknowledgments

I would like to acknowledge Dr. Judy Bond for having invited me to give a keynote presentation that first got me to organize my thoughts on this topic; Stan Haskins for reading an early version of this work; and my current and former colleagues and students at the University of Miami and Northwestern University, whose ideas have shaped this work. This chapter is based on an online article I wrote in Spanish for the *Laboratorio de investigación en formación y profesionalización Universidad de Granada* called Convocando un espíritu creativo e innovador en la preparación de educadores de música.

Notes

1. This idea came from Dr. Eve Harwood at the University of Illinois.

2. The following programs were selected because of my familiarity with them. These courses (required or offered at the time of writing this chapter) serve only as examples and are not in any way meant to be comprehensive.

References

Abril, C. R. (2009a). School music education in the United States: Beliefs, conditions, and implications. *Diskussion Musikpädagogik, 43*(9), 43–53.

Abril, C. R. (2009b). Responding to culture in the instrumental programme: A teacher's journey. *Music Education Research, 11*(1), 77–91.

Abril, C. R. (2010). Opening spaces in the instrumental music classroom. In A. Clements (Ed.), *Alternative approaches in music education* (pp. 3–14). Lanham, MD: Rowman & Littlefield Education.

Abril, C. R., & Bannerman, J. (in press). Percieved factors impacting school music programs: The teacher's perspective. *Journal of Research in Music Education.*

Abril, C. R., & Gault, B. (2008). The state of music in secondary schools: The principal's perspective. *Journal of Research in Music Education, 56*(1), 68–81.

Amabile, T. M. (1996). *Creativity and innovation in organizations* (pp. 1–15). Cambridge, MA: Harvard Business School.

Beveridge, T. (2010). No Child Left Behind and fine arts classes. *Arts Education Policy Review, 111*, 1, 4–7.

Campbell, M. R., Thompson, L. K., & Barrett, J. R. (2010). *Constructing a personal orientation to music teaching.* New York: Routledge.

Campbell, P. S., Connell, C., & Beegle, A. (2007). Adolescents' expressed meanings of music in and out of school. *Journal of Research in Music Education, 55*(3), 220–236.

Clements, A. C. (2010) (Ed.) *Alternative approaches in music education: Case studies from the field.* Lanham, MD: Rowman & Littlefield Education.

Clements, A., & Campbell, P. S. (2006). Rap, rock, and rhythm, music and more in a methods class. *Mountain Lake Reader, 4*, 16–22.

Darling-Hammond, L. (2006). Constructing 21st-century teacher education. *Journal of Teacher Education, 57*(3), 300–314.

Elpus, K. (2013). Is it the music or is it selection bias? A nationwide analysis of music and non-music students' SAT scores. *Journal of Research in Music Education, 61*(2), 175–194.

Elpus, K., & Abril, C. R. (2011). High school music ensemble students in the United States: A demographic profile. *Journal of Music Education Research, 59*, 128–145.

Erault, M. (1975). Promoting innovation in teaching and learning: problems, processes and institutional mechanisms. *Higher Education 4*(1), 13–26.

Fitzpatrick, K. R. (2013). Blogging through the music student teaching experience: Developing visual communities of practice. *Research Studies in Music Education.* doi: 10.1177/1321103X13509350.

Gay, G. (2010). *Culturally responsive teaching: Theory, research, and practice.* New York: Teachers College.

Greene, M. (1995). *Releasing the imagination: Essays on education, the arts, and social change.* New York: Jossey-Bass.

Hickey, M. (2012). *Music outside the lines: Ideas for composing in K–12 music classrooms.* New York: Oxford University Press.

IFPI. (2013). *IFPI digital music report 2013: Engine of a digital world.* Retrieved from http://www.ifpi.org/content/library/DMR2013.pdf.

Johnson, N., Oliff, P., & Williams, E. (2011, February 9). An update on state budget cuts. Retrieved from http://www.cbpp.org/cms/?fa=view&id=1214

Kavilanz, P. (2013, February 12). *5 hot franchises.* Retrieved from http://money.cnn.com/gallery/smallbusiness/2013/02/12/hot-franchises/index.html.

Kot, G. (2010, July 21). Old Town School readies $18 million expansion, new concert hall. *Chicago Tribune.* Retrieved from http://archive.is/lgFs.

Koza, J. (2008). Listening for whiteness: Hearing racial politics in undergraduate school music. *Philosophy of Music Education Review, 16*(2), 145–155.

Kratus, J. (2007). Music education at the tipping point. *Music Educators Journal, 94*(2), 42–48.

Kuhn, T. S. (1970). *The structure of scientific revolutions* (2nd ed.). Chicago: University of Chicago Press.

Myers, D. (2008). Lifespan engagement and the question of relevance: Challenges for music education research in the twenty-first century. *Music Education Research, 10*(1), 1–14.

National Association of Music Merchants (NAMM). (2011). *2011 The NAAM global report.* Retrieved from http://www.nxtbook.com/nxtbooks/namm/2011globalreport/#/0.

National Center for Education Statistics (NCES). (2012). *Arts education in public elementary and secondary schools: 1999–2000 and 2009–2010.* Washington, DC: US Department of Education.

Rabkin, N., & Hedberg, E. C. (2011). *Arts education in America: What the declines mean for arts participation.* Washington, DC: National Endowment for the Arts.

Sawyer, R. K. (2006). Educating for innovation. *Thinking Skills and Creativity, 1*(1), 41–48.

Shulman, L. S. (2005). Signature pedagogies in the professions. *Daedalus, 134*(3), 52–59.

Strand, K. (2006). Survey of Indiana music teachers on using composition in the classroom. *Journal of Research in Music Education, 54*(2), 154–167.

Wagner, T. (2012). *Creating innovators: The making of young people who will change the world.* New York: Scribner.

Williams, D. A. (2011). The elephant in the room. *Music Educators Journal, 98*(1), 51–57. doi: 10.1177/0027432111415538.

What If…?

A CURRICULUM IN SUPPORT OF TECHNOLOGY, CURIOSITY, AND PLAY IN MUSIC TEACHER EDUCATION

Gena R. Greher

A fundamental purpose of arts education is to enlarge the number of active participants in the art forms, not just the number of passive spectators.

— (Hope, 1987, p. 34)

What If…?

What if music teacher education could become a conduit for all students to unleash their natural curiosity, their need to express themselves, and tap into their natural love of music? What if the music teacher education curriculum placed an emphasis on musical exploration and play, in addition to musical skill building? What if the focus of music teacher education was more relevant to the students our students will actually be teaching? What might such a curriculum look like and what might the role of technology play in that curriculum? What if this could be accomplished without necessarily adding to the credit load, but rather it could be accomplished by modifying existing courses and taking a more holistic approach to teaching and learning? What if this curriculum could better reflect student culture today, and into the future?

If you accept the premise that music education should be considered an essential component of a well-rounded public school curriculum, the concerns I will address in this chapter have to do with the disconnect between the music teacher education curriculum and who today's students are, with regard to how media and technology impact their culture and how we in music teacher education might better serve the musical interests of our current generation, as well as future generations, of students. I offer this as just one possible pathway into how we might change the music teacher education paradigm to better equip future music teachers for a diversity of student populations and teaching situations.

In this chapter I will propose a more central role for the inclusion of the tools of technology as a route toward developing creative and critical thinking skills. While I do not believe technology will solve all ills, I do believe it needs to play a more prominent role in the music teacher education curriculum. In fact, I would even suggest we rethink our music teacher licensing policies to include competency in "teaching *with* technology" as an integral component to being a highly qualified music teacher, right alongside the instrumental, choral, and general music requirements that are the standard licensure routes in most states (Greher, 2011).

The More Things Change...

Digital technology is permeating all aspects of our lives, culture, and educational institutions. Our students are at the center of this cultural shift, and in many cases their interactions with technology are spearheading many of the current innovations, whether it is for gaming, musicking, or socializing. Though music technology is now part of most music teacher education curricula, it is usually in the form of an obligatory intro to technology class. Most likely the emphasis will be on learning about some basic music software applications rather than fully incorporating and embedding music technology into the core of the music teacher education curriculum.

The biggest hurdle for beginning music teachers in any setting is being able to apply what they are learning. Moving away from the traditional teacher-centric model that has often been the standard for how the role of "music teacher" is perceived is difficult enough, without the added layer of teaching with technology. Novice teachers need multiple experiences embedded into their course work for exploring, working creatively, and thinking with technology at the college level (Greher, 2011), so that teaching and thinking with technology is as natural as picking up one's instrument. Even then, it may not be so until they see for themselves how younger students can engage with music at a more intuitive level through the use of innovative approaches involving technology (Greher, 2003; Ruthmann, 2007). When they have those experiences, they are more receptive to adapting their teaching toolkit to bring technology into their classrooms (Croft, 2007; Quinn, 2007). Whatever the area of specialization, a teacher's comfort level working with technology plays a large part in choosing whether or not they will embrace technology (Barry, 2003; Bauer, 2007; Cuban, 2001; McGrail, 2006; Noxon, 2003; Taylor, 2003; Zhao et al., 2002).

Technology in schools, if it is offered at all, is usually relegated to a subset of the general music curriculum (Greher, 2011). Ruthmann (2007) points out that at the middle school level, many students in general music classes perceive themselves as "failed" musicians. Yet he discovered a great deal of innate musicality amongst his students, that were it not for his intervention, would have gone untapped. With a major focus in music teacher education on teaching *about* technology as opposed to thinking *with* technology (Doering, Hughes, & Huffman, 2003), there will inevitably be a disconnect between what the teacher is comfortable delivering and what will actually engage the students. This is further compounded by the faulty assumption that demonstrating proficiency with technology will automatically bestow upon the folks who successfully complete the course work an ingrained ability to teach with technology (Mishra & Koehler, 2006).

Musical Play: It's Not Just for Kids

Our current tradition of compartmentalizing content knowledge courses as separate and apart from pedagogy courses, with a technology course as a single outlier course, teaches about music, teaches about pedagogy, and teaches a very little bit about some technology applications, with little focus on applying any of this knowledge as a teacher would; which is always context specific (Pogonowski, 2002). As Mishra and Koehler (2006) suggest, "The addition of a new technology is not the same as adding another module to a course. It often raises fundamental questions about content and pedagogy that can overwhelm even experienced instructors" (p. 1030). In the Technology Pedagogy Content Knowledge (TPCK) model proposed by Mishra and Koehler, the authors believe that "rather than treating these as separate bodies of knowledge, this model additionally emphasizes the complex interplay of these three bodies of knowledge" (p. 1025).

The curricular approach being proposed in this chapter integrates content, pedagogy, and technology into comprehensive learning experiences that foster creative solutions to problems posed in order to develop musical knowledge and thinking skills. In so doing we will consider how technology can support, expand, and enhance this effort. We need to also think about how we define technological proficiency. As suggested by Mishra and Koehler (2006), just knowing how to use a piece of hardware or software does not necessarily guarantee that "teachers will be able to successfully incorporate technology into their classrooms" (p. 1031). One dedicated course to learn about the various software applications that can be used in the classroom is no longer sufficient, given the rapid pace of technological change. As expressed by Mishra and Koehler (2006), as well as Heines and colleagues (2011), it is safe to assume that a great deal of the technology our students may need to know has yet to be invented.

To compound the issue for many of our students is the fact that rather than treat the study of music holistically, much of the teaching and coursework is compartmentalized. In a very poignant essay, Tod Machover (2011)[1] reflects on how "there is much in musical education that encourages the dissociation of thought and touch" (p. 17). He goes on to express that his formal "musical training has separated sound and touch, thought and feeling, concrete and abstract" (p. 18). He writes about his first encounters with music making as a toddler exploring the sounds around his house with his musician mother, and his relationship to the cello. Those first informal musical experiences planted the seeds that music making, musical expression, structure, and form could be found anywhere. When he began to study music formally, he felt the range of the cello combined with the physicality needed to play the instrument afforded him the perfect instrument with which to master the full range of musical expression. Machover goes on to discuss the tensions that ultimately ensued between his classical training and his falling into the grip of pop culture and rock music. When he began electrifying his cello it opened him up to "composing, improvising and experimenting with tape recorders" (p. 16). The very concreteness of touch and the physicality required to play the cello, along with a trip to India where the Western tonal system sounded strange to many of the musicians he encountered, helped him to bring those dichotomies together and to eventually imagine and seek out new instruments and new tonalities for making music. As he states, he eventually found himself at the intersection of digital technology, human interaction, and music making (Machover, 2011).

Before digital technology engulfed all aspects of music, from instrument creation to the recording and distribution process, music technology in an educational setting was a rather cumbersome, technically complex, experimental, and expensive affair. Music technology courses were generally referred to as *electronic music* courses, and were mostly limited to the college setting due to the complexity of learning programming languages and the need to understand a good deal of the science behind sound production. Since most schools did not have the budgets or the hardware capabilities to include music technology in their curriculum, it was not imperative for colleges and universities to alter their music teacher education curriculum, which had served them so well for so many years. Eventually, Jeanne Bamberger, through her work with Seymour Papert at MIT's Media Lab on the design of *Music Logo* and *Impromptu*, was at the forefront of developing child-friendly and low-cost music technology for use in school settings.

In my own education as a music student, a slight detour from the traditional conservatory path occurred in college as a result of taking an elective course in *electronic music*. The music produced in the lab focused on generating and processing sounds via music synthesizers such as the Minimoog and Buchla Electric Music Box, as well as relying on creative tape manipulation of recorded sounds. Computer-generated music was also possible during this time, though it consisted of learning a music programming language based on Fortran, developed by Hubert S. Howe Jr.[2] We submitted our program to the mainframe computer (which was housed in another building) via punch cards, and then waited days for a digital-to-analog tape readout. One misplaced comma could result in a composition run amok.

While we now might think of this as a great interdisciplinary course, since there was a huge learning curve in terms of understanding the science behind how to generate and process sounds, there was definitely a sense of experimentation and discovery. Playing around with sounds became a central goal that permeated my own sessions in the lab. Since there was no such thing as a preset sound at that time, I had to keep careful notes regarding what sound waves I used and how I processed them in order to recreate what I had done in future sessions.

I bring you this brief journey down memory lane to underscore the fact that up until taking this class, just "playing" with sound and freely creating something based on these sound explorations was something that was not generally encouraged in a formal study of music. At least not in the music world I inhabited from middle school through college, which was largely based on the music conservatory model. And unlike Tod Machover's early musical explorations, which he continued doing with his cello, playing with sound was certainly something I never considered doing with my violin. When I picked up my instrument there was always a purpose: to master a technique, work on learning a new piece of music, or perform in a concert. Mastering the violin was one of the main avenues for developing my musicianship, yet oddly enough those exploration and discovery experiences that were my main focus in the electronic music laboratory, were clearly absent from the rest of my formal musical studies. Those sound exploration experiences however, ended up having a bigger impact on me and my future development as a musician. This was the one space in my musical education where everything came together for me.

After one of my electronic compositions was presented at an afternoon student concert, it was a bit of a shock to receive compliments from several of my professors. That was a revelatory moment. Unlike my composition class where I was applying theoretical constructs to create what resulted in fairly unmusical academic compositions, in the electronic music studio I was creating music from a purely intuitive perspective. The only rules I followed were those dictated by my ears and my own sense of what I felt "worked" or "did not work." It was a liberating experience on many levels. Now think for a moment how this type of sound exploration might benefit our own and future students, and how the current state of technology could facilitate those experiences.

The Challenge and Potential of Technology

Due to the current explosion of low-cost user-friendly digital options available that will allow students at any level to engage with music creatively, students today can and do play with sound and explore a much vaster sonic palette with greater ease than ever before. They can do this with minimal expense and without the huge and often frustrating learning curve that comes with the acquisition of a new symbol system. They can even create music and videos on their cell phones and tablet devices. They just do not generally do this within the confines of a school setting.

Unlike the early days of music technology, students now have the potential to take on the roles of music creators, producers, and distributors in much the same manner as music professionals, through low-cost software options and cloud-based music technology sites. At the moment however, only a small fraction of students across the country actually get to have these experiences inside a school building. The lack of a budget to invest in new technology and the serious lack of time allotted to the arts in most public schools certainly contribute to the problem. However we should not discount the negative attitudes toward technology's role in music education that is harbored by many music students, performers, and teachers. While our music education students may all be connected through email, texting, and a variety of social networking sites outside of our classes, oddly enough for many students, that tech-savvy behavior seems to be left at the door when they enter our music pedagogy or music methods classes. The pervasive orientation toward performance-based music instruction causes many of my own students to see technology as an either/or proposition. Technology is certainly not something that our future ensemble directors think they need to embrace, nor even care too much about. Of the instrumental and vocal students who are hoping to become ensemble directors, several of them take a negative view of technology, as something that is "a not quite as good as the real thing" version of a musical instrument. And there is this implied assumption that to be an ensemble director means you will be working with the "musically gifted" students. Whereas teaching the general music or technology classes mean you are most likely working with the "nonmusical" students. Is it any wonder that Ruthmann's students saw themselves as failed musicians?

Burnard (2007) underscores these biases when she asks her readers to "Imagine a music pedagogy that builds upon assumptions about creativity and the instrumental use of technology as unrelated concepts, treated separately or at best where one was made to 'fit in' to the other's way of working" (p. 37). While many students may grudgingly admit technology can be useful in some circumstances, they often make comparisons to "real" instruments, noting technology cannot do what "real" instruments can do and it does not sound like "real" instruments. They often complain that they cannot get the technology to do what they want, though one has to wonder if they have even explored each technology enough to understand its limitations, challenges, and benefits. Rather than finding out what a certain piece of software or hardware can do, and what musical concepts can be taught with a particular technology to engage students, many pre-service teachers merely throw up their hands at the first road-block that presents itself and then will attempt to shoehorn the technology into a preexisting model of a lesson.

But perhaps thinking of technology as a substitute for the "real thing," or comparing technology to more traditional expectations of what constitutes "real" music, misses the point entirely. Music technology is in many instances its own "thing" and it can help one create music that can be far beyond the scope of traditional acoustic instruments. There are many software programs and music apps that allow students easy entry into the creation and performance process with little to no formal training. The abundance of instructional videos currently on the market and available through YouTube makes it possible for students to learn how to play a variety of instruments on their own. These experiences more often than not contribute to a student's interest in pursuing a more formalized study of music. But more to the point, they are very useful tools to engage those students who just may not identify with school music ensembles as the default route to music making and self-expression through music. In some cases the introduction of music technology can serve as a transformative tool.[3] As with all educational tools, the teacher needs to create well-crafted projects to maximize their learning objectives.

To be fair, our students invest a great deal of time, emotion, and personal identity in learning to play an instrument, along with developing their musician personas, which are oftentimes based on their instrument or vocal choices. For many students a focus on technology places them clearly out of their comfort zones and requires a great deal of rethinking of what they know in terms of representational and organizational structures, and what it means to teach. For students who have a vision of the teacher as the center of all knowledge and the person in control of the classroom, technology will quickly upend that scenario in favor of a less teacher-centric, more democratically oriented, studio-based approach to instruction.[4]

… And Action!

In my proposed technology-infused music teacher education curriculum, I would first eliminate the different tracks we slot our music education students into. We are educating music teachers who should be able to embrace all aspects of teaching music. While some students may shine in one aspect of music making over another, eliminating the artificially imposed distinctions during their course of study will hopefully dispel the notion that there's a music teaching hierarchy. My goal in this is to suggest to students that all the pedagogy and methods course work will have relevance to them, no matter what they end up teaching or what they ultimately may see as their individual music teacher niche. I would also propose that opportunities to think with technology and make music with and through technology should infuse the entire music curriculum, not just the one or two music education courses dedicated to technology. While that might be a harder sell with your non-music education colleagues, you could point out how they would be missing out on some great teaching and learning moments by not taking advantage of the tools available to us.

A recent journal reflection from one of my students would confirm that.[5] She had been working on creating an interactive computer program that would require certain events to be triggered by certain parts of a song. In programming the song based on notation that was available online, she and her teammates discovered it did not sound right. They checked and double-checked the notation against their programming and confirmed that they had translated the notation correctly into MIDI values. But the song as programmed was definitely off. They finally decided to reprogram the notes based on what sounded right to their ears. At that moment she turned to me laughing about her "ah-hah" moment. Her journal reflection for that project brought it all together. She writes:

> I learned that ear training is actually used outside of the Aural Skills classroom. Who knew?! Also this answers a question that another one of my classes posed about the future of music and technology, or it at least offers a possible path that future will take.

Given the fact that getting your non-music education colleagues on board may not be entirely realistic, for the purpose of this chapter I will just focus on reimagining the music education curriculum.

Technology and the Music Teacher Education Curriculum

As you may recall from the outset of this chapter, I claimed this could be done without adding courses and that ideally the pedagogy, the music content, and the technology should all be integrated across the entire spectrum of pedagogy and methods classes. A good place to start with a curricular overhaul would be to think about developing a project-based approach to teaching, learning, and thinking with technology. A well-defined project with an open-ended outcome can provide learning opportunities for a diverse group of students with a variety of learning styles, ability levels, and outcomes. You should strive to create projects that encourage divergent thinking and promote divergent outcomes, allowing each student or team of students to approach each assignment in a personally meaningful way. Each project should be designed to allow for multiple learning goals in terms of letting students demonstrate their mastery of the specific subject matter being addressed, the specific technology tool or tools they are working with to accomplish this task, their ability to communicate effectively, and their pedagogical ability to engage and educate whatever age group that is being targeted.

A project-based approach sets up problems for students to solve. In this case, learning to explore a specific type of technology, and how to use this technology to communicate what the student needs to express, is one of the major problems to be solved. This type of approach immerses students in learning the technology on an as-needed basis. Rather than teach about the technology, where the technology becomes the subject, such as learning to work with video-editing software, you may wish to create a video project where the technology becomes a means for demonstrating mastery of the music content and the ability to engage and educate an audience of learners.

Learning to work with one's peers is an important educational goal, no matter what age group is involved. Students planning on becoming music teachers need to understand the dynamics of collaborative work. A mix of individual and collaborative projects will help your students understand both the benefits and challenges to this type of work. They will begin to learn how beneficial it is to the learning process to promote their students' social nature, in spite of the many challenges that might pose. Putting your students in the same types of position they would be asking of their own students in the future can help them develop the skills needed to support their own students in navigating the challenges.

At this point in time, laptops, tablets, and smartphones are the most common forms of digital hardware, and many schools are now also upgrading to "smart" classrooms. Ideally it would be great but it is unrealistic to assume that every student in a preK–12 classroom has access to either a laptop or a tablet in your classrooms. We can also assume that not every school will have the budget to purchase the latest digital audio, video-editing, notation, and music-creation software on the market. Therefore you may wish to develop your curriculum around projects your students can accomplish with a limited number of computer workstations, laptops, or tablet devices, using freeware, shareware, and software that comes with the computers they are using, or through free or low-cost apps. This may be a bit more challenging, but what is the point of bogging down your music education students with learning the specifics of a particular program if they ultimately may have to use something else. However, there are certain procedures and features that are universal. For instance, if you are asking your students to create a video, no matter what operating system or software package they are using they will need to know how to:

- Import and export their videos,
- Use transitions to move from one scene to the next,
- Create titles and video effects, split and duplicate tracks,
- Separate the audio from the video to have greater control of each aspect of the video,
- Mix and equalize their audio tracks,
- Understand the difference between saving a project, which is most likely program specific, and saving a file which can be played on multiple systems.

Plus, many of the web-based software programs allow students to collaborate on their projects and share them with their classmates. It also affords them the ability to work on the project outside the classroom setting, allowing more time in class for problem solving, sharing, and feedback from peers as well as the teacher.

Would You Watch It on YouTube? Multimedia and Musical Literacy

A quick tour around YouTube will reveal countless instances of musical creativity, and examples of melodic, harmonic, and rhythmic acuity to rival anything that is going on in a typical music class.[6] What is literacy in our mediacentric age and do we need to broaden what it means to be literate beyond just the traditional artifacts of reading and writing? Greg Dimitriadis (2001) used the viewing of various films representative of black urban life as a springboard for the construction of personal narratives among the adolescents he was working with at an urban community center. As he indicates, popular culture provides key narratives in helping this population validate their identities, yet official institutions, such as schools, do not necessarily endorse popular culture (Dimitriadis, 2001, p. 96). Researchers such as Valerie Kinloch (2012) and Elizabeth Moje (2000) point to the fact that students can often demonstrate an ability to manipulate language through the exploration of rap texts, indicating their motivation to express themselves while exploring language. These practices however, are not supported or valued by the school community, contributing to their sense of being on the fringes of school. Peppler (2010) suggests that learning through media-art making that takes place out of school "could be leveraged for learning in other traditional content areas" (p. 2020). In our case music literacy traditionally refers to the ability to read from traditional notation, write down what you are hearing, and perform from a written score. As with other areas of education, narrowly defining musical literacy to traditional forms of sight-singing, dictation, and the music literature canon misses a whole wealth of musical opportunities for students to demonstrate what they intuitively know and understand.

It is now not uncommon to ask students to act out, create a video, write a song, or create a commercial: all to demonstrate a student's understanding of a passage from a book or poem. These are all great projects for your general methods students to create, in that they have the added benefit of linking music-making activities to creative thinking, critical thinking, and literacy development. You can invite your students to turn a passage from a book into either a blues composition or a rap, complete with a video recording of their performance where they have to be in character or update a character, based on those in the book or story. If iPads are available to you, your students can use them to perform their musical arrangements. There is a multitude of music apps available that are too numerous to mention here but that would lead one to believe that the iPad is actually a musical device. From music-creation apps, to musical games, to music-productivity apps, you and your students can devise a host of lessons to bring into the classroom.

Your students can create public-service announcements as either an audio or video production. These can cover a range of issues that schools are dealing with, such as developing anti-bullying awareness, learning to eat more healthfully, learning to read, or needing to exercise more. This audio or video project should be sixty seconds long and should include original music, either as a short catchy song or jingle, or as background music for the action or narrative. Video and audio presentations that give a specific time limit are useful devices for getting students to be articulate and concise.

In our program, as part of our partnership with a variety of schools, our students are assigned a project to create a video introducing themselves to the class they will be working with for the semester. They are assigned to teaching teams and are asked collaboratively to create, perform, and edit a video in a manner that is geared specifically to the age group of the students they will be working with. Through this activity they are learning to understand the importance of knowing who their students are, and giving serious thought as to how best to engage them. Over the past few years my students have channeled everything from their inner Kermit the Frog to Hannah Montana, among the many cultural icons at their disposal.

In your instrumental or vocal pedagogy classes, for instance, you may wish to have your students create some short, simple, how-to video guides for their students. What are some of the issues they are encountering with learning to play or sing, which for many of your students may be a secondary study? What are some tips they are learning and how might they demonstrate these tips via perhaps a video podcast that other students might benefit from? How might they accomplish this in an engaging, rather than a dry manner? How might they accomplish this within a specified time frame?

We all have our favorite methods books that we like to use in our classes, and they serve a really important function. Why not have your students in their instrumental or vocal pedagogy classes analyze several of the exercises as to their structure and pedagogical goals in order to compose their own exercises and études? They can also arrange some compositions for specific skill levels. For some great real-world feedback, perhaps you can arrange with a local school or outreach program to have their students play these exercises and comment on their usefulness. Requiring the students to use a web-based notation program[7] will allow your students to more easily share and collaborate with other members of the class. Noteflight is a nonplatform-specific system and a more cost-effective approach to learning the basics of a notation program. It may not have all the bells and whistles of the more professional applications, but students will learn the basics of how to use notation software regardless of which program they will have in their future schools.

What ensemble director does not want a good-quality recording of their concert? And more important, wouldn't it be great to record rehearsals so students can actually hear their progress, or lack of? Learning to record and edit the tracks, adjusting for volume, extraneous noise, and equalization issues is an invaluable skill for our future music teachers to have. Incorporating recording projects using simple microphones, either external or built-in, along with a variety of different devices from laptops to cellphones can give students multiple opportunities to listen to and analyze the issues inherent with each device, as well as to learn about microphone placement and how to maximize the sonic quality with limited technological means. Working with a basic digital audio tool such as Audacity,[8] students can learn the basic principles of recording, editing, and mixing tracks. You can start with some simple remixing projects, perhaps by asking them to take several current pop tracks that have some questionable language and to remix it into an entirely new school-appropriate version. In addition to being part of a dedicated introduction to technology class, these recording projects can be integrated into conducting classes, instrumental and vocal pedagogy classes, music methods classes, and small ensemble classes.

For assessment purposes it is relatively easy to set up criteria regarding musical content, pedagogical content, and mastery of the technology. This is something you and your students can work on together. In fact it is a good idea to have these projects be self-assessed and peer-assessed, in addition to your assessment, so that students gain more experience critiquing their own work as well as the work of others. These are more or less objective measures that you can set.

Making a judgment call on someone's level of creativity however can become problematic, with the potential of undercutting someone's willingness to take risks in the future. To that end I try to lighten things up and frame the creative and more subjective portion of the assessment in language the students can all relate to. The criterion I generally use is simply this question: Would they want to watch this on YouTube? Why and why not? It plays to students' sensibilities of what is engaging, interesting, and novel without necessarily pasting a potentially debilitating label on them, that one student or group of students is more or less creative.

That's a Wrap!

Our obligation today is to find ways of enabling the young
to find their voices, to open their spaces, to reclaim their
histories in all their variety and discontinuity.

—(Greene, 1995, p. 120)

When the music teacher education curriculum is infused with technology projects, your students and ultimately their students learn not only how to use technology but how to concisely put their ideas together. They can get immediate feedback from you and their peers on what does and does not work. We as professors not only need to model uses of technology in our own classes, we also need to help our students understand how what we do in our college classes can be applied across all age groups and types of learning situations.

I am certain there are some folks out there who are wondering why we need to offer music technology in a school setting if our students are already creating music with technology outside of school. To those of you getting ready to sharpen your budget ax, I say, "Not so fast." As opposed to the more traditional paper-and-pencil assessments and the host of standardized tests our students are routinely asked to endure, these types of technology-based projects will provide an additional medium through which students can not only express themselves, but can demonstrate what they know and understand in a manner that is personally meaningful.

When Bamberger (1995) worked with students who were considered unsuccessful based on the traditional benchmarks used in schools, she discovered that they demonstrated a great deal of critical and analytical thinking when they were building and creating things and building upon their own intuitions: musically and nonmusically. Music technology has the capacity to widen a student's field of interest to include the multiple possibilities of creating, designing, and producing things, whether it is through artistic or technical endeavors, or by a merging of both. Educating music teachers capable of enabling their students to realize their musical and creative potential, and as Pond (1980) would argue, not "alienate them from their own musical beings" (p. 41), should be the focus of music teacher education.

Notes

1. Tod Machover is a composer and head of the MIT Media Lab's Opera of the Future Group; for more information see http://www.media.mit.edu/people/tod.

2. Hubert S. Howe Jr. is a composer and Professor of Music at the Aaron Copland School of Music at Queens College, CUNY.

3. For but one example of the transformative power of music technology, see the following website for Dan Ellsey: http://www.ted.com/speakers/dan_ellsey.html.

4. See Hetland et al. (2007) for an example of a studio-based approach to arts education.

5. Based on work done in our interdisciplinary course in Computing + Music we call "Sound Thinking." More information can be found at http://www.performamatics.org.

6. For examples, see Clip Bandits: http://www.clipbandits.com/; ThruYou: http://thru-you.com/#/intro/; iPad Band: http://www.youtube.com/watch?v=aSC2QS1VOZo&feature=related.

7. Such as http://www.noteflight.com.

8. http://audacity.sourceforge.net/download/.

References

Bamberger, J. (1995). *The mind behind the musical ear.* Cambridge, MA: Harvard University Press.

Barry, N. (2003). University music education student perceptions and attitudes about instructional technology. *Journal of Technology in Music Learning,* 2(2), 2–20.

Bauer, W. I. (2007). Research on professional development for experienced music teachers. *Journal of Music Teacher Education,* 17(2), 12–21.

Burnard, P. (2007). Reframing creativity and technology: Promoting pedagogic change in music education. *Journal of Music, Technology and Education,* 1(1), 37–55. doi: 10.1386/jmte.1.1.37/1.

Croft, S. (2007). Finding flow through music technology. In J. Finney & P. Burnard (Eds.), Music education with digital technology (pp. 41–51). London: Continuum.

Cuban, L. (2001). *Oversold & underused: Computers in the classroom* (2nd ed.). Cambridge, MA: Harvard University Press.

Dimitriadis, G. (2001). *Performing identity/performing culture: Hip hop as text, pedagogy, and lived practice* (Vol. 1). New York: Peter Lang.

Doering, A., Hughes, J., & Huffman, D. (2003). Presevice teachers: Are we thinking with technology? *Journal of Research on Technology Education,* 35(3), 642–362.

Greene, M. (1995). *Releasing the imagination: Essays on education, the arts, and social change.* San Francisco: *Jossey-Bass.*

Greher, G. R. (2003). Multimedia in the classroom: Tapping into an adolescent's cultural literacy. *Journal of Technology in Music Learning,* 2(2), 21–43.

Greher, G. R. (2011). Music technology partnerships: A context for music teacher preparation. *Arts Education Policy Review,* 112(3), 130–136. doi: 10.1080/10632913.2011.566083.

Heines, J., Greher, G. R., Ruthmann, S. A., & Reilly, B. L. (2011). Two approaches to interdisciplinary computing + music courses. [Special Issue on Computers and the Arts]. *IEEE Computer,* 44(12), 25–32. doi: 10.1109/MC.2011.355.

Hetland, L., Winner, E., Veenema, S., Sheridan, K. M., & Perkins, D. N. (2007) *Studio thinking: The real benefits of visual arts education*. New York: Teachers College Press.

Hope, S. (1987). An overview of the strategic issues in American arts education. *Journal of Aesthetic Education,* 21(4), 25–40.

Kinloch, V. (2012). *Crossing boundaries: Teaching and learning with urban youth.* New York: Teachers College Press.

Machover, T. (2011). Objects of design and play: My cello. In S. Turkle (Ed.), *Evocative Objects* (pp. 12–21). Cambridge, MA: MIT Press.

McGrail, E. (2006). "It's a double-edged sword, this technology business": Secondary English teachers' perspectives on a school-wide laptop technology initiative. *Teachers College Record* 108 (6): 1055–1079.

Mishra, P., & Koehler, M. J. (2006). Technological pedagogical content knowledge: A framework for teacher knowledge. *Teachers College Record,* 108(6), 1017–1054.

Moje, E. B. (2000). "To be part of the story": The literacy practices of gangsta adolescents. *Teachers College Record,* 102(3), 651–690.

Noxon, J. (2003). Music technology as a team sport. *Journal of Technology in Music Learning,* 2(2), 56–61.

Peppler, K. A. (2010). Media arts: Arts education for a digital age. *Teachers College Record,* 112(8), 2118–2153.

Pogonowski, L. (2002). The role of context in teaching and learning music. In E. Boardman (Ed.), *Dimensions of musical learning and teaching: A different kind of classroom* (pp. 21–37). Reston, VA: Rowman & Littlefield/Music Educators National Conference.

Pond, D. (1980). The young child's playful world of sound. *Music Educators Journal,* 66(7), 38–41.

Quinn, H. (2007). Perspectives from a new generation secondary school music teacher. In J. Finney & P. Burnard (Eds.), *Music education with digital technology* (pp. 21–29). London: Continuum.

Ruthmann, S. A. (2007). The composers' workshop: An approach to composing in the classroom. *Music Educators Journal,* 93(4), 38–43.

Taylor, J. A. (2003). Proceedings from the Fourth National Symposium on Music Instrudction Technology:The Status of technology in K–12 music education. *Journal of Technology in Music Learning:,* 2(2), 67–73.

Zhao, Y., Pugh, K., Sheldon, S., & Byers, J. L. (2002). Conditions for classroom technology innovations. *Teachers College Record,* 104(3), 482–515.

11 }

21st Century Musicianship through Digital Media and Participatory Culture
Evan S. Tobias

How is musicianship applied and expressed in the twenty-first century? Along with musicianship being socially constructed, it might be contextualized in terms of how society has evolved since music teacher education programs first began preparing young adults to become music educators. One can only imagine how Lowell Mason might have addressed remixing or how Julia Crane might have integrated MIDI controllers and composing software. In an age where one can create music with virtually limitless timbres on a mobile device or collaborate with musicians located thousands of miles away, musicianship, along with music teaching and learning, is increasingly mediated through digital technology. Music teacher-educators face a critical challenge in preparing pre-service music educators to address twenty-first-century cultural milieux and the evolving ways people engage with music.

This chapter situates a twenty-first-century pre-service music education program in two aspects of contemporary society: (1) digital media, and (2) participatory culture (Jenkins, 2006). After presenting three vignettes representative of how people leverage digital media and enact participatory cultures, I outline conceptual frameworks for understanding these aspects of contemporary musical engagement. I then discuss how five key characteristics of digital media relate to musicianship and might inform a closer alignment between music teacher education and contemporary society. The five characteristics addressed in this chapter (digital, networked, interactive, hypertextual, and virtual) serve as starting points for expanding, modifying, and potentially restructuring pre-service music education programs. While acknowledging a need for including specific types of contemporary musicianship related to idiomatic practices such as creating mashups, producing original music, or digital DJing in undergraduate music programs, I focus on how musicianship in its broadest sense might be applied in ways that connect to digital media and participatory cultures.

Three Vignettes of How People Are Applying Musicianship in the 21st Century

The following three vignettes situate emerging ways that people engage with music in contemporary society. Each example outlines how digital media afford ways for people to interact with music and apply musicianship in a participatory culture characterized by:

> Relatively low barriers to artistic expression and civic engagement, strong support for creating and sharing one's creations with others, some type of informal mentorship whereby what is known by the most experienced is passed along to novices, where members believe that their contributions matter, and members feel some degree of social connection with one another (at the least they care what other people think about what they have created). (Jenkins et al., 2009, pp. 5–6)

Music teacher-educators might look to such examples of applied musicianship to inform decisions regarding preparing pre-service music educators for an evolving landscape of how people know and do music.

TIMBALAND STEALS MUSIC!? A CASE OF COLLECTIVE FORENSIC MUSICOLOGY

Thomas Crowne, a.k.a. Timbaland, is a popular hip hop producer and emcee or rapper in the United States. In January of 2007 a number of people around the world leveraged a range of digital media to accuse Timbaland of lifting or stealing other people's music in his production without giving proper credit or sharing royalties. Many focused on the song "Do It," sung by Nelly Furtado and produced by Timbaland, accusing the producer of using the song "Acidjazzed Evening," arranged by Glenn Rune Gallefoss (GRG) and composed by Janne Suni (Tempest). A video uploaded to YouTube titled "Timbaland rips song from finnish [*sic*] musician?"[1] articulated this case by combining video and audio footage with text, comparing "Acidjazzed Evening" to the Timbaland-produced "Do It." The video creator engaged as a forensic musicologist—albeit in public online rather than as a professional—analyzing the music to determine issues such as whether it contained content from other music.

Over time, questions about whether Timbaland did indeed steal someone's music were woven into a public investigation, generating a body of knowledge and perspectives regarding Timbaland's production and supposed exploitation of others' music. Participants in this process drew upon research or knowledge of varied music and analysis to create videos comparing Timbaland's productions to other music he may have "stolen." Several people applied their knowledge of digital software, equalizing and filtering aspects of the music to draw attention to particular points. Individuals and communities with particular expertise expanded and broadened public understanding of the issue. For example, some on a forum dedicated to music created on the Commodore 64 added information specific to the software used to create Gallefoss's song, highlighting aspects of Timbaland's "Do It" they felt used recorded audio from "Acidjazzed Evening."

The discourse flowed through various media including blogs, websites, and forums, with comments ranging from discussions of ethics and aesthetics to factual disputes and analyses of the music. The phenomenon surfaced throughout the Internet and eventually in mainstream media sources across the world, forcing Timbaland to address the issue in interviews. Even after the case was officially closed in 2007 (according to a statement by the original composer of "Acidjazzed Evening"), the discourse continued through text-based comments and video responses posted on YouTube or related sites, a process that continues years later. Through their individual, collaborative, and collective efforts, people effectively drew upon their musicianship and leveraged digital media to frame discourse of Timbaland's production practices in popular culture.

CROWDSOURCING, COLLABORATING, AND CREATING MUSIC

Crowdsourcing, or inviting the public to contribute content or ideas to a project, is increasingly being applied in music creation and performance. Eric Whitacre's (n.d.) "virtual choir" projects invited people to send him video recordings of themselves singing parts from his vocal compositions that were then compiled into composite virtual choir performance and recordings. Orchestras such as the Pittsburgh Symphony and Calgary Philharmonic are adopting this social networking tactic in ways ranging from hosting a concerto competition on YouTube (PSOblogs, 2012) to encouraging people to send twitter messages of lyrics to be sung to the music of Orff's "O Fortuna" from *Carmina Burana* (Adams, 2012).[2]

Imogen Heap (n.d.) engaged in an extended process of crowdsourcing and collaborating with the public through the entire duration of her process in creating the song "Lifeline." Over several days Heap invited the public to send her "sound seeds," or recordings of sound and music, and "lyrical word sparks," images and video footage to inspire her songwriting process. She also encouraged people to record and submit a solo performed over her music. Heap opened her process to the public by live streaming and recording video of her listening to and discussing the submitted content, as well as demonstrating and discussing her process of creating the song such as playing parts over produced versions of the recorded samples. By leveraging digital media one could witness or take part in the development of Heap's song as it was being created. The videos are archived for those who still wish to observe the process unfold.

SHARING CLASSICAL MUSIC WITH THE WORLD FOR INFINITE POSSIBILITIES

Though much of the Western art music canon is in the public domain, recordings are largely copyrighted, limiting what one can do with this music. In an era when people engage with and recontextualize music by creating arrangements, remixes, mashups, sample-based beats, and countless variations on these musical forms (Tobias, 2013), one might imagine the possibilities were recordings of classical music made available without copyright limitations. Such an initiative is underway. In two separate instances the organization Musopen raised capital through the crowdsourced funding site Kickstarter to hire professional musicians and record classical music. Understanding the potential of providing the public with free and uninhibited access to recordings and scores of classical music, Musopen released the music with creative commons licensing, allowing people to use, transform, and engage with the music in any way they saw fit.

Whether serving as excerpts in music lessons, added to an MP3 device for one's enjoyment, or used as musical content in one's musical creations, creative commons licensed music plays a significant role in contemporary musical culture. The musician woo tangent, for instance, created music using recordings from the Musopen project, writing the following on a personal blog: "I took one of the shorter (and more frantic) pieces—Mozart's The Marriage of Figaro—and extracted a few short elements, stretching them out to create a short ambient electronic (the genre I affectionately call 'artwank') track" (Dyer, 2012). Musopen's initiative of recording music and making it available with creative commons licensing speaks to an era in which people wish to interact, engage, and participate with music beyond its consumption. Furthermore it serves as a model for musicians and ensembles with the means to do the same.

From an Evolving Society to an Evolution of Music Teacher Education

The aforementioned vignettes offer starting points for thinking about musical engagement in the context of contemporary culture. Each vignette draws upon affordances of digital media, acknowledges and represents aspects of a culture in which people participate with music in a multifaceted fashion, and is social in nature. How might these ways of engaging with music relate to music teaching and learning? What might pre-service music educators learn from participating in such practices and how might that translate in their future teaching? What would a pre-service music education program look and sound like if contemporary forms of musical engagement were fully integrated across schools of music? To answer such questions and forward pre-service music education, we might consider the development and application of musicianship in contemporary society—what we might consider twenty-first-century musicianship—in the context of digital media and participatory culture.

Considering Participatory Culture(s)

Participatory culture is a key aspect of how many people interact with the world in the twenty-first century (Gee, 2010; Jenkins, 2006; Jenkins et al., 2009). Though not reliant on technology, participatory culture flourishes and is supported by affordances of digital media. Linking participatory culture to new technologies, Jenkins and colleagues (2009) state that "participatory culture is emerging as the culture absorbs and responds to the explosion of new media technologies that make it possible for average consumers to archive, annotate, appropriate, and recirculate media content in powerful new ways" (p. 8). As Gee (2010) argues:

> Digital tools are changing the balance of participation and spectatorship. More and more, people do not have to play just the role of the spectator because they now can produce their own music, news, games, and films, for example; these practices once were reserved for professional or elite musicians, filmmakers, game designers, and journalists. (p. 35)

Such engagement is often social or collaborative in nature. Even when people engage in participatory culture as individuals, their processes and products occur in a larger social context and may be shared with others through social media.

Given the affordances of digital media, participatory culture is characterized by a blurring of distinctions, such as professionals and amateurs or producers and consumers (Bruns, 2008; Gee, 2010; Jenkins, 2006; Jenkins et al., 2009). Gee (2010) highlights how pro amateurs, or pro-ams, leverage technology to expand their expertise in areas about which they are passionate and at times work together to accomplish large tasks or solve large problems by pooling their skills and knowledge in ways that extend beyond any one individual's contributions. Bruns (2008) articulates a similar sociocultural phenomenon he labels "produsage," characterized by: (1) open participation with fluid and distributed leadership and communal evaluation; (2) the ability for all participants to "make a worthy contribution to the project"; (3) unfinished artifacts and continuing process; and (4) common property and individual rewards (pp. 27–28).

Such phenomena suggest "a transformation of the audience or consumer experience, from a static role of *viewer* to a role as *active, mobile user* or *participant* within the creation" (Miller, 2011, p. 31). If music teacher education programs are to evolve along with society, it is incumbent on music teacher-educators to consider relationships between musicianship and participatory cultures along with helping pre-service music educators do the same. This includes addressing how people learn and do music through collaborative, social, and participatory cultural contexts mediated by digital technology. Such an approach necessitates an understanding of digital media and its potential relationship to musicianship.

Digital Media, Musicianship, and 21st Century Pre-service Music Education

Digital media are best considered in terms of content and process. Gere (2008) suggests that "digital refers not just to the effects and possibilities of a particular technology. It defines and encompasses the ways of thinking and doing that are embodied within that technology, and which make its development possible" (p. 17). Castells (2010) echoes this notion, asserting that "new information technologies are not simply tools to be applied, but processes to be developed. Users and doers may become the same" (p. 31). In describing an emerging area of education scholarship addressing digital media and learning (DMAL), Gee (2010) argues that:

> The emerging area of digital media and learning is not just the study of how digital tools can enhance learning. It is, rather, the study of how digital tools and new forms of convergent media, production, and participation, as well as powerful forms of social organization and complexity in popular culture, can teach us how to enhance learning in and out of school and how to transform society and the global world as well. (p. 14)

Music teacher education might benefit from taking part in this scholarship and assisting pre-service music educators develop the skills, understanding, and dispositions to weave together musicianship with digital media and participatory cultures. This necessitates an understanding of digital media's characteristics, processes, and the cultural contexts in which they are situated.

The following section draws upon the work of digital and new-media scholars (Lister et al., 2009; Manovich, 2002; Miller, 2011) to outline basic aspects of digital media content and processes in relation to musicianship and participatory culture. The section is meant to serve as a starting point

rather than an exhaustive account of digital media. Though the five characteristics are discussed separately for purposes of clarity they should be seen
as overlapping and interwoven. Each aspect of digital media outlined in the
section refers back to the aforementioned vignettes and is followed by a discussion of potential applications in pre-service music teacher education situated in terms of studying Bach chorales.

The focus on Bach chorales throughout this chapter is only to provide
a concrete example of how undergraduate music programs might integrate
digital media and participatory culture across schools of music. In this way
music teacher education might intersect with pre-service music educators'
work in ensembles, studios, and music courses in a fashion similar to how
Jenai Jenkins (2008), a public school music educator, facilitated a school-wide
exploration of the Harlem renaissance. In this case, a theme, topic, essential
question (Wiggins & McTighe, 2008), or organizing principle can be woven
throughout students' experiences with digital media and participatory culture
mediating their engagement. Readers might substitute their own, colleagues',
or students' interests in place of Bach chorales to imagine possibilities for
leveraging affordances of digital media in relation to musicianship, music
teaching, and learning.

DIGITAL MEDIA AS DIGITAL

The terms "digital media" and "new media" are often used interchangeably.
Both concepts stress how "media are translated into numerical data accessible for the computer. The result: graphics, moving images, sounds, shapes,
spaces, and texts become computable, that is, simply sets of computer data"
(Manovich, 2002, p. 25). The digital nature of media and music made up of
code facilitates a broad range of ways that people can engage and interact
with such content. Lister and colleagues (2009) explain that such media and
digital data "exist in a permanent state of flux in that, freed from authorial
and physical limitation, any net user can interact with them, turning them
into new texts, altering their circulation and distribution, editing them and
sending them" (p. 19). Understanding the affordances of media in digital
form is critical to imagining possibilities of musicianship that may otherwise
be time-consuming, difficult, or impossible.

Consider a musical recording in digital format. One can store this recording along with hundreds of thousands of other recordings on a small
device or in the cloud to be accessed anywhere with the ability to connect
online. The ability to easily access, share, and distribute music in digital form
was evident in how Imogen Heap's fans recorded and uploaded sounds online. Digital music can be manipulated, augmented with additional content,
or recontextualized. Thus, one can analyze and process music to hear it in
new ways, as some did when investigating Timbaland's music, or juxtapose

creative commons licensed orchestral recordings with additional music, video, and text to generate new multimodal works (Kress & Van Leeuwen, 2001). The plasticity of digital media thus affords creative and educational possibilities limited only by a student's access to resources, skill, and literacies in working with digital media.

RE-ENVISIONING PRE-SERVICE MUSIC
EDUCATION PROGRAMS AS DIGITAL

Imagine that pre-service music educators are engaging with chorales composed by J. S. Bach. As a first step in leveraging digital media, students might identify and curate existing media relevant to a Bach chorale. During this process they might be expected to assess the veracity, relevance, and quality of the information and media they find while using a web-based bookmarking system such as diigo.com to organize relevant and quality resources. Students might also be expected to create high-quality additional digital media relevant to the Bach chorale from a variety of perspectives and in a variety of musical roles. For instance, students might create multimedia works, combining audio of the chorale, visual representations of the music such as notation or other imagery, and analysis of the music. As part of this process, students might perform and record each part of the chorale on voice or instrument and upload the recordings to a service such as soundcloud.com that allows people to comment on, store, stream, and share the digital files online.

Some students might generate recordings of the chorale that contain inaccuracies, ranging from obvious intonation issues to subtle rhythmic errors, that can be used for others to engage in error detection. Others might record high-quality performances of individual parts and upload them to soundcloud.com with creative commons licensing for use by the public in a remix contest. Some students might create and upload video recordings to YouTube and use the videoscores component of MuseScore.com to synchronize the YouTube video with corresponding notation. Others might create MIDI versions of Bach chorales and synchronize the MIDI data with animated iconic notation using the MIDI Animation Machine software (Malinowski, n.d.) or Synthesia (n.d.) keyboard tutorial software. Still others might determine how Bach chorales could be performed using the Smule Ocarina mobile app (Smule.com) and submit corresponding iconic notation to the Smule Ocarina songbook (n.d.) for people to perform. Some students might opt to create more traditional listening maps that can be scanned, digitized, and displayed online.

Students might generate analyses of the music through digital media, ranging from engaging in panel discussions that are recorded and shared online as podcasts to creative video productions that emulate talk shows or other popular culture formats. Other students might provide historical context and information about the music by creating animated versions of imagined conversations with Bach by using animation applications such as the service goanimate.com. Some music teacher-educators might curate a range of media related to Bach's music and compositional techniques and have students discuss the media and respond to their peers' perspectives via text, audio, or video recordings using a service such as VoiceThread.com. The ability to access, share, and modify digital content makes this type of media a powerful tool for music teaching and learning.

DIGITAL MEDIA AS NETWORKED

Digital media consist of data or code that can be copied or linked to multiple spaces online, such as when one clicks a "share" button or copies and pastes "embed code" to place a video or audio file located in one part of the Internet to a website, blog, or other location online. As Manovich (2002) describes, "a new media object is not something fixed once and for all, but something that can exist in different, potentially infinite variations" (p. 36). Digital text, audio, images, and other media can thus be reproduced, reconfigured, modified, shared, and networked across space and time via the Internet. Similarly, people can connect with one another both asynchronously and in real time, regardless of physical proximity, through technological infrastructure. Thus, along with being networked, digital media facilitate networks.

Networks can be conceptualized in terms of the technological infrastructure that supports the movement of data and the connection between nodes and hubs or "specific places, with well-defined social, cultural, physical, and functional characteristics" that link up other places (Castells, 2010, p. 443). Networks can also be understood as the information, people, ideas, and media connected through such infrastructure. Miller (2011) explains that networks consist of "more than two *nodes* (or points), multiple *ties* (or links) between them, and the *flows* between the nodes and along the ties which maintain the network" (p. 60). Flows, according to Castells (2010) are "purposeful, repetitive, programmable, sequences of exchange and interaction between physically disjointed positions held by social actors in the economic, political, and symbolic structures of society" (p. 442).

Imogen Heap's collaborative project with fans was enabled by technology and media that facilitated the networking of people, media, and processes. Her website and Facebook page served as hubs connecting activity, music, and discussions related to the song "Lifeline." Networks, however, by their very nature can be decentralized, nonlinear, and infinitely expanding as related content and discussions continue over time. As Castells (2010) articulates, "networks are open structures, able to expand without limits, integrating new nodes as long as they are able to communicate within the network" (p. 501). While Heap's website and Facebook consolidated and linked to a range of media related to her project, they could not possibly encompass all communication, activity, and related interaction that occurred across society and the Internet. Related conversations on fans' Facebook walls or in physical spaces, online articles, or video commentary on YouTube could be seen as part of the network related to Heap's "Lifeline" project, in which case her Facebook page and website were nodes among a network of other nodes.

This does not mean, however, that all networks are without structure or that one cannot attempt to organize aspects of networks. Though media can be decentralized and located in an unorganized manner across the Internet, people can provide structure and reframe or connect media through platforms such as websites, blogs, and aggregation tools. Musicians can create hubs and nodes to provide a sense of order and connection between otherwise disconnected information, media, ideas, conversations, and resources. Databases and wikis, such as the ChoralWiki (n.d.), Wind Repertory Project (n.d.), or Musopen.org, function as hubs to organize information and media related to musical works. These websites allow people to add or modify content, such as information related to the included music, and in some cases audio recordings and scores of works in the public domain or with creative commons licenses. Such networks provide musicians with resources and are open for ongoing development as people add content and value over time.

Digital media also enable people to form communities and networks around shared musical interests. Beer (2008) demonstrates how fans of musician Jarvis Cocker use aspects of networks and affordances of Web 2.0 such as wikis, mashups, and social networking sites to form communities (p. 227). Beer argues that musicians can use such networks to increase their proximity to the public and fans, reconfiguring the relationship between performers and their audiences. Furthermore, Beer articulates how in such networks the flow of communication is not necessarily from the performer to audience or vice versa but between members of the network.

Salavuo (2006) found that members of an online music community primarily sought opportunities for musical practices such as sharing, listening to, or reviewing music. Partti and Karlsen (2010) articulate how this same site supported people developing and enacting musical identities through sharing and discussing their music and musical experiences. They frame the online community as a community of practice (Lave & Wenger, 1991; Wenger, 1998) since members had opportunities to learn through their interactions supported by the site.

Networks and communities can also serve to connect people interested in specific musical foci such as Old Time and Bluegrass banjo music (Waldron, 2009, 2011b) or Irish music (Waldron, 2011a; Waldron & Veblen, 2008). Waldron (2011a) identified how those involved in an online community focusing on Irish music: (1) discussed music; (2) uploaded and downloaded media; (3) connected with others; (4) learned to play from others via YouTube videos; (5) took live lessons via Skype; and (6) engaged in hybrid scenarios, such as instructors performing in jam sessions streamed online, providing an online interface for community members to text to instructors questions and messages which were read aloud and responded to on camera (pp. 194–195). Salavuo (2006) argues that those inexperienced with online communities are at a disadvantage and suggests that "music educators should teach their students new skills to cope in these environments" (p. 267). Given the opportunities for musical engagement and learning through networks and online communities, music teacher-educators ought to assist pre-service music educators to understand how networks function and might be engaged with in terms of musicianship and music education.

RE-ENVISIONING PRE-SERVICE MUSIC EDUCATION PROGRAMS AS NETWORKED

As pre-service music educators research, study, perform, and create opportunities for learning in relation to Bach chorales, they might identify databases and wikis such as the ChoralWiki (n.d.), Wind Repertory Project (n.d.), and Musopen.org to draw upon existing resources along with contributing information and media they create over the course of their engagement with Bach's music. Pre-service music educators might also develop unit plans or project ideas that can potentially be shared online. As part of these projects, they might develop a website focusing on Bach chorales as a hub connecting existing resources with the content they generate.

Music teacher-educators who choose to collaborate with colleagues within their institutions or from other institutions might assist students in developing the dispositions and skills involving networking principles to facilitate collaborative projects that span time and place. Along with serving as an opportunity to develop undergraduate students' musicianship and knowledge, such projects could serve as contributions to the larger community. Educators and students ought to discuss decisions regarding if or how work might be shared along with issues of privacy, quality, and related concerns. Students should have a say in decisions as to whether or not their work is shared publicly and if or how they wish to be acknowledged. Music teacher-educators ought to be cognizant of the Family Educational Rights and Privacy Act (FERPA) (US Department of Education, n.d.), regulations and related policies to inform decisions in which students' work intersects with aspects of participatory culture. Discussing such issues with undergraduate students may help them develop understanding of how they in turn might address similar concerns in their future teaching.

Along with creating networks to augment their experience with musical works, pre-service music educators might engage in existing networks related to the project, such as dedicated "Bach" groups on Facebook, Google Groups, or Yahoo Groups. After reading and analyzing original content ranging from videos of people performing Bach chorales posted on YouTube and corresponding comments to discussions in online communities, pre-service music educators might contribute their perspectives with the option to post under a pseudonym. Such engagement may assist pre-service music educators develop skill in responding to media such as YouTube videos with constructive feedback and following expected etiquette when interacting with others across networks via social media and web-based forums.

Music teacher-educators ought to encourage their students to engage in similar networking among their peers and practicing educators via ongoing professional development networks, for example by posing questions to friends and colleagues on Facebook and Twitter, meeting virtually via Twitter to discuss teaching and learning,[3] or participating in dedicated forums or networks where they can read and post questions or responses to issues pertaining to music teaching and learning (Bauer, 2010; Ruthmann, 2007; Ruthmann & Hebert, 2012). This type of engagement might extend to physical collaboration and networking in their school or local community. The ability to negotiate a range of networks and ways of communicating and collaborating with others is critical if pre-service music educators are to facilitate their future students' engagement in similar networks (Jenkins et al., 2009).

DIGITAL MEDIA AS INTERACTIVE

From a technical standpoint, interactivity can be understood as "a measure of media's potential ability to let the user exert an influence on the content and/or form of the mediated communication" (Jensen, 1999, p. 59). Kiousis (2002) proposes that interactivity be considered in terms of mediated environments in which people can communicate synchronously and asynchronously while perceiving these experiences as interpersonal communication (p. 372). For instance, digital media such as websites can enable people to post comments for others to read, which may in turn lead to dialogue.

Miller (2011) explains that interactivity might also be thought of as the "responsiveness of a media object or piece of information to the preferences, needs or activities of the user" (p. 16). Kiousis (2002) frames this aspect of interactivity in terms of the ability of individuals to "manipulate the content, form, and pace of a mediated environment in some way" (p. 367). Lister and colleagues (2009) similarly explain that "being interactive signifies the users' (the individual members of the new media 'audience') ability to directly intervene in and change the images and texts that they access" (p. 22). The ability to interact directly with digital media contributes to expanding ways in which people can engage with music and participate as listeners, creators, performers, and audience members, often in an overlapping and hybrid fashion. In creating interactive media or situating existing examples in musical and educative contexts, this aspect of digital media holds great potential in terms of musicianship and music education.

For example, online spaces such as Audiotool.com allow one to create music through interactive digital media, in this particular case through digital versions of analog music gear that one can add to, control, record, mix, and engage with via a website. The *Build a Pop Song* interactive feature on the *New York Times* website (Spangler et al., 2012) enabled people to engage as producers, by choosing recorded vocal performances to include in a composite recording, to share their version via social media, and to compare their version with the one chosen by vocal producer Kuk Harrell.

Musicians such as Imogen Heap are leveraging interactive aspects of digital media to connect with the public in ways extending beyond performing for audiences. Heap's fans listened to her music, created additional music that could be added to her song, and posted blog, Facebook, and Twitter comments on her creative process. Musopen's decision to release classical music to the public with creative commons licensing invites people to interact with the music in ways that extend beyond listening to the recordings. That people wish to interact with media and enact musicianship in multifaceted ways is evident in the videos of those who manipulated and juxtaposed Timbaland's music with other music to demonstrate similarities.

Web-based platforms such as Indaba Music (Indabamusic.com) provide infrastructure for musicians to listen to, comment on, create, and share music in a collaborative environment. Creative opportunities hosted on the site range from invitations for people to upload musical performances to be voted on by judges and the public to contests where the public can remix professional musicians' music. These forms of musical engagement are mediated by digital technology and rely on the interactive aspects of digital media. While interactivity is often framed in terms of technical or enabling aspects of digital media, people are active in the meaning-making process (Deuze, 2006). This means that one can interact with media regardless of the technical components designed to enable interaction. For instance, people can discuss a television program and one can write notes in the margin of a text, though neither might be in digital format. Digital media, however, facilitate additional types of participation and can afford participation in ways that might otherwise be difficult.

RE-ENVISIONING PRE-SERVICE MUSIC EDUCATION PROGRAMS AS INTERACTIVE

By thinking imaginatively, analytically, and pedagogically with an understanding of how digital media allow for interactive musical engagement, pre-service music educators might design resources situating analysis and learning in musical contexts. In this case pre-service music educators would be encouraged to think in terms of participatory culture and how they might design opportunities for people to engage with music in new and emerging ways. Even the process of envisioning musical possibilities that are beyond a student's technical proficiency may be helpful in developing expanded ways of thinking about teaching, learning, and musical engagement. Developing these dispositions and conceptual frameworks early in pre-service education can serve as a foundation to inform the development of multimedia resources at a point when one has necessary technical proficiency or by collaborating with others.

It may be helpful for students to observe and engage with interactive media, ranging from the aforementioned examples to those available as part of Michael Tilson Thomas and the San Francisco Philharmonic's Keeping Score initiative (San Francisco Symphony, n.d.). In some contexts pre-service music educators might learn how to leverage tools for developing interactive media ranging from HTML5 to YouTube video annotation, while in other settings they might collaborate with others who have expertise in developing such content. Perhaps students could create a website similar to the aforementioned *New York Times* interactive vocal production feature, which could allow them to choose how parts of a Bach chorale are voiced in a composite recording or to adjust the mix or volume of each independent vocal part.

Pre-service music educators might develop interactive aspects of the website focused on the Bach chorale, including prompts to generate discussion or options for the public to contribute their own chorales to which others listen and provide feedback. Perhaps a dedicated Twitter hashtag, such as #Bachchorale2014, might be deployed to generate and consolidate related conversations at concerts or in reference to the website.

The public might be invited to engage in error detection by interacting with recordings created for this specific purpose or to choose and discuss their favorite recording of a Bach chorale available online. Undergraduate students might engage in or host a remix contest by making available individual vocal or instrumental chorale parts as stems for people to remix in styles of their choice. Select submissions might then be played on a local radio station or in a lobby or concert hall before and after a concert.

Some students might approach rehearsing Bach chorales in a way similar to Imogen Heap's creative process, by uploading videos of their process or of reflective commentary on their progress, inviting feedback and discussions from peers or the public. Creating opportunities for the public to interact with media and musicians may require an evolution in the way education and musicianship are conceptualized as well as how a musician functions in society. Pre-service music educators ought to have opportunities to think through related issues and consider their own perspectives on the benefits and challenges associated with generating, engaging with, and providing interactive media to others.

DIGITAL MEDIA AS HYPERTEXTUAL

A critical aspect of digital media allowing for the type of interactivity discussed above is hypermedia or hypertext. Lister and colleagues (2009) define hypertext as "a work which is made up from discrete units of material, each of which carries a number of pathways to other units. The work is a web of connection which the user explores using the navigational aids of the interface design. Each discrete 'node' in the web has a number of entrances and exits or links" (p. 26). Snyder and Bulfin (2007) explain how "hypertext provides a set of possibilities through which many different arguments or lines might be traced or arranged" (p. 1301). The aforementioned wikis function as hypertexts, where one can search for a particular musical work, click the name of the composer, and have access to available works of that composer on a different page.

The process of tagging or adding categories to organize media that can be hyperlinked is critical to leveraging the potential of interactive media databases. By leveraging hypertext, sites allow one to select a categorical label or tag to filter information so that only related media with that tag are visible. For instance, when selecting the tag "Beethoven" on the Musopen site, one would be presented with links to music composed by Beethoven. While in some cases organizational structures are predetermined by a particular site or person, platforms ranging from social bookmarking sites such as Diigo. com to personal blog systems such as wordpress.com allow individuals to apply their own tags, choosing how they might wish to leverage hypertext. Musicians might consider the countless ways a musical work could be categorized—such as by composer, genre, tempo, instrumentation, degree of difficulty, tonality, or any number of other characteristics—to assign corresponding tags. Given the options, types of expertise, and contexts in which people engage with music and enact musicianship, musicians might tag works differently from one another. This process has tremendous musical learning and teaching potential when approached in creative ways, particularly when addressing the thinking behind how one leverages hypertext.

Hypertext allows for information, content, and media to be accessed and engaged nonlinearly and nonhierarchically. Miller (2011) explains how the networked, interactive, and hypertext aspects of the internet allow for nonlinear experiences with media and content in a way that aligns with Deleuze and Guattari's (1987) concept of the rhizome (p. 26). For instance, while engaging with media associated with the "Timbaland steals music" phenomenon, the choices one makes as to what media to interact with and in what order may affect one's overall experience. There is no correct, hierarchical, or predefined order. Those interested in suggesting particular trajectories for accessing media across the Internet might create a hypertext as a form of organizing and curating media.

Waldron (2011b) demonstrates how those involved in online communities such as The Banjo Hangout leverage hyperlinks to develop networks of overlapping blogs, websites, and YouTube videos, and forum posts creating complex hypertexts. Waldron identifies this phenomenon as "overlapping communities of practice." Members of this type of community leverage hypertext to weave together a range of resources, discourse, and media in a collective effort to share and learn music.

Along with creating and interacting with hypertext to engage in music, musicians might use hypertext as a metaphor to conceptualize musical works in terms of infinite connections, relationships, and ways of navigating between ways of doing and knowing music. In discussing the notion of active readers and very active readers, Landow (2006) demonstrates how the process of creating links, materials, and websites related to a text shift the role of one from reading to a form of writing. One might consider similar shifts in musical roles when engaging with music as hypertext. By imagining and realizing hypertexts related to music, one has opportunities to engage with the music in new and potentially meaningful ways. Experiencing and making sense of music in a rhizomatic fashion or as hypertext has potential for preparing students to think broadly about how they might incorporate music in their teaching and the types of musicianship they might develop and foster.

RE-ENVISIONING PRE-SERVICE MUSIC EDUCATION PROGRAMS AS HYPERTEXTUAL

As pre-service music educators explore the possibilities of integrating hypertext in their musical practice they might conceptualize Bach chorales in terms of relationships and connections to other works, related social and cultural context, how people make meaning of the work, counterpoint, cadences, and other information that might augment or deepen the experience and understanding of, and meaning making through, engaging with the work. Students might consider a Bach chorale in relation to other Bach chorales, chorales by different composers, other music by Bach, instrumental arrangements of chorales, music with similar harmonic progressions, the concept of functional harmony, the historical context in which Bach created chorales, or performance practices in relation to chorales.

Students might then contextualize these ways of thinking about Bach chorales in terms of larger explorations of musical ideas, themes, and curricular content. Students might also consider their own questions related to Bach chorales. All of the content and media generated to address these ways of thinking about and engaging in Bach's music could be realized in digital form and transformed into hypertext on the websites students create. To accomplish this, students might work collaboratively to develop rich resources and media that expand beyond what any one person might be able to accomplish on her own. Applying principles of networking and curating along with musical understanding, undergraduate music students might tag their digital media accordingly and link them together in ways that can benefit their peers, future students, music educators, and the public.

Along with providing others opportunities to engage with music in new ways, pre-service music educators' generation of hypertext to augment music may contribute to their own musical understanding and thinking about music education. By generating and transforming layers of information related to music into hypertext, tags, and hyperlinked websites, pre-service music educators might think in terms of relationships and connections between music, musicianship, and their life experience. This type of musical engagement has potential to encourage undergraduate students to think rhizomatically and in ways that connect and synthesize what they learn throughout their undergraduate experience.

DIGITAL MEDIA AS VIRTUAL

In describing how digital media allow for audiences and users to engage with media in new ways, Miller (2011) highlights the potential for immersive relationships between media and those engaging with media. He suggests such relationships between people and media are "embodied in the features of telepresence, virtuality and simulation, which can be considered fundamental immersive elements of digital media" (p. 31). Telepresence is the idea that one can be present or experience presence in an environment through a communication medium when one is physically located elsewhere (Lister et al., 2009; Miller, 2011; Steuer, 1992). For instance, one can feel present in a digital environment, particularly one that contains a high degree of vividness, as Miller (2011) describes, when a "technology [produces] a rich environment for the senses in terms of sensory depth and breadth" (p. 32). The virtual thus ought to be considered in relation to the physical rather than contrasted with the "real" (Miller, 2011).

Lister and colleagues (2009) describe virtual realities as "simulated environments and immersive representational spaces" (p. 13). One can log onto an online virtual world, such as Second Life, represented by a graphic avatar or visual representation of the person one wishes to portray, and engage with others in a range of environments including performance spaces or classrooms. Projects such as Eric Whitacre's (n.d.) virtual choir, where people submit video recordings of themselves singing his music, leading to a composite version of the performances, raise interesting issues for music educators to reconcile in terms of what constitutes a performance, ensemble, and musical experience, given the increasingly sophisticated and accessible digital spaces where people can create, perform, discuss, and engage with music virtually without being physically present with one another in terms of both time and space. Thus, the notion of performing together or live may not be limited to situations where people are located in a single physical space at the same time. Telepresence or telematic musicking and immersive qualities of media trouble notions of liveness, presence, virtuality, and togetherness, particularly in terms of musicking as technology and digital media support creating and performing with others asynchronously and synchronously via the Internet.

The ability for people to leverage digital media to create immersive and engaging virtual environments has great potential when combined with musical expertise. Whereas one might learn about Baroque music by reading a traditional text and listening to musical excerpts, a team of experts in music, music education, history, virtual-world building, and related disciplines might collaborate to develop an interactive virtual world, videogame, or simulation of a particular place during the Baroque period that contains a range of multimedia to explore with an avatar and learn through the engagement.

Digital media also provide opportunities to create alternatives to physical objects or environments. Though fans never stepped foot in the physical space of Imogen Heap's studio, they gained virtual access through the live streaming of the artists' processes as she worked in the studio. Similarly, while some are physically present at a live performance, others might feel present though they are accessing a live feed online through a computer or mobile device. In both cases, those experiencing the concert might express their perspectives and communicate with one another via a virtual communicative layer, such as Twitter. Lister and colleagues (2009) acknowledge how technology enables and mediates "shifts in the personal and social experience of time, space, and place (on both local and global scales) which have implications for the ways in which we experience ourselves and our place in the world" (p. 13).

Similarly, music educators might think in terms of virtual layers that might be connected to physical spaces or objects through technologies that facilitate augmented reality. Azuma and colleagues (2001) explain that an augmented reality system "combines real and virtual objects in a real environment, runs interactively and in real time; and registers (aligns) real and virtual objects with each other" (p. 34). Augmented reality allows a connection between physical and virtual space, typically mediated by mobile devices that can scan QR codes, access GPS data, or superimpose digital visual information via the device's screen (Azuma, 1997; Azuma et al., 2001; Squire & Klopfer, 2007). QR codes are small graphics that can be linked to websites or other digital media, printed in paper format if needed, and scanned by mobile devices. Upon scanning a QR code the mobile device accesses the file or website to which the code is linked. Using mobile devices in combination with augmented reality software such as ARIS (n.d.) or SCVNGR (n.d.), one can also trigger digital media existing in a virtual layer while located in physical space through global positioning system (GPS) data built into many mobile devices.

One might leverage aspects of digital media mentioned throughout this chapter to create hypertext related to a specific musical work that can be accessed with a computer or mobile device when engaging with the work in physical space. A QR code placed on sheet music, for example, might link to a corresponding page on the Musopen site containing information about the music developed by music educators and others with links to additional media and resources. When scanned with a mobile device the QR code could provide immediate access to the related information and media providing one with an augmented reality or blend of physical and virtual engagement with the music.

Partti and Karlsen (2010) suggest that music educators acknowledge how music education occurs in both physical and virtual spaces, arguing that "we are now in a situation in which the 'global reality' of online communities and similar virtual and digital worlds, as well as the 'local reality' of the schools, bands and other music groups in which students participate, provides platforms through which people engage with and learn music" (p. 377). An understanding of how virtual spaces might be leveraged and connected to physical spaces may open exciting possibilities for music teacher-educators and pre-service music educators to augment music or physical interactions with music and realize new types of musical experiences.

RE-ENVISIONING PRE-SERVICE MUSIC EDUCATION PROGRAMS AS VIRTUAL

As pre-service music educators weave together their musicianship with aspects of participatory culture and digital media, they may envision and create virtual layers that connect to and mediate musical experiences. In some cases this might take the form of virtual ensembles performing Bach's music in a similar vein to Whitacre's virtual choir, while in other cases they might perform with others live via the Internet. Some students might wish to collaborate with experts in virtual-world building to design a video game where Bach chorales play a key role or a virtual world where one can interact with media to explore Bach's life and music.

By leveraging aspects of digital media such as hypertext, networks, interactivity, and virtual or augmented reality, students might collaboratively develop virtual layers of information, interactive opportunities, and immersive experiences discussed throughout this chapter pertaining to Bach's music. Pre-service music educators might imagine how interactive media and websites related to Bach chorales can function in relation to physical engagement with Bach's music for concertgoers, students, or performers. Students might create and print QR codes linked to the digital media devised in relation to Bach's music and apply the codes to physical media such as sheet music or concert programs, essentially augmenting or annotating the music or program as hypertext. Students might also create digital documents such as PDF files and websites containing hyperlinks to corresponding information and media related to the work. Digital representations of music might link to the same media via hyperlinks.

Students might also leverage the affordances of mobile devices and augmented reality to create immersive musical experiences in a hybrid of physical and virtual space. After recording Bach chorales and uploading the files to sites such as SoundCloud.com, students could create QR codes that when scanned result in a chorale being streamed to a mobile device, providing a soundscape to particular places around a campus or community. Additional QR codes might lead to information about Bach or opportunities for people to upload and share their own chorales with others. The musical experiences enabled by these types of virtual layers may transform one's relationship to the physical environment and Bach's music.

The ability to augment physical space through accessing digital media can also be applied in musical situations such as concerts. Concertgoers might be invited to communicate in real time virtually while experiencing the performance, by the setting up of a dedicated chatroom or Twitter hashtag for those with access to mobile devices. Pre-service music educators might participate in the conversation by asking questions and providing insights, essentially playing new types of roles as musicians and educators. Ensembles that have experimented with this type of engagement, such as the Cincinnati, Indianapolis, and San Francisco symphonies (Lewin & Wise, 2012) and instrumental ensembles at Arizona State University (Tobias, 2008; Turner, 2008), have provided a dedicated physical space in the concert hall, sometimes referred to as "tweet seats" (Lewin & Wise, 2012), so as not to distract those who choose to engage solely as listeners without using technology during the concert. Similarly, live performances can be streamed online using platforms such as Ustream.com, Justin.tv, or Stageit.com that facilitate web-based conversations among those who are not physically present at the performance.

By thinking in terms of the virtual extensions that can be made to musical works, pre-service music educators might imagine expansive ways that they can apply their musicianship. Similarly, through creating virtual layers of musical engagement around musical works, pre-service music educators might develop facility and flexibility in their musical thinking and teaching.

Considering Challenges of Integrating Digital Media and Participatory Culture

The approaches to integrating digital media and participatory culture outlined throughout this chapter offer possibilities for musical engagement and learning but are not without challenges. Resistance to the ideas discussed in this chapter might pose a key challenge. Such resistance often occurs when technology or digital media are framed as replacing or marginalizing acoustic music and musical practices. A central tenet of this chapter is how digital media, participatory culture, and aspects of musical engagement typical in schools of music can coexist and intersect. Identifying and creating models for such an approach can be challenging but critical in alleviating a sense of anxiety that existing musical traditions may be replaced by digitally mediated musical engagement and learning.

A similar challenge relates to misguidedly focusing on technologies and media without considering if and how they might mediate musical engagement and learning. Focusing solely on technology, devoid of social, cultural, musical, or educational contexts, often leads to misapplications of technology or to technological deterministic discourse and associated decision making (Ruthmann et al., 2014). From a technological deterministic perspective, technology itself causes social practice (Bimber, 1994; Grint & Woolgar, 1997). Both those in favor of and those against the integration of digital media and technology in terms of twenty-first-century musicianship can act and speak from a perspective of technological determinism. Addressing this challenge necessitates nuanced perspectives informed by research and experience and by keeping people central to considerations of digital media in the context of musicianship. This challenge might be addressed by situating digital media, participatory culture, and musicianship in social, cultural, musical, and educational contexts along with the development of related skills and understanding that can inform practice.

This chapter promotes an approach to the undergraduate experience that fosters students' ability to synthesize and make connections between what they learn and what they experience. The often compartmentalized nature of curricular and other structures in schools of music poses challenges to the integrated and interdisciplinary approach discussed in the aforementioned scenarios. While developing collaborative projects that span and connect multiple courses, ensembles, and other aspects of schools of music is ideal, such endeavors may be difficult to develop and may require buy-in by multiple faculty members along with supporting infrastructure. In addition to forging collaborative relationships with colleagues, those interested in the types of projects discussed above might identify places in their own programs and courses to integrate digital media, participatory culture, and twenty-first-century musicianship. The use of a digital hub such as a portfolio can be helpful in archiving and connecting students' varied experiences and projects (Bauer & Dunn, 2003; Berg & Lind, 2003).

Embracing Digital Media and Participatory Culture: Toward 21st Century Pre-service Music Teacher Education

Assisting pre-service music educators to connect their musicianship to aspects of digital media and participatory culture discussed throughout this chapter necessitates providing opportunities for them to engage with music in ways that leverage, are mediated by, and at the very least acknowledge digital media in contemporary society. While technical knowledge is important when working with digital media, one's musical knowledge and musicianship provide a foundation for deciding how best to leverage digital media. Music teacher-educators thus ought to encourage undergraduate music students to consider and articulate how they apply aural skills, music literacies, performance skills, learning theory, pedagogy, and musical understanding in their creation and use of digital media. Such an approach ensures that students' integration of digital media is situated in terms of music teaching and learning and interwoven with their musicianship.

While creating classes that specifically address digital media and participatory culture may benefit students, the approaches addressed throughout this chapter might be integrated in collaborative projects that span undergraduate curricula. In this case, music teacher-educators might facilitate large-scale interdisciplinary projects (Barrett, McCoy, & Veblen, 1997; Jenkins, 2008) in ways that help students connect theory, practice, musicianship, and pedagogy. Aspects of digital media and participatory culture might be embedded as components of recitals or concerts with preparation and development encompassing multifaceted ways in which music can be shared, presented, and engaged with in addition to rehearsing and performing.

Evidence of students' ability to leverage digital media and connect to participatory culture in relation to their developing musicianship, skills, and understanding throughout their studies might be integrated in portfolios over the course of their tenure in a music program. Such an approach might provide students with opportunities to reflect on and synthesize the varied courses, ensembles, and musical experiences that they engage in over their time in a music program and demonstrate development in their sophistication as musicians and future music educators.

Embracing digital media and participatory culture does not mean the end of live or acoustic music. In fact, it may heighten students' awareness of the unique experience that live acoustic music provides. However, twenty-first-century music teacher education programs ought to acknowledge how music is increasingly mediated through digital means. The framework proposed in this chapter thus looks to re-envision undergraduate music education through a paradigm of digital and participatory culture rather than focusing on adding a project or two to a technology-related class. This means thinking of digital media, participatory culture, media skills, musicianship, pedagogy, and curriculum as overlapping and intertwined. Assisting pre-service music educators to think imaginatively about musicianship and education in relation to digital media and participatory culture is fitting for contemporary culture, music teaching and learning, and the young people who will look to them as their music teachers.

Notes

1. To view this video see http://www.youtube.com/watch?v=M4KX7SkDe4Q.

2. At the time of writing, the PSO online concerto competition had concluded without a winner, leading to a range of perspectives expressed across the Internet, including on the PSO's blog.

3. http://musicedmajor.net/musedchat/.

References

Adams, D. (2012). A twitter chorus: Calgary philharmonic orchestra sings tweets. *Bit Rebels*. Retrieved from http://www.bitrebels.com/social/a-twitter-chorus-calgary-philharmonic-orchestra-sings-tweets/.

ARIS. (n.d.). ARIS. Retrieved from http://arisgames.org/.

Azuma, R. (1997). A survey of augmented reality. *Presence: Teleoperators and virtual environments, 6*(4), 355–385.

Azuma, R., Baillot, Y., Behringer, R., Feiner, S., Julier, S., & MacIntyre, B. (2001). Recent advances in augmented reality. *IEEE Computer Graphics and Applications, 21*(6), 34–47.

Barrett, J., McCoy, C. W., & Veblen, K. K. (1997). *Sound ways of knowing: Music in the interdisciplinary curriculum.* New York: Schirmer.

Bauer, W. I. (2010). Your personal learning network: Professional development on demand. *Music Educators Journal, 97*(2), 37–42. doi: 10.1177/0027432110386383.

Bauer, W. I., & Dunn, R. E. (2003). The electronic portfolio in music teacher education. *Journal of Music Teacher Education, 13*(1), 7–20.

Beer, D. (2008). Making friends with Jarvis Cocker: Music culture in the context of web 2.0. *Cultural Sociology, 2*(2), 222–241.

Berg, M. H., & Lind, V. R. (2003). Preservice music teacher electronic portfolios integrating reflection and technology. *Journal of Music Teacher Education, 12*(2), 18–28.

Bimber, B. (1994). Three faces of technological determinism. In M. R. Smith & L. Marx (Eds.), *Does technology drive history? The dilemma of technological determinism* (pp. 79–100). Cambridge, MA: MIT Press.

Bruns, A. (2008). *Blogs, Wikipedia, Second Life, and beyond: From production to produsage.* New York: Peter Lang.

Castells, M. (2010). *The rise of the network society* (2nd ed.). Chichester, UK: Wiley-Blackwell.

ChoralWiki. (n.d.). ChoralWiki. Retrieved from http://www1.cpdl.org/wiki/index.php/Main_Page.

Deleuze, G., & Guattari, F. (1987). *A thousand plateaus: Capitalism and schizophrenia*. Minneapolis and London: University of Minnesota Press.

Deuze, M. (2006). Participation, remediation, bricolage: Considering principal components of a digital culture. *The Information Society, 22*(2), 63–75. doi: 10.1080/01972240600567170.

Dyer, L. (2012, June 4). Sketchbook: musopen musings. Retrieved from http://wootangent.net/tag/argotlunar/.

Gee, J. P. (2010). *New digital media and learning as an emerging area and "worked examples" as one way forward*. Cambridge, MA: MIT Press.

Gere, C. (2008). *Digital culture* (2nd ed.). London, UK: Reaktion.

Grint, K., & Woolgar, S. (1997). *The machine at work: Technology, work, and organization*. Malden, MA: Blackwell.

Heap, I. (n.d.). Lifeline. Retrieved from http://heapsong1.imogenheap.com/.

Jenkins, H. (2006). *Fans, bloggers, and gamers: Exploring participatory culture*. New York: New York University Press.

Jenkins, H., Purushotma, R., Weigel, M., Clinton, K., & Robison, A. J. (2009). *Confronting the challenges of participatory culture: Media education for the 21st century*. Cambridge, MA: MIT Press.

Jenkins, J. N. (2008). A kaleidoscopic view of the Harlem renaissance, *Music Educators Journal, 94*(5), 42–49.

Jensen, J. F. (1999). The concept of interactivity in interactive television and interactive media. In J. F. Jensen & C. Toscan (Eds.), *Interactive television: TV of the future or the future of the TV* (pp. 25–66). Aalborg, Denmark: Aalborg University Press.

Kiousis, S. (2002). Interactivity: A concept explication. *New Media & Society, 4*(3), 355–383. doi: 10.1177/146144480200400303.

Kress, G., & Van Leeuwen, T. (2001). *Multimodal discourse: The modes and media of contemporary communication*. London: Arnold.

Landow, G. P. (2006). *Hypertext 3.0: Critical theory and new media in an era of globalization* (3rd ed.). Baltimore, MD: Johns Hopkins University Press.

Lave, J., & Wenger, E. (1991). *Situated learning: Legitimate peripheral participation*. Cambridge, UK: Cambridge University Press.

Lewin, N., & Wise, B. (2012, March 28). Attraction or annoyance? Orchestras invite audiences to use their smartphones. *WQXR*. Retrieved from http://www.wqxr.org/articles/conducting-business/2012/mar/28/attraction-annoyance-orchestras-invite-audiences-use-smartphones/.

Lister, M., Dovey, J., Giddings, S., Grant, I., & Kelly, K. (2009). *New media: A critical introduction* (2nd ed.). New York: Routledge.

Malinowski, S. (n.d.). Music animation machine MIDI player. Retrieved from http://www.musanim.com/player/.

Manovich, L. (2002). *The language of new media*. Cambridge, MA: MIT Press.

Miller, V. (2011). *Understanding digital culture*. Thousand Oaks, CA: Sage.

Partti, H., & Karlsen, S. (2010). Reconceptualising musical learning: New media, identity and community in music education. *Music Education Research, 12*(4), 369–382.

PSOblogs [Pittsburgh Symphony Orchestra]. (2012). PSO concerto competition. Retrieved from http://www.youtube.com/watch?v=94O_uZpjwvI.

Ruthmann, S. A. (2007). Strategies for supporting music learning through online collaborative technologies. In J. Finney & P. Burnard (Eds.), *Music education with digital technology* (pp. 131–141). New York: Continuum.

Ruthmann, S. A., & Hebert, D. G. (2012). Music learning and new media in virtual and online environments. In G. E. McPherson & G. F. Welch (Eds.), *The Oxford handbook of music education* (Vol. 2, pp. 567–583). New York: Oxford University Press.

Ruthmann, S. A., Tobias, E. S., Randles, C., & Thibeault, M. (2014). Is it the technology? Challenging technological determinism in music education. In C. Randles (Ed.), *Music Education: Navigating the Future.* New York: Routledge.

Salavuo, M. (2006). Open and informal online communities as forums of collaborative musical activities and learning. *British Journal of Music Education, 23*(3), 253–271.

San Francisco Symphony. (n.d.). Keeping score. Retrieved from http://keepingscore.org/.

SCVNGR. (n.d.). SCVNGR. Retrieved from http://www.scvngr.com/.

Smule. (n.d.). Smule ocarina songbook. Retrieved from http://www.smule.com/songbook/scores.

Snyder, I., & Bulfin, S. (2007). Digital literacy: What it means for arts education. In L. Bresler (Ed.), *International handbook of research in arts education* (pp. 1297–1310). Dordrecht, Netherlands: Springer.

Spangler, C., Myint, J., Davis, L., & Bloom, J. (Producer). (2012). Build a pop song. [Interactive media] retrieved from http://www.nytimes.com/interactive/2012/06/29/arts/music/build-a-pop-song.html.

Squire, K., & Klopfer, E. (2007). Augmented reality simulations on handheld computers. *Journal of the Learning Sciences, 16*(3), 371–413.

Steuer, J. (1992). Defining virtual reality: Dimensions determining telepresence. *Journal of Communication, 42*(4), 73–93.

Synthesia. (n.d.). Synthesia. Retrieved from http://www.synthesiagame.com/.

Tobias, E. S. (2008, September 19). Liveblogging a concert experience. Retrieved from http://evantobias.net/2008/09/19/liveblogging-a-concert-experience-3/.

Tobias, E. S. (2013). Toward convergence: Adapting music education to contemporary society and participatory culture. *Music Educators Journal, 99*(4), 29–36.

Turner, C. (2008). Audience chats online and out loud at concert. *State Press.* Retrieved from http://www.statepress.com/archive/node/1070.

US Department of Education (US ED) (n.d.). Family educational rights and privacy act (FERPA). Retrieved from http://www2.ed.gov/policy/gen/guid/fpco/ferpa/index.html.

Waldron, J. (2009). Exploring a virtual music 'community of practice': Informal music learning on the Internet. *Journal of Music, Technology, and Education, 2*(2–3), 97–112.

Waldron, J. (2011a). Conceptual frameworks, theoretical models and the role of YouTube: Investigating informal music learning and teaching in online music community. *Journal of Music, Technology, and Education, 4*(2–3), 189–200.

Waldron, J. (2011b). Locating narratives in postmodern spaces: A cyber ethnographic field study of informal music learning in online community. *Action, Criticism and Theory for Music Education, 10*(2), 32–60.

Waldron, J. L., & Veblen, K. K. (2008). The medium is the message: Cyberspace, community, and music learning in the Irish traditional music virtual community. *Journal of Music, Technology, and Education, 1*(2–3), 99–111.

Wenger, E. (1998). *Communities of practice: Learning, meaning, and identity.* Cambridge, UK: Cambridge University Press.

Whitacre, E. (n.d.). The virtual choir. Retrieved from http://ericwhitacre.com/the-virtual-choir.

Wiggins, G. P., & McTighe, J. (2008). *Understanding by design.* Alexandria, VA: Association for Supervision and Curriculum Development.

Wind Repertory Project (WRP). (n.d.). The wind repertory project. Retrieved from http://www.windrep.org/.

EPILOGUE

At the beginning of this book we raised the question, "What is a music educator?" While answers to that question have always been multiple, it seems clear that a plethora of new answers is on the horizon. The emerging nature of music education needs to be constantly considered in light of the diverse people, tools, spaces, and time frames that shape the contemporary educational landscape. Music teacher education programs must find ways to lead the profession forward—or become mere conservators of the past.

We believe that it is important to resist the notion of one best practice or way forward for all music teacher education programs. Rather, we believe that it is critical to the health and sustainability of our field to explore and offer a variety of models. This approach seems to hold great potential for those teacher-educators ready to draw on their own creative scholarship. Restructuring teacher preparation programs clearly requires both scholarship and creativity.

We hope that teacher-educators who are searching for ways to embrace evolution within their own programs find this collection of chapters inspiring. The ideas shared by the contributors to this volume are not meant to be adopted wholesale. Instead, they have the potential to inspire creative thinking and sensitive, responsive action within the specific contexts of each teacher education program. Adaptation and evolution, rather than adoption and revolution, are the appropriate models in the very diverse teacher education contexts of the United States.

Much more like a recipe book than a technical "how to" manual, this volume is provocative and proactive. It moves the profession beyond mere criticism of current practice toward possible solutions. Good cooks know how to adapt a recipe to make it their own. It is our hope that thoughtful teacher-educators will do the same with the ideas in this book.

We are fully aware that not all of the "recipes" will hold equal appeal and expect there will be divided reaction to much that is here. We encourage dialogue about these ideas, and the extent to which this occurs will be the real test of the books' success. The point remains that musical culture is evolving and teacher education needs to adapt accordingly.

It should also be clear from the essays that there is no single way to be a music educator. This, too, has always been true. We live in a complicated time when the predominant model of state certification and national accreditation demands that we prepare future music educators to teach preK–12 everything—including literacy skills, socially acceptable behavior, patriotism, and the "Common Core"—oh yes, and band, chorus, orchestra, general music, and anything else that can be tossed into the state certification requirements. This, accompanied by a tendency toward a perhaps more narrow range of musical practices and behaviors, is certainly deeply entrenched, but may be inappropriate when measured against the broader range of musical practices and preferences that are most valued in twenty-first-century society. Clearly older models that add more and more on to what a music educator is and must do are broken and in need of a fresh reconsideration.

At core, we must ask ourselves and our colleagues how long our profession can continue to ignore the educational needs and interests of the vast majority of secondary school students and still survive as a school subject. Can we continue to create music teachers who choose to remain only in rehearsal halls with a smaller number of students who are interested in only large performing ensembles? This seems like an unlikely strategy for the long-term survival of music education. Yet this is precisely what many music education programs prepare teachers to do for students who have reached the point of elective music study in grades 6–12. There are many other secondary school students with a deep interest and curiosity about music. Their educational needs are of equal importance. They, too, deserve a music education.

By embracing the tensions inherent in the power relationships, learning spaces, political expediencies, and current educational structures listed in the opening chapter, music teacher-educators can bring about powerful change. The authors who contributed to this volume have already begun this process as they have made—and continue to make—changes within their own programs.

This book is a call to action. We hope that others in our profession will take up these challenges and engage in the creation of additional promising practices to advance music teacher education in the twenty-first century.

CONTRIBUTOR BIOGRAPHIES

Frank Abrahams is Associate Dean for the Arts and Professor of Music Education at Westminster Choir College of Rider University in Princeton, New Jersey. A native of Philadelphia, Dr. Abrahams holds degrees from Temple University and New England Conservatory. In addition to his work in music education and administration, he enjoys an active career as a pianist and choral conductor, and in musical theater. He is the founder and conductor laureate of the Westminster Conservatory Youth Chorale and is the founder and conductor of the Westminster Conservatory Collegiate Chorale. For twenty years he has been the director of the Summer High School Music Theatre Workshop on the main campus at Rider University. Dr. Abrahams has pioneered the development of a critical pedagogy for music education. This teaching model encourages music teachers and ensemble conductors to adapt instruction and rehearsal technique to address individual differences in learning styles and empowers students to be musicians. He has presented research papers and taught classes in the United States, China, Brazil, Taiwan, Hungary, Israel, Italy, and the United Kingdom. Dr. Abrahams is the curriculum facilitator for the Society for Music Teacher Education. He is editor of the Westminster Conservatory Youth Chorale Jewish Music Series, published by Transcontinental Music Publications (Hal Leonard), and senior editor of *Visions of Research in Music Education*. He has been a member of the editorial board of the *Music Educators Journal*. With Paul Head, he is co-author of *Case Studies in Music Education* (GIA Publications) and *Teaching Music through Performance in Middle School Choir* (GIA Publications).

Carlos R. Abril is Associate Professor and Director of Undergraduate Music Education at the Frost School of Music at the University of Miami, where he teaches courses in cultural diversity in music, music in childhood, and philosophy of music education. Prior to this appointment he served as an associate professor and the coordinator of music education at Northwestern University. Abril's research focuses on sociocultural issues in music education, music education policy, curriculum, and music perception. His work can be found in books, journals, and his newly created blog. Recently completed work includes a study of hardcore band members for the *Oxford Handbook of Children's Musical Cultures* and a chapter on movement and music learning in the *MENC Handbook of Research on Music Learning* (Oxford University Press). He coedited the book *Musical Experience in Our Lives* (Rowman &

Littlefield) and is currently coediting a book critically examining general music teaching approaches and methods (Oxford University Press). He serves on various editorial boards in the United States, Spain, and South America, including the *Journal of Research in Music Education, Enseñar Musica: Revista Pan Americana De Investigación*, and *Bulletin of the Council for Research in Music Education*. Abril recently received the Provost's Research Award at the University of Miami.

Cathy Benedict is currently the Area Coordinator of Music Education at Florida International University (FIU). Before coming to FIU she played trombone in many different musical settings. As a Level III Orff-certified teacher with a master's degree in Kodály she also taught elementary music education for fifteen years in New York City. In the university setting she has taught classes such as elementary pedagogy, Orff Schulwerk, curriculum design, critical readings in music education, and courses addressing music education for students with special needs. Her scholarly interests lay in facilitating music education environments in which students take on the perspective of a justice-oriented citizen. To this end, her research agenda focuses on the processes of education and the ways in which teachers and students interrogate taken-for-granted normative practices. She has published in such journals as *Philosophy of Music Education Review, Music Education Research*, and *Research Studies in Music Education*, the Brazilian journal *ABEM*, and most recently she coedited the journal *Theory into Practice* and the 2012 *National Society for the Study of Education Yearbook* (Teachers College Press).

Mark Robin Campbell is Professor of Music Education at the Crane School of Music, SUNY Potsdam. His study of music teacher education, emphasizing personalized learning built upon empirical research and principled practice, has established him as a leader in the field. Known for its substance and significance, Campbell's work has led to involvement in numerous educational projects around the nation. He has most recently collaborated with colleagues to design professional learning experiences using the idea of inquiry-based learning and change agency as a basis for living a creative and vitalized life in music teaching. Campbell regularly appears at national conferences, and his published work can be found in handbooks and journals ranging from classroom teaching to curriculum and research design. He is coauthor of *Constructing a Personal Orientation to Music Teaching* (Routledge), editor of *Musicality and Milestones* (University of Illinois), and coeditor of *Advances in Music Education Research* (Information Age Publishing). Campbell's teaching has been recognized as important in helping young music teachers clarify reasons for teaching and for creating powerfully effective pedagogical repertoires for student learning. Raised in a musically active family in the

Midwest, and a "music maker and taker" of all kinds, Campbell is a committed and lifelong "student of music teaching."

Gena R. Greher is Professor and Coordinator of Music Education at the University of Massachusetts, Lowell. She teaches undergraduate and graduate level music classes in music methods; world music for the classroom; popular culture; curriculum design; Sound Thinking, an interdisciplinary course in Computing + Music; and technology applications in music education. Her research interests focus on creativity and listening skill development in children and examining the influence of integrating multimedia technology in urban music classrooms, as well as in the music teacher education curriculum. Recent projects include: *Performamatics*, an NSF CPATH grant linking computer science to the arts; an NSF TUES type 2 grant, *Computational Thinking through Computing and Music*; a music technology mentor/partnership with UML music education students in local preK–12 schools; *Soundscapes*, a technology-infused music intervention program for teenagers with autism spectrum disorders. She has coauthored a book with Jesse Heines titled *Computational Thinking in Sound: Teaching the Art and Science of Music & Technology* and has been published in *Arts Education Policy Review, International Journal of Education and the Arts, Journal of Technology in Music Learning, Journal of Music Teacher Education, Music Educator's Journal, General Music Today, Psychology of Music.*

Frank Heuser is Associate Professor at UCLA, where he oversees all aspects of the music education program. His research focuses on developing ways to improve music pedagogy. Dr. Heuser's publications have appeared in the *Medication Problems of Performing Artists, Music Education Research*, and other journals. He has contributed chapters to numerous books and served on a variety of arts education committees for the state of California, as well as on evaluation panels for the National Endowment for the Arts. He frequently serves as an adjudicator and guest conductor and has taught at the Idyllwild Arts summer music festival.

Michele Kaschub serves as Professor of Music and Coordinator of Music Teacher Education at the University of Southern Maine School of Music. Her teaching responsibilities include courses in music education philosophy, research and curriculum as well as preK–12 choral and vocal methods, and composition methods. Publications include articles in the *Arts Education Policy Review, Choral Journal, Music Educator's Journal, Research Studies in Music Education*, and others. She has contributed chapters to several books, while clinics, papers, and workshops have been presented at multiple state, national, and international conferences. Dr. Kaschub has recently coauthored *Minds on Music: Composition for Creative and Critical Thinking* (Rowman & Littlefield) and coedited *Composing Our Future: Preparing Music*

Educators to Teach Composition (Oxford University Press). She also serves as the Immediate Past President of the Maine Music Educators Association, as a member of the NAfME Composition Council, and as a member of the MEJ Editorial Committee.

Patrick Schmidt is Associate Professor of Music Education and the Associate Director of the School of Music at Florida International University, where he teaches courses in philosophy, research, curriculum, and policy, as well as courses such as choral methods, secondary methods, introduction to music education, hip hop, and music education in urban schools. His most recent publications can be found in the *International Journal of Music Education, Arts Education Policy Review, Journal of Curriculum Theorizing, Theory into Practice, Philosophy of Music Education Review, Action, Theory and Criticism*, the *Finish Journal of Music Education*, and the *Journal of ABEM* of Brazil. He is the coeditor of the 2012 *NSSE Book* (Teachers College Press) and is currently working on the coeditorship of the *Oxford Handbook for Social Justice and Music Education*. Further information can be found at http://patrick-schmidt.wordpress.com.

Janice Smith is Professor of Music Education and undergraduate coordinator of music education at the Aaron Copland School of Music, Queens College, City University of New York. Her teaching responsibilities include courses in music education philosophy, general music methods, and composition pedagogy. She has presented at numerous state, division, and national conferences and published articles addressing composition in music education and working with unpitched singers. She is the research chair for the New York State School Music Association. In addition to various book chapters in edited publications dealing with urban education and/or composition pedagogy, she is the coauthor of the book *Minds on Music: Composition for Creative and Critical Thinking* (Rowman & Littlefield) and coeditor of *Composing Our Future: Preparing Music Educators to Teach Composition* (Oxford University Press).

Evan S. Tobias is an Assistant Professor of Music Education at Arizona State University (ASU), where his research interests include creative integration of digital media and technology, social justice, expanding beyond traditional music curricula, and integrating popular culture and music in music classrooms. He is recently published in *Arts Education Policy Review, Music Education Research, Research Studies in Music Education, Music Educators Journal*, and the *Oxford Handbook on Music Education*, vol. 2 (Oxford University Press). He is on the editorial board of *College Music Symposium: Instructional Technologies and Methodologies Component* and the advisory board of *Music Educators Journal*. He teaches varied courses in contemporary curricular and pedagogical approaches. Tobias heads the Consortium for Digital, Popular, and Participatory Culture in Music Education at ASU (http://cdppcme.asu.edu) and serves on the NCCAS Media Arts Standards Writing Team. Tobias is also a member of the ASU Music Education Music, Learning, and Society Research Group. Prior to his appointment at ASU, he taught courses in technology in music education at DePaul University and middle school instrumental and general music in New York. He is a frequent presenter at state, national, and international conferences. Tobias holds an MM and PhD in music education from Northwestern University and bachelor of music in music education from the Crane School of Music at SUNY-Potsdam. He maintains a website and professional blog at http://evantobias.net.

David A. Williams is an Associate Professor of Music Education and the Associate Director of the School of Music at the University of South Florida (USF) in Tampa. He joined the faculty at USF in the fall of 1998. Before this he taught at Morningside College in Sioux City, Iowa, and in the public schools of Florida. Dr. Williams holds a PhD in music education from Northwestern University. His research interests center on the enhancement of teaching and learning situations in music education involving student centered pedagogies and informal learning strategies.

INDEX